POLITICAL
LEADERSHIP

POLITICAL LEADERSHIP

Towards a General Analysis

JEAN BLONDEL

⑤ SAGE Publications
London ● Beverly Hills ● Newbury Park ● New Delhi

SAGE Publications Ltd
28 Banner Street
London EC1Y 8QE

SAGE Publications Inc.
275 South Beverly Drive
Beverly Hills, California 90212
and
2111 West Hillcrest Drive
Newbury Park, California 91320

SAGE Publications India Pvt Ltd
C-236 Defence Colony
New Delhi 110 024

British Library Cataloguing in Publication Data

Blondel, Jean
   Political leadership: towards a general analysis.
   1. Political leadership
   I. Title
   306'.2   JF2111

ISBN 0-8039-8036-1

Library of Congress Catalog Card Number 87-060197

Printed in Great Britain by J.W. Arrowsmith Ltd, Bristol

Contents

Preface   vii

Introduction   1

1   What is political leadership and how can it be
    assessed?   10

2   The role of political leadership past and present   36

3   A conceptual assessment of the impact of political leaders   80

4   The influence of personal characteristics on political
    leadership   115

5   The influence of institutions on political
    leadership   148

6   The future of the study of political leadership   181

7   Conclusion   195

Bibliography   204

Index   211

Preface

This book on political leadership is both logically related to and different in character from the previous volumes on comparative executives. It constitutes, so to speak, the Introduction to the last volume that is to appear in the series, concerning the impact of governments. The overall aim of the series is to describe the ways in which the national executive operates in the world today and to examine the reasons for similarities and differences. Such an approach presupposes that there is clarity and, indeed, consensus as to what the object of the analysis should be — an assumption that is valid, by and large, with respect to the assessment of what constitutes a national executive, but one that turns out to be less founded, if founded at all, when we come to consider what executives may or may not achieve.

We are accustomed to believe that actions of governments have some effect; we do indeed blame governments — and occasionally praise them — for what we believe to be the consequences of their actions. But we are equally prone to think that governments are constrained by the environment in which they operate — so much so, indeed, that we are sometimes inclined to conclude that they have no room for manoeuvre and that their behaviour is entirely dictated by the environment. This inconsistency in our mind is reflected in the debate between those who believe that governments matter and those who think that they do not 'make any difference', a debate that is fuelled more by ideology — and, one may add, by prejudices in favour or against particular governments — than by a close analysis of the extent to which certain outcomes can be attributed to the deeds of various executives.

Given this situation, it becomes impossible to proceed to an analysis of the impact of governments before clarifying what this impact can be expected to be, in order to assess whether it is reasonable to believe that governments do make a difference. But the question is further complicated because, within the government, leaders appear to be, prima facie at least, rather special. They appear special because their status is different from that of the other members of the government; they appear special also because they are felt to be endowed, at least in some cases, with the potential to attract the emotional and even almost religious support of their followers: personalized or 'charismatic' leadership is thus deemed to be able to achieve results on a level that is clearly different in kind from what ordinary ministers can obtain, although ordinary ministers, of course, may well benefit from the vast protective mantle that leaders may deploy around them.

As the problem of the impact of governments is compounded by that of the impact of leaders, there seems to be no alternative but to pause in the sequence of the analysis of contemporary executives and to examine more closely the phenomenon of political leadership. This is the object of the present work, which, given the complexity of the subject, does not pretend to provide more than a partial answer to this controversial problem; rather, the aim is to indicate the ways in which enquiries into the impact of leaders — and therefore of governments — can be conducted, as well as the limits within which it is reasonable to expect to discover hard findings, at least at present. It is hoped that this book will stimulate research in both the methodology and the instruments with which to analyse the impact of leadership, while making it possible to undertake (in a subsequent volume) an analysis of what governments do achieve:

This book could not have been written without the extraordinarily generous support of the Russell Sage Foundation of New York, where I was fortunate to be a Visiting Scholar during the academic year 1984–5. The magnificent working conditions and the exceptionally congenial atmosphere of the Foundation, as well as the stimulating intellectual environment of New York City, made the preparation and early drafting of this book a wholly enjoyable affair: it is hoped that the outcome will be thought to justify the trust which the Foundation placed in me. I wish therefore to thank most warmly the President of the Foundation, Marshall Robinson, the Trustees and the staff for having given me this unique opportunity. I wish particularly to thank the Vice-President, Peter de Janosi, whose constant encouragement and infinite patience truly made this work possible. I wish also to thank the many colleagues and friends with whom I discussed aspects of this work, and in particular Ronald King of Cornell University for his continuous help, Robert Merton of Columbia University and Russell Sage Foundation, Pierre Tabatoni of the University of Paris, Robert Dahl and Robert Lane of Yale University and Barbara Kellermann of Fairley Dickinson, for their advice and encouragement as well as, in the case of the latter two, for being prepared to read an earlier draft of the manuscript. I wish to thank David Brooks and David Hill of Sage Publications for having allowed me to make this detour in the series on comparative executives. I wish to thank my wife, whose patience was often brought close to the limit. To all, I want to record my warmest gratitude for their having helped to render less imperfect a study that is, in many ways, an attempt at reconnoitring an extremely rich and complex terrain.

Florence, Italy   May, 1986

Introduction

Leadership is as old as mankind. It is universal, and inescapable. It exists everywhere — in small organizations and in large ones, in businesses and in churches, in trade unions and in charitable bodies, in tribes and in universities. It exists in informal bodies, in street gangs and in mass demonstrations. It is not, indeed, confined to the human race: it can be found in many animal societies, precisely where animals form a society. Leadership is, for all intents and purposes, the no. 1 feature of organizations. For leadership to exist, of course, there has to be a group: but wherever a group exists, there is always a form of leadership.

Among the various aspects of leadership, political leadership, in particular in the nation-state, occupies a special position. It is not that it is intrinsically different in kind or character from leadership in other organizations, but it is vastly more visible and, ostensibly at least, vastly more important. Within each nation, political leadership can command and reach out widely and extensively; and the rulers of the most important nations have a resonance that carries an echo to all corners of the world. Thus far, political leadership at the international level, save in some areas and in a limited number of fields, continues to depend on the leadership of the most important states, while at the regional and local level, in most countries at least, it is an essential, but also rather limited, element in the framework of public life. If one reduces politics to its bare bones, to what is most visible to most citizens, it is the national political leaders, both at home and abroad, that remain once everything else has been erased; they are the most universal, the most recognized, the most talked about elements of political life.

Given this recognized importance of political leadership, it is prima facie surprising that a general analysis of the phenomenon should be so little advanced. As R. M. Stogdill notes in his comprehensive survey published in 1974, 'Leadership in various segments of the population (students, military personnel, and businessmen) have [sic] been heavily researched, while others (politicians, labour leaders, and criminal leaders) have been relatively neglected' (Stogdill, 1974: 5). There has been some change in, and indeed a marked awakening to, the importance of the subject from the mid-1970s, but the political scientists who have since devoted their attention to leadership (and there are still not many), in particular G. D. Paige, J. M. Burns, B. Kellerman, M. Rejai and R.C. Tucker, note how little research has been carried out in the field, as the survey undertaken by L. Seligman for the *International Encyclopedia of the Social Sciences* amply demonstrates (Sills, 1968: 106–13).[1] We shall have to examine the reasons for such a neglect, which is rather paradoxical, since, from the Greeks to the modern period, many political theorists have been concerned with the elaboration of mechanisms designed to improve on the methods of appointment of rulers and on the conduct of these rulers when they were in office.

What is political leadership? There is in reality no generally accepted definition of the concept, a characteristic that seems to apply also to leadership in general. Stogdill, for instance, finds that the many definitions given by social scientists fall within nine different groups, some of which, admittedly, partly overlap; they range from personality to structure and from roles to forms of effectiveness (Stogdill, 1974: 7–16). Nor do recent works in political science provide clear guidance: no single definition of political leadership is given in the writings of Paige, Burns or Kellerman, although each of these authors is emphatically concerned with the general phenomenon of political leadership. There is an effort to survey the field, to map out the directions in which the study of political leadership needs to be undertaken; but there is limited concentration on what might be the core element of the concept. Perhaps this is because there is concern not to lose sight of the many ways in which leadership should be examined; it is indeed important that we should focus on personality while not forgetting the role of the environment, that we should give attention to behaviour while not ceasing to be interested in the roles and the institutional structures that are embedded in these roles, or, indeed, that we should study the characteristics of leaders while not losing sight of the problems posed by their aims and their achievements.

Yet it is not permissible to undertake broad, indeed general, studies of a subject without attempting to delineate, as precisely as possible, the boundaries of that subject. Thus, a definition of leadership must be sought even if, because it has to be general, it is of necessity rather vague and may demand further elaboration over time. Moreover, a definition needs to be given in order to clarify the distinction between what should be described as the core, the central aspect of leadership, and elements that are tributaries of or dependent on this core. We have to differentiate between what leadership is and what its origins or sources are, what its various modes may be and what its consequences or effects consist of. Part of the difficulty that writers in this field have experienced in recent years with respect to such a definition seems to come from the fact that not enough has been done to elaborate these distinctions, and thus that causes, modes and effects of leadership seem to be discussed on the same plane as the phenomenon of leadership itself.

What, then, is political leadership? It is manifestly and essentially a phenomenon of power: it is power because it consists of the ability of the one or few who are at the top to make others do a number of things (positively or negatively) that they would not or at least might not have done. But it is not, of course, just any kind of power.[2] It appears to be power exercised from the top down, so to speak: the leader is, in various ways, 'above' the nation (in the case of national political leadership), and can give orders to the rest of the citizens. However, a moment's reflection suggests that all power is from the 'top down', since it implies that A can make B do something and, therefore, that A is in some sense superior to B. Thus, what differentiates the power of leaders from other forms of power is not so much the nature of the relationship between the leader and the rest of the nation but the fact that, in the case of leadership, the 'A' who gives the order, who has power, exercises this power over a large number of 'Bs', that is to say, over the whole nation. Thus, while power relationships are always unequal (they can of course be reciprocal, if A makes B do something and, later, B makes A obey him; but even then there is inequality, although the roles are subsequently reversed), the power relationship exercised in the leadership context is particularly unequal in that leaders are able to make all others in the group (and, in the case of the nation, all the citizens) do what they would otherwise not have done, or might not have done. It might be added that this ability of the leader is also durable and indeed, in some cases, can be exercised for a long period.[3] Thus it seems possible to define political leadership, and specifically national political leadership, as the power exercised by one or a few in- dividuals to direct members of the nation towards action.

The potential immensity of such a power of leaders is, of course, immediately apparent; this indeed already provides an insight into what might be one of the reasons why national political leadership poses fundamental questions about its origins, its mode of operation and its effect. Indeed, the potential, and on occasion the actual immensity of the power, also reveals in part why, at first sight surprisingly, political theorists have not studied leadership directly and systematically. As Hobbes would have put it, political leadership is a Leviathan, a frightening beast, which it is perhaps more urgent to tame than to dissect. It frightens because it appears so dangerous; there is therefore some reluctance to approach it calmly and objectively, while there is, on the contrary, a great urge to ensure that means are discovered to diminish its effects. Thus the study of leadership has tended to be viewed in terms of an examination of the mechanisms by which the actions of leaders would be sufficiently constrained so as not to encroach unduly upon the lives of citizens.

Yet, after generations in which efforts were devoted to 'taming' the 'beast', the time may have come to consider all aspects of leadership, not merely in order to ensure that the lives of citizens are more secure but in order to see how the power of leaders can be positively harnessed for the good of mankind. For, if the power of leaders can be exercised to control, dominate and subjugate, it can surely also be exercised to uplift, improve and develop. As it is manifest that the condition of mankind deserves amelioration, and as leadership appears to be a power that can affect mankind, it is clearly valuable — indeed, imperative — to see how this power can help to bring about a 'better' state of affairs in our societies. This is particularly so since political leadership appears to be one of the clearest ways in which men and women can be induced to work jointly for the improvement of their lot; leadership seems able, by virtue of what it is, both to bring citizens together in a concerted effort and to do so over time by gradual achievements aimed at a common goal. Thus, while leadership may be a 'beast' which can frighten mankind, it can also be one of the most powerful means of leading to collective action, not just severally and in a discreet manner, but in a common endeavour over substantial periods: it can thus result in development for the whole society.

This is not of course to deny that the results of leadership can differ widely and, specifically, that these can be bad as well as good — indeed, that they can vary markedly from excellent to abysmal. But it is precisely because they can vary so much that they have to be considered in their entirety. If leadership is to be harnessed for the common good and for development, and if this harnessing has to occur because there are no obvious alternatives readily available to mankind, then it is imperative to study leadership in its generality; and it is essential to assess how far, and under what conditions, leadership is likely to be good. This is why all types of political leadership need to be classified and categorized and to be related to the situations in which they emerge as well as to the consequences that result from them. This is also why, starting from the general definition that national political leadership is the power exercised by one or a few individuals to direct the actions of the members of the nation, one has to ask three questions in succession. First, what are the origins of this power? Second, what are the instruments by which this power is exercised? Third, and obviously most important, what difference do leaders make?

Let us examine these questions to see whether the problem of leadership can be approached in this manner. It is clear that we are interested in the impact of leaders: we want to know to what extent they modify the society they rule. But by mentioning this impact, we are immediately raising two problems: the actions of the leaders, and the nature of the response. The impact of leaders depends on the environment, at any rate in the sense that the actions of leaders must be related to the character of the environment. Leaders have to adapt to the problems of their societies; they cannot raise matters as they come to mind and expect to be successful. Thus, the question of the effect of leaders is inextricably linked to the state of the environment; some have even said that leaders are prisoners of that environment, in that they can do only what the environment 'allows' them to do. Even if this viewpoint is exaggerated, it is difficult to counter, at any rate until we have examined closely both the nature of the environment and the character of the leaders' actions.

Assuming for the moment that leaders have an effect on their environment, we seem justified in stating that this effect is the result of both the personal origins of these actions and the instruments by which these actions can be implemented. By and large, the origins would seem to lie in the person of the leader, while the instruments stem from the nature of the institutional structures that are at the disposal of the leaders. But the distinction is more analytical than real; it is difficult to distinguish the person from the position which that person occupies, for instance; the instruments also appear to be in part at least a source of the power of leaders. Thus, although we must maintain the analytical distinction, we must be prepared to recognize that the two elements are in part intertwined and that it is somewhat theoretical to ask what exactly are the sources and what exactly are the instruments.

The three questions that the power of leaders seemed originally to raise should therefore probably be rephrased in a different way. When looking at leadership, we have to consider first the personal origins of the leaders' power, second, the institutional instruments that help (or constrain) leaders, and third and fourth, the actions of the leaders and the characteristics of the environment in which these actions take place.

Little needs to be said at this point about the question of the personal origins of leaders' actions, as anyone who believes that leaders have an influence would readily recognize that personality has a part to play; we will find in the course of this book that what is meant by 'personality' may not always be clear and that the measurement of the phenomenon is still in its infancy. But, in principle at least, the role of the personality of the leader in starting the process of influence appears unequivocal.

We encounter more difficulties when we come to attempt to circumscribe the instruments that help leaders to be effective. To begin with, these instruments include the 'position', especially the legal and constitutional position, which the leader holds: leaders appear to 'have power' because they are 'in power'. However, not all leaders occupy a constitutionally defined position: they may have taken office as a result of a coup, for instance, and it is therefore as a result of an ill-defined situation that they 'have' power. Moreover, even the leaders whose position is constitutionally and legally defined owe elements of their power to customs, habits and special circumstances. Thus, while the position occupied by the leader helps in a large number of cases to determine in broad terms what power this leader has, this is true in general terms only, and it may even not be important in some cases.

A further complication results from the fact that the position the leader occupies can both establish and curtail the power of the leader. The curtailment may in turn result from the constitution or the law, or from custom and habit. Thus not only are constitutional presidents, for instance, forbidden to exercise certain types of powers, but these powers may be reduced (or indeed increased) as a result of practice. The curtailment can even almost completely abolish the power: monarchs in parliamentary systems often may be no longer able to wield any political power although 'technically' (i.e., constitutionally) they may still have some powers. This is only an extreme example of the many ways in which, often as a result of the pressure of publicists and theorists, the power of leaders has been limited and constrained; however, as these arrangements are not necessarily effective, as they may be set aside or may fall into disuse, or as some individuals may be stronger or weaker, the power exercised by a given leader may turn out to be greater or less than that of his predecessors or his successors.

To a large extent, the analysis of the 'position' of leaders has been hampered by the much greater emphasis traditionally given to the determination of a 'theoretical' set of powers than to the empirical analysis, on a comparative basis, of the effective basis of the power of leaders. Indeed, by concentrating on discovering means of curtailing the powers of leaders, and by undertaking this analysis on the basis of theoretical principles, students of leadership have too often given a low priority in the past to the elaboration of the typologies and classifications that are necessary if the instruments of the power of political leaders across the world are to be realistically assessed and related to different types of societies.

Moreover, the 'position' is only one of the instruments through which leaders can exercise their power. As a matter of fact, the whole of the political system and even of the social system, to the extent that it impinges on political life, is part of the instruments that leaders have at their disposal. This is why leadership is often viewed in terms of 'regimes', of institutional styles characterizing polities under given rulers; for what is important, besides the position, is the way in which the relationships are organized between leaders and their immediate 'entourage', in particular the government, and also with the more distant subordinates and indeed with the nation as a whole. Thus the instruments of leadership cover a wide range of types of linkages, all of which affect, in some manner, the operation — and therefore, presumably, the results — of leadership. It is manifest that only a detailed — and laborious — examination of these instruments across the world can truly reveal which of them is the most suitable for each society.

Yet the main question raised by leadership is that of its effect; it is also the most difficult question to handle, in large part because, as we saw, it encompasses two separate matters, that of the actions of the leaders and that of the character and reactions of the environment. Within this context, a series of complex problems arises. We stated earlier that leaders exercise their power to direct members of the nation towards action: what constitutes the 'actions' of the citizens for the purpose of political life is of course amenable to a wide variety of interpretations, as the notion can be construed broadly or narrowly. The actions of the citizens can encompass both public matters and the most private activities, such as life within the family. In practice, the scope of activity of leaders hovers between extreme positions. It includes not merely foreign affairs and internal order, which tend almost everywhere to be considered as minimum requirements, but also a substantial number of questions in the economic, social and cultural fields. However, the involvement of leaders in these matters can vary to a marked degree. Leaders may be concerned merely with the drawing-up of general guidelines; on the other hand, they may delve fully into the regulation and mobilization of the activities of all the citizens.

We may find it difficult to determine the actions of the citizens from the point of view of an analysis of their reactions to leadership; the actions of leaders may therefore seem easier to circumscribe. This is doubtful, however, as even the actions of a single leader are so numerous and so varied that it is difficult to imagine that one could even begin to list them; in practice, some means will have to be found to reduce their number. But even if such a means is found, there are further problems arising from the interdependence between the leaders and the environment. It is true, of course, that a leader may decide to put greater or less emphasis on a particular problem, for instance in contrast with his or her predecessors; as a matter of fact, almost any leader is likely to differ somewhat from predecessors in this respect, as this is often how leaders make their mark on political life.

The scope of activities of leaders is conditioned by their 'environment', however. First, the environment structures this scope by establishing some 'habits' or an 'ideology': there are thus matters that are felt to be within the province of leaders, either directly or indirectly, because they are deemed to be part of the questions that the state should deal with: for instance, it may or may not be the case that the leader intervenes deeply in economic or social questions. Among the means that structure the scope of activity of leaders is a variety of constitutional and legal arrangements which determine the frontiers between what is and is not the role of the state in society and the role of the leader within the state. There are also customary and de facto boundaries that result from practices of previous leaders, of the bureaucracy, and of the citizens. Indeed, as is well-known, legal and constitutional arrangements are often, perhaps usually, unable to ensure that the scope of the intervention of leaders is effectively determined.

One of the reasons why legal arrangements are inadequate in this respect is because the environment also affects the activities of leaders as a result of the circumstances that leaders have to face. Internal and external crises are likely to have an important effect, as leaders have to respond to 'unforeseen' situations. These crises can then markedly constrain leaders and force them to act in a particular direction or to concentrate in a particular field; but they can also occasionally give leaders new opportunities; crises may even indirectly enable leaders to expand their scope of intervention in other fields as when a development in foreign affairs, for instance, suddenly changes the position of the ruler vis-à-vis the nation and specifically the rest of the political class.

The role of the leaders' own perspective, alongside the role of the environment, in determining what the 'affairs of the nation' consist of, therefore needs to be carefully examined in each case if an assessment is to be made of the effect of leadership. To achieve real progress, a systematic study must explore widely the range of occurrences across the world, including changes that take place as situations alter and as the views about what leaders should do also alter. But such an empirical analysis cannot of course be undertaken without a general framework: alongside the effort to obtain a wide variety of empirical data, efforts must be made to develop a model of the scope of activities of leaders and of the ways in which the situation can variously interfere with this scope. In order to be practically useful to the categorization of empirical data, this framework must go well beyond simple typologies and, in particular, dichotomies and trichotomies: one must look for continuous dimensions, as only these will provide a suitable tool for assessing the extent to which the scope of activities varies among leaders as well as the complex manner in which the 'circumstances' are likely to affect this scope of activities.

The present study constitutes a move in the direction of such a general analysis. After having examined the current state of political leadership studies and considered the extent to which answers have been given to the general problems posed by the power of leaders, in particular in terms of the development of a classificatory framework, I shall attempt to categorize the leaders of the world by reference to their activities. This categorization will take into account both the goals of the leaders themselves and the constraints and opportunities resulting from the environment. I shall then consider the personal sources of the power of leaders and assess how rapidly one can make some progress in the determination of their role. An effort will then be made to examine the instruments at the disposal of leaders, to see to what extent the position of leadership, as well as the relationship between leaders and subordinates and between leaders and citizens, can have an effect on the influence of leaders. This study is a starting point, designed to provide a basis for subsequent and cumulative analyses. The aim is to go beyond statements about what leaders might or should be like in order to examine what they are actually like, not only by describing them individually but by comparing them generally. This is the only realistic way in which, ultimately, it will be possible to discover how the power of leaders can be best organized if it is to be used to the full for the development of human societies.

Notes

1. See Bibliography for a list of works on leadership.

2. See K.F. Janda, 'Toward the Explication of the Concept of Leadership in Terms of the Concept of Power', in Paige (1972: 45–64); see also Blondel (1980: 11–15).

3. Strictly speaking, one could conceive of a group that has almost no duration at all: leadership in street demonstrations can be of this kind. In practice, however, some duration is required in the large majority of cases; indeed in many cases, in particular of course that of the state, the duration of the organization is very long and that of leaders can also be long.

1

What is political leadership and how can it be assessed?

'Can we distinguish *leaders* from mere power-holders?' asks J. McGregor Burns at the end of the Introduction of his book on *Leadership* (Burns, 1978). This question echoes those that many writers on leadership have asked and that are also asked by the interested public. Are we right to call 'leaders' most of those who run our governments? Are they not often mere 'managers', enjoying the trappings of power but not really having the effect that we feel they should have? We are looking for great men and women who, to use Burns's expression, will 'transform' the character of political life:[1] do we not merely have, most of the time, office-holders?

Paradoxically, though perhaps not too surprisingly, we also seem often to think that 'great' leaders are a thing of the past. We seem sometimes to hold the view that we are constrained, in Western democracies at least, to have only managers as leaders. The complexities of political and administrative life in advanced industrial countries appear to result in rulers being 'merely' able to modify, by very small touches, the arrangements of society. As in Wagnerian dramas, we seem to be experiencing the end of heroes.

This view is a little suspect, in part because it is clear that people have always felt that the leaders in the past who were deemed to be great were, indeed, greater than life; in part also because we so quickly forget the many limitations, defects and failures of dead 'heroes'. They were arrogant and selfish — but they are no longer here for us to be the subject of this arrogance; they were often mistaken — but we do not suffer daily from the consequences of their errors; nor are we the targets of their repressive acts, or taxed unduly to finance their grandiose projects. There is a French saying, 'Que la République etait belle sous l'Empire!' ('How great was the Republic now that we are under the Empire!') Isn't it the same with leaders whose 'epic' characteristics come to be truly perceived only after they have died? The apotheosis, after all, always takes place after the part has been played!

Indeed, a moment's reflection suggests that none of the great 'heroes' were without their bad — indeed, very dark — sides. Perhaps Lycurgus was truly a wise man or a saint: our knowledge of his deeds is rather limited. [2] But we know enough about the leaders of more recent periods to be more cynical: is there no controversy about Cromwell, Napoleon, Bismarck, Lenin or Mao? They permitted or engineered killings, by war or otherwise; their economic and social achievements are, to say the least, in part questionable. They may have caught the imagination of whole populations — both during their terms of office and since — and this is not to be discarded as being without its importance; but the negative aspects must at least be examined alongside apparent successes. And while Washington, Lincoln, Franklin D. Roosevelt or Churchill cannot be faulted on the same scale, they too made their mistakes and had their limitations. Perhaps other policies might have led to fewer deaths in war or less misery at home; perhaps they could have achieved the same results by different and 'softer' means, had they been more farsighted, less stubborn, better prepared. Meanwhile, at the other extreme, the 'great villains' — the Hitlers and the Stalins, to quote only from the dead of the relatively recent past — may have had some positive achievements, or at least may have responded to some 'needs', to some twisted urges, in the populations they ruled.

Whether or not views about a golden 'heroic' age are correct, the feeling does remain that, most of the time, we seem to be ruled by men and women who do not appear to measure up to the requirements of 'real' leadership. The evidence seems to be that large numbers of presidents and prime ministers or other heads of states and governments are not the heroes we think they should be. This is an intuitive feeling, which may of course be incorrect, as seems probable, with respect to both the past and the present. But since this intuitive feeling exists, it cannot be expected to disappear unless a powerful demonstration is made that, indeed, the feeling is wrong. There must therefore be an analysis of what leaders, past and present, do achieve, from which it will have to be concluded that some at least do not deserve the 'bad' judgements passed on them while others may not deserve the posthumous praise that they are given. As long as there is no such analysis, there cannot be any real ground for hoping that misconceptions about leaders will be redressed, if this is what the intuitive feeling truly is.

There is therefore a need for a systematically conducted empirical analysis of the achievements of leaders, an analysis that so far has not been done except in a partial manner about some revolutionary leaders (see Rejai and Phillips, 1979, 1983). Why it has not been undertaken has much to do with the 'unease' about leadership which we shall examine in the next chapter; but it also has to do with methodological difficulties. Comparisons across time and space raise major problems, especially when attempting to assess the characteristics of leaders, since one needs to discover tools by which to control for differences in their environments and in the background and socialization processes they underwent. This has not yet taken place, in large part no doubt because so few scholars have found it imperative to devote themselves to the task.

But the assessment of the leaders' worth does not merely require an operation of data-gathering guided by a framework and by tools of comparative analysis. It requires, first and foremost, a better conceptualization of the problem at hand. It may seem strange that this should be the case after political scientists have for so long been concerned, at least indirectly, with the notion of rule, but there is still little conceptualization of what leadership entails: the idea is more intuitive than systematically circumscribed; yet without such a conceptualization, progress can scarcely be made.

The first task must therefore be to discover the characteristics of leadership and to find criteria that help to distinguish 'real' leaders from 'mere' managers or office-holders. While doing so, we shall discover that it is incorrect to divide rulers in a dichotomous manner between the 'real' and the unsuccessful, or indeed between 'good' and 'bad'. As a matter of fact, these simple distinctions, perpetuated by many classical theorists, who, often for normative reasons, painted leaders in either very dark or shining colours, have in part contributed to the limited development of an analytical framework for the study of leadership. In this chapter therefore we shall first survey the elements that enter into the definition of leadership; we shall see how far continuous dimensions can be substituted for dichotomies; and we shall examine the basis on which to distinguish leadership from other forms of rule, in particular from coercion or imposition.

What is 'real' leadership?
In the first place, greater rigour has to be introduced into the definition of the concept of leadership. There are difficulties, however, partly because the contours of the concept emerged gradually in the English language alongside other words describing various forms of rule. It is not irrelevant to note that the word 'leader' is difficult to translate. In French, for instance, there is no direct equivalent: 'chef' is somewhat more autocratic than 'leader' and suggests not merely a hierarchy, but a structure of command which the word 'leader' encompasses, but does not necessarily entail; 'decideur', a rather recent acquisition, is much too closely related to decision-making and therefore too narrow; 'guide' — an expression that was dear to De Gaulle — is simply not commonly used in political life (except perhaps with sinister connotations): its usage is confined primarily to the context of mountaineering or to visits to museums or other buildings of artistic interest. 'Dirigeant' is perhaps the closest to the English word, but it is used primarily in a collective context: one rarely refers to a single 'dirigeant', rather to a 'dirigeant' among others who jointly participate in the leadership process. Not surprisingly, even in France, where the suspicion is high with respect

to the introduction of English words, the word 'leader' itself has been adopted by the political literature and even beyond.

If the word 'leader' is thus difficult to translate into other languages, it must be that the concept is to some extent culture-bound. This does not mean that it should not be used, or indeed that its introduction has not contributed to the enrichment of the analysis by helping to describe a specific role better or by linking together a set of roles; but the fact that the word 'leader' is used in such a contingent manner does account in part for the difficulty of apprehending its precise meaning.

Position and behaviour

Perhaps the most important contribution of the concept, both in political life and elsewhere, is that it helps to draw a distinction between position and behaviour — a distinction that has to be made sharply if we are to apprehend fully the characteristics of political and indeed other forms of rule. Leadership is a behavioural concept. This is one of the reasons why the French words 'chef' and 'dirigeant' are unsatisfactory translations, since both of them are associated with the holding of positions in a particular structure. A leader is someone who influences a group whether or not he or she happens to be formally at the head of that group. Thus, not only are there leaders in informal bodies, but the real leader of a constituted organization may well be someone who does not occupy a formal position in the group.

The distinction is obviously important: it makes the concept of leadership broader, more subtle and more flexible; but in turn it creates major difficulties because there is a relationship, in practice, between leadership and the positions that are held; furthermore, in view of the particular part that institutions play in political life, for both empirical and normative reasons, the difficulties are correspondingly greater in the political context than in other arenas.

The relationship between leadership as a mode of behaviour and the holding of a 'top' position poses two types of problems. First, 'real' leadership has to be distinguished from purely formal office-holding, since the two concepts overlap but do not coincide. Some leaders do not hold top positions; some holders of top positions are not leaders. A head of state — monarch or president in a prime ministerial system — is not a political leader if his or her activities are limited to being wholly symbolic. In Britain, for instance, the Queen is not a political leader; nor is the president in West Germany. The English monarch was a political leader in the past, but the gradual abandonment of powers has restricted his or her powers in public affairs to such an extent that there is no scope left for political leadership. Conversely, the secretary general of the Communist Party of the Soviet Union is a political leader not merely within the party, but in the nation as a whole, in view of the fact that, at least since Stalin, the party general (or first) secretary has continuously been recognized as the top decision-maker. Admittedly, under Brezhnev and his two immediate successors, the CPSU secretary has also been appointed president of the country (and a similar development occurred in several other communist states); but, while the position of president has given the CPSU leader a formal leadership position in the nation, only because — and as long as — the position of president has been occupied by the CPSU secretary has that position come to be important. Under Stalin and Kruschev (and even when Brezhnev was president for the first time), the position of head of state in the Soviet Union was purely symbolic and resembled that of president in West Germany. It came to have the same character under Gorbachev in the early years of his regime as he decided in the first instance not to be president as well as party secretary.

Formal position has to be distinguished from 'real' power. But the concept of leadership is also difficult to handle because formal position and real power often — indeed, nearly always — have an effect on each other: someone is likely to become a leader *as a result* of the fact that he or she obtains a particular position; the politician who is chosen as leader of a political party in Britain becomes prime minister as a result of that party's dominance in a general election. Leadership is thus in part *the product* of office-holding. The situation may change over time, moreover: an office that did not result in leadership may do so in the future after someone who was a leader (in the real sense) occupied that office. We do not know whether this will happen to the Soviet presidency eventually; but it did happen to the French presidency, which de Gaulle gave an importance that it did not have before, an importance that went beyond what the Constitution stipulated and was inherited by his successors;[3] conversely, by becoming chancellor rather than president, Adenauer contributed to the reduction in the 'standing' of the German presidency to the point where it became as symbolic as the position of the monarch in the countries of north-western Europe.

This means that it is not permissible to ignore positions and concentrate exclusively on 'real' leadership. This is probably true in all organizations; it is particularly the case in the political arena, however, as institutions are often given great prestige precisely in order to ensure that they have an effect: specifically, political theorists have repeatedly devised mechanisms designed to supervise or limit leadership. There is therefore a long tradition of efforts aimed at ensuring that the contours of behavioural leadership be determined by positional leadership, efforts which, of course, have often been only partly successful.

Power and political leadership

Leadership is a behavioural concept: the definition of leadership must therefore be behavioural. But if this is so, how does one determine who the leaders are? We can easily discover who the *positional* leaders are, but the determination of *behavioural* leaders is not so simple. Prima facie, leadership appears related to power: a leader (in the behavioural sense) is a person who is able to modify the course of events. But the operationalization of power is elusive, as is well known. The operationalization of behavioural leadership is consequently equally difficult to achieve.

Moreover, not all exercises of power are instances of leadership. Power that occurs in a once-and-for-all context is not leadership; nor is leadership the reciprocal or successive influence of a variety of members of a committee. Leadership suggests continuity, not merely the occasional use of power. This means that leadership will tend to be exercised in the context of well organized groups, which is why it is critically important in bodies such as the state, though, of course, it is also relevant in other institutions and, at the limit (but only at the limit), in very informal bodies.[4] Finally, political leadership is a special type of power in that it is exercised over a wide range of subject-matters. While many of us have power over a group, perhaps for relatively long periods, and may be leaders as a result, political leaders exercise this power over an area comprising foreign affairs, defence, the economic and social well-being of citizens, and even culture and the arts. There are, admittedly, substantial variations, not merely because of the environment (as there can be with respect to population and time), but also for personal reasons. The leader may not wish to be concerned with all the affairs of the nation. Perhaps he or she feels incompetent in a particular field; perhaps he or she feels that it is not right to intervene in a particular area, for instance in family matters, religion or the arts. But, at least in principle, political leadership is broad and might be all-embracing: decisions that could be taken by the leader might cover any subject.[5]

Thus, political leadership is almost certainly broader than any other form of leadership, and for this reason too it is a special kind of power. There are, of course, variations, as we have just noted. The breadth of political leadership cannot be expected to be the same from leader to leader, from country to country or from period to period. We are thus already encountering grounds for substantial variations likely to affect the character of political leadership. But, despite these variations, political leadership is almost certainly one of the most exalted and most general forms of power. Power is the central ingredient of leadership; but this ingredient has to be examined carefully before we can determine the extent to which it results in leadership.

The components of political leadership

Let us attempt to circumscribe the concept a little more and see whether we can 'decompose' the power of leadership into a number of elements. 'Leadership', writes R.C. Tucker, 'is direction' (1981: 15). It is direction in that it is ultimately geared towards action. But leadership will be effective and 'real' only if the direction makes sense with respect to a given situation, to what the 'moment', so to speak, 'demands'. This is why Tucker analyses leadership in terms of three elements which are analytically successive, although they may not occur in chronological order in every situation. These three phases are the 'diagnosis', the 'prescription of the course of action', and the 'mobilization' of those who will be involved in ensuring that the action does take place. The existence of these aspects, which give leadership 'purpose', is the reason why Tucker believes that political activity must be defined not in terms of power, but in terms of leadership (1981: 26): as was suggested earlier, it is probably more correct to view leadership as a subset, or a special form, of power; but Tucker's contribution is important in that it helps to determine a number of elements, or phases, which correspond to the stages through which 'demands' (inchoate or not) or needs (latent or not) are transformed into a course of action. Because leadership, and particularly political leadership, is exercised over a substantial period, within a group and in a wide variety of fields, the successive elements become truly distinct.

The 'diagnosis' is the phase during which the leader grasps the situation intellectually and assesses what is wrong, in his opinion, and therefore what has to be redressed. The leader then devises a course of action designed to meet these problems; or at any rate he comes to a conclusion, often based on advice, to be sure, as to what the better course of action should be. But this second element is not sufficient for what is ultimately essential in implementation: as Tucker also rightly points out, this can be achieved only through mobilization. Mobilization has to be conceived broadly: it covers the mobilization of subordinates, immediate or distant (within the bureaucracy, for instance), and of the population as a whole, or at any rate the fraction of the population that is relevant to the course of action. This may mean ensuring that the rank-and-file of the government party supports wholeheartedly the measure proposed and in turn acts in such a way that the rest of the population becomes supportive; it may mean that appeals are made to the nation to achieve a substantial level of consensus; it may mean, in wartime, that the leader ensures that the morale of the troops and of the country is high. Even in the most mundane actions, and even where the regime is autocratic, some amount of mobilization has to occur, albeit with respect to a narrow group. Leadership is always more than analysis and decision-making: it consists also in affecting the minds and energies of those who have a part to play in the implementation. 'Ideal' leadership thus always implies combinations of the three elements, even if the forms that this combination takes vary greatly from one situation to another.

Leadership and the environment

While examining the successive phases of the leadership process, we came to discover repeatedly that the actions of leaders were directly related to the situations they faced. In fact, leadership cannot be dissociated from the environment in which it takes place: this is one of the main reasons why it is difficult to assess and has proved even more difficult to measure. Indeed, we found the environment figuring at every point of the analysis. When discussing the distinction between behavioural and positional leadership we referred to it, since the environment determines both the formal positions and the effective strength of these positions — that is to say, the institutions — in the specific context of a leader.

In a strict sense, no two positions are exactly the same over time and over space: the formal powers of the presidents of West Germany and Italy may not be very different; they are none the less somewhat different, and the strength and weight of these positions also differ. The powers of the president of the United States were broadly the same in the 1980s as they were in the 1880s; but they were also somewhat different; the strength and weight of the United States presidency has also changed. The environment also plays a part in relation to the determination of the 'power' of the leader, since the relative strength of the various actors changes continuously over time and is also different from one country to another at a given point in time. This relative power also includes the role of political leaders of other countries, who play a different part, depending on circumstances, in either strengthening or reducing the power of each leader internally. We also saw that the environment was central to each of the phases into which leadership is to be decomposed: diagnosis means surveying the environment; determining a course of action means taking into account the environment and the instruments that the leader has at his or her disposal; and mobilizing the population consists in knowing what the configuration of forces is in a specific context and in being able to understand how these forces are likely to operate if they are pushed in a particular direction.

It is because the influence of the environment is so vast that it has been argued that leadership does not really count and is merely an epiphenomenon. The environment structures the situation with which the leader has to cope and from which s/he cannot escape; the means at the disposal of the leader also structure the response and the implementation process; finally, the leader, by being part of the environment, is socialized in such a way as not to be able to distinguish himself or herself from the environment: s/he breathes a certain 'air' and this makes the leader continuously dependent on what the environment proposes, suggests, even dictates.

Presented in this general way, the case against the real importance of leaders is difficult to combat successfully; and, to the extent that the 'falsification' of historical events is impossible, the supporters of the 'leaders-do-not-matter' thesis appear to have an unanswerable case, but one as unanswerable as the case of those who felt that the arrow could not reach its target, or who felt that the hare would never overtake the tortoise. The prima facie case for analysing and discussing the role of leaders must rest on a combination of intuitive standpoints and gradually improved empirical tests; these tests, in turn, require the development of a comparative framework, a framework that is still largely undetermined. Since it is generally believed that leaders do matter, whatever the weight of the environment, it is reasonable to explore the problem further; since the only tools at our disposal are somewhat blunt or rough, there is no alternative but to try and sharpen them while also examining closely what these tools, so far, help us to discover.

Yet the environment does matter, and it matters markedly. If we are to assess realistically the relative importance of leaders, and, to begin with, if we are to see whether someone is a 'mere' office-holder or a 'real' leader, we must do so after taking into account the magnitude of the problem with which the leader was faced. The leadership that Churchill exercised in 1940 was not of the same nature as that which he exercised in 1951 when he returned to power, or that which Mrs Thatcher exercised in the 1980s, as the situation was different in each of these cases.

Strangely, perhaps, it seems easier to compare leaders when there are relatively small differences in the situations they face. Indeed, 'ordinary' discussions about leaders often concentrate on these small differences; one is often tempted to do the same in the scholarly literature. But it is more urgent and more important to compare leaders who exercise 'their' power in vastly different environments — for instance Third World leaders with communist or Western leaders, war leaders with leaders in peacetime — as these differences are more revealing about leadership and its role. In this respect, judgements have so far been rapid and vague. This may be inevitable given the present state of development of political leadership studies; this is therefore probably where the bulk of the effort should take place.

The conceptualization of political leadership thus entails an attempt at characterizing more accurately the situation that leaders are confronted with or, perhaps more accurately, are a part of. This aspect of leadership has so far been little studied, in part because it poses difficult methodological problems, but also because it may seem paradoxical that the study of the environment should be one of the main routes by which to come to assess the real strength of leaders. Of course, one should not ignore the personal characteristics of leadership. We are far from having obtained a satisfactory level of knowledge of these characteristics; efforts in this direction are therefore badly needed. But the analysis and classification of the types of situations with which leaders are confronted are at least equally urgent tasks. By and large, those who have studied the environment have done so in order to demonstrate that leaders count little or are interchangeable. Those who wish to show, on the contrary, that leaders are important are therefore apt to concentrate primarily on the study of psychological characteristics. The danger, then, is that the same phenomena will be examined on two different planes of analysis and that no satisfactory resolution of the argument will result. By improving the means of comparing different environments, on the other hand, it will become possible to assess the relative contributions of leaders, not merely in particular cases, but in general.

The strength of the argument that leaders do not matter results fundamentally from the fact that, as long as means are not found to classify situations, the insuperable hurdle of historical 'falsification' makes any conclusion suspect: by improving the means of comparing different environments, by elaborating classifications or typologies of situations, it will become possible to determine more accurately the extent of the contribution of leaders, as the sculpture gradually emerges from the block of marble under the hammer of the artist.

The unwarranted dichotomy between 'heroes' and 'mere' office-holders

The prevailing dichotomy in the analysis of the impact of leadership

Such is the background that has to be adopted if the study of leadership is to advance; it suggests that leaders are of many kinds and should therefore be categorized with care and on the basis of many variables. Yet it has been common, to the extent that there are indeed classifications, to divide leaders into two broad groups, from the point of view of their impact on society: (1) the 'real' leaders, the 'heroes' (or 'villains'), and (2) the 'office-holders', the 'managers', the ordinary men and women who have little or no effect on the course of events.

This dichotomy prevails in the literature on leadership. It is so diffuse and so latent that it is not seriously challenged. From Plutarch to the present day, it has apparently been accepted that there are 'heroes', 'illustrious men' (or, alternatively, 'great villains'), who shaped the course of history; and throughout the centuries it has also been assumed that there was very little to be said for or about the great majority of leaders, who remained largely anonymous and are at most, occasionally, the subject of ephemeral biographies or autobiographies.

The distinction is so widely and so unconsciously adopted that few have attempted to examine the basis of, and to give grounds for, the dichotomy. R.C. Tucker, for instance, seems to accept as a given the point that leaders are either 'real' leaders or managers (1981: 16). It seems to be assumed that only leaders, in the sense that Tucker gives the word, exercise the functions of diagnosis, action-preparation and mobilization that were outlined earlier. This seems strange, since it is manifest that at least the first two of these activities have to be fulfilled by managers in relation to any decision they take and the third, mobilization, also has to be fulfilled by managers, albeit perhaps in a less grandiose manner, if these managers wish to see their decisions implemented.

J. McGregor Burns is the contemporary writer on leadership who has most consciously attempted to give a theoretical basis for the dichotomy (Burns, 1978: Parts III and IV). His book on leadership is devoted to the successive analysis of what he considers to be two types: *transforming* and *transactional* leadership. It is not altogether clear whether there is a further, residual, category (the 'mere' power-holders); given that he does not discuss this group, however, it must be assumed that all the leaders, in his opinion, are either 'transforming' or 'transactional'. As a matter of fact, even if he were to view leadership as divided into three rather than two types, the main difficulty of the approach would scarcely be diminished.

The essential value of Burns's distinction is that a ground is given for the division. One group of leaders, the 'transforming' group, having a vision of the society, sets about doing something to implement that vision; the 'transactional' leaders, on the contrary, merely operate trade-offs or exchange one advantage for another. They act in the here-and-now and focus on details, without any global perspective as to how society should be ultimately. This distinction is manifestly important; it seems to correspond to differences which we feel intuitively exist among leaders and which seem to be borne out by the evidence drawn from biographical material: Lenin or Franklin D. Roosevelt each had a vision of the society he wanted to promote; Harold Wilson, on the contrary, except during a short period preceding the time of his first election as UK prime minister in 1964, seemed to live from day to day; his time-horizon was short in the extreme. Admittedly, the distinction did not originate entirely from Burns: Pareto's division of leaders into lions and foxes (Pareto, 1963) — which Burns had used, indeed, in his 1963 study of Franklin D. Roosevelt — had similar connotations. But Burns is more systematic in the examination of the characteristics and consequences as he looks at the various groups in society in which one or the other type of leader emerges.

Burns also relates (as Pareto had done earlier) the transforming or transactional character of the leadership to the situation in which the leaders find themselves. There are long developments in his work describing the various institutional and behavioural characteristics that will result in one or the other of the two forms of leadership. Leadership arising out of party political activity, in normal circumstances at least, will be transactional; leadership arising out of revolutions, on the contrary, will have a transforming character.[6] Although Burns stops short of elaborating a tight scheme which would provide a universal and necessary relationship between environmental situations and one or the other type of leadership, there are clear indications that there is at least a definite propensity for certain situations to result in transforming or transactional leadership.

Thus, Burns's analysis constitutes a significant advance over a mere distinction between 'real' leaders and 'others'; but it is a limited advance only, inasmuch as it seems clear that the reality is markedly richer and cannot be comfortably compartmentalized into these two categories. Nor, for that matter, would a trichotomy be very helpful. Among the trichotomies that have sometimes been elaborated, that of Weber seems to 'stick' even less closely to the reality than Burns's analysis. In fact, Weber consciously refers to ideal-types, rather than to categories of existing leaders.[7] It might be argued, admittedly, that Burns's 'transforming' leadership bears many similarities to the characteristics of leaders in a charismatic context, while bureaucratic authority may be felt to give rise naturally to transactional leaders, the case of the traditional leaders remaining uncovered, perhaps because Burns sees little cause for giving much emphasis to this group in the contemporary world. While Weber's analysis deserves closer examination (and has of course given rise to much exegesis), in part because of the ambiguity attached to the concept of charisma, Burns's presentation is a more determined attempt than Weber's at developing a model that will result in categorizing leaders; but his attempt remains unsatisfactory because it does not break away from the straitjacket of the dichotomy.

Why the dichotomy has prevailed

Why has Burns, together with other political scientists, continued to adopt a dichotomous approach to leadership, while the diversity of leaders in both the 'heroic' and the 'ordinary' groups is glaring? It seems obvious that Napoleon's leadership differed from that of Hitler, and Lenin's from that of Franklin D. Roosevelt. It seems equally obvious that not all the 'transactional' leaders belong to the same group: should J.F. Kennedy or Harold Macmillan, Brezhnev or Gomulka, be placed alongside the ephemeral prime ministers of Greece, France or Egypt of the late 1940s and early 1950s?

Part of the answer seems to relate to a widespread practice in political science, in which there appears to be a penchant for dichotomies or trichotomies. For generations, political scientists have distinguished between liberal and authoritarian states, democracies and autocracies, centralized and decentralized countries. Only gradually, and indeed recently, has there been a trend to substitute dimensions for these sharp divisions. The simple distinctions die hard partly out of habit, regimes having been classified and described in this manner for very long periods; they correspond to a language that has become familiar both in the scholarly community and beyond; they have also resulted in part from the influence of law, which naturally divides situations into two, three or at most a few categories. But, while constitutional law creates the classifications, as in the case of the opposition between presidential and parliamentary systems, political science has to monitor and analyse characteristics occurring in the world. It should not therefore import methods from a prescriptive discipline such as law and hope that they will be satisfactory in an empirical context.

The maintenance of dichotomous distinctions in the field of leadership studies does not stem merely from general traditions in political science, however; it also results from broader considerations, including normative standpoints. For it is not only in political science that the simple division of leaders into 'heroes' and 'mere' office-holders has occurred; it has also been commonly used in history. As B. Mazlich points out,

> The first thing to be said [about the way historians deal with leadership in their work] is that historians have always been attracted to the 'great men in

history' theory. Biography is a major adjunct of history, as is the 'cult of personality'. What I am calling traditional history, generally devoid of causal analysis other than the account itself, frequently 'explained' a whole period or a major event in terms of some leading personality. (Mazlich, 1984: 1-2)

These 'great men' have been very 'good' or 'villains', but the stress was on their major impact.

Thus, political science was confronted with a tradition that gave leaders a commanding position in the explanation of events; as historians (traditional ones at least) were typically concerned only with the period they studied and with 'explanatory' factors of the events of that period, there was no comparative dimension that might have led to an effort to rank these leaders. There was normally a gallery of portraits, examined successively, discretely, and in such a detailed manner that there was little or no possibility to grasp the material in a comprehensive manner.

The approach was of course shaken by the 'leaders-do-not-matter' school. Sociologists, but also some historians — social and economic historians in particular — came to reject leaders. As Mazlich (1984: 2) points out, 'the mass, not the leader, is the new hero'; but although, as he further states, 'even social historians are in the ironic position of discovering that masses are not leaderless' (1984: 2-3), the chasm between the two schools was too great for an accommodation to occur, at least for long periods. This resulted in a stalemate, a cold war between the two approaches, and perpetuated the distinction.

The acceptance of a few great leaders on the one hand and of a mass of 'ordinary' leaders on the other was indeed comfortable for scholars in both schools. No one seems prepared to deny the influence of very great leaders, not even the Marxists, who of course are somewhat embarrassed by the fact that at least Lenin and Mao, and possibly other communist leaders also, have to be placed in the category of superior leadership, as well as by the fact that, in the Soviet Union and in other communist states, the phraseology places immense emphasis on the part played by some leaders. More generally, it seems so difficult to undermine totally the role of great leaders, who appear as immense Moore-like statues in the landscape of politics, that it seems practically easier to drill into the material that makes up the 'gnomes' who more commonly run our affairs. Thus, as a modus vivendi, social and political scientists usually have simply concentrated on situations in which countries were ruled by lesser heads of governments and ministers; and, as only a small minority would be so daring as to challenge the general thesis of the large part played by 'underlying forces', for which there is indeed a great weight of admittedly partial evidence and which is supported by a large body of theoretical literature, analyses have proceeded without a real confrontation having fully taken place.

Moreover, the relatively peaceful coexistence between the two interpretations can be regarded as being maintained at least in part by theoretical argument, and especially by Weber's tripartite model of authority. By distinguishing sharply between two types of situations where traditional or bureaucratic rulers prevail and a third, where the personalized authority of charismatic leaders obtains, Weber goes a long way towards justifying the view that the two interpretations can be simultaneously adopted. For in Weber's analysis, only leaders endowed with charisma have the opportunity to make a truly large personal mark on the political and social system; but this mark is very large indeed (see Chapter 2). In other situations, the structures of the society, be they political, social, economic or a combination of all three, are the real elements sustaining the system. Although Weber himself notes the part played by leaders outside the charismatic context, he certainly allows social scientists to view societies in which traditional or bureaucratic authority prevails as being controlled primarily by the 'underlying forces', while stressing that this cannot be the case when charismatic rule obtains.

Weber does help to give a theoretical basis to the sharp dichotomy between two types of leadership since he describes the conditions under which charisma may occur. These conditions are effectively summarized in one broad characteristic: the break-up of the structures that used to tie together the members of the population and the consequential need for the emergence of a new set of social and political relations. Thus, the idea of a dichotomy becomes grounded in a general model of the relationship between leadership and social and political life: when the conditions are 'normal', ordinary (i.e., not personalized) leadership obtains, but when there is a social chasm, the weaving together of the society again depends on personalized leaders. Strong leadership can therefore have a place without it being untenable to adopt the view that, in normal situations, leaders may matter little.

Thus, the distinction between 'heroes' and 'ordinary' leaders is not merely the result of an oversimplification: it runs deep in the traditions of social science and of political science in particular. It is precisely because it runs so deep that it has played a significant part in making a more empirically based and more systematic analysis of the characteristics of leadership difficult to undertake. What has to be done therefore is to turn away from the very idea of a dichotomy and, by recognizing that the reality is vastly more complex, slowly to elaborate models and develop methodological techniques that will make it possible to grasp more realistically the contours of leadership.

The need to study variations in leadership on the
basis of dimensions

Political leadership consists of actions designed to modify the environment. Its specific character depends, as I noted in the Introduction, on the combination of three aspects: the personal characteristics of the leaders, the instruments they have at their disposal, and the situations they face. It is manifest that all three aspects have to be defined broadly. The personal characteristics of leaders include not merely the 'personality' of these leaders, but the sum of the elements that 'describe' the leaders at a particular moment. They include 'personality' elements, to be sure, and in particular energy, drive and the ability to grasp problems quickly; but they include also other aspects, which may usually be defined as 'sociological': studies of voters, for instance, include both 'sociological' and 'psychological' characteristics. Thus the examination of the social background and of the careers of leaders is an important aspect of the 'personal' elements of leadership.

The instruments that leaders use must also be defined broadly. They include groups, parties, the bureaucracy, courts and legislatures, all of which may help or hinder the actions of leaders; also the media, which may enable leaders to have a more or less direct relationship with the population. The level of institutionalization (that is to say, the extent to which institutions are truly 'alive'), the degree of centralization or decentralization of the system and the loyalty of the members of these bodies are among the characteristics that are essential if one is to differentiate realistically among the means that are at the disposal of leaders.

Instruments are part of the environment; they are to a large extent 'givens'. But they can also be organized by the leaders or moulded by them. They can at least be used in a manner that leaders may think more appropriate to the furtherance of their aims. In the strict sense, therefore, the environment covers the set of problems with which leaders are confronted and which they wish to solve (or at least begin to solve). These problems may be vast or limited; they may be concerned with the transformation of the society or may relate to the improvement of the welfare of a small section; they may affect the very existence of the nation; equally importantly, they may relate to 'objective' conditions or to the 'mood' of the population — for instance, if there is a high degree of discontent or if the level of integration is low. Thus, the leader is confronted with a state of affairs that may be 'calm' or, when there is a crisis, with a crisis that may vary in intensity or immediacy. The types of cases are thus very numerous and cover an extremely wide range.

Even a rapid presentation of personal characteristics, instruments and situations thus suggests that the nature of political leadership is not only complex, but cannot realistically be grasped on the basis of simple distinctions and in particular on the basis of dichotomies or trichotomies. There are manifestly many types — perhaps an infinite number of types — of personal characteristics, instruments and situations. It follows that a rigorous analysis of leadership entails a recognition that dimensions have to be discovered on the basis of which it will be possible to draw comparisons that will give an accurate picture of the reality.

Political behaviour rarely, if ever, has a dichotomous character. In many cases an approach based on a dichotomy, after having had a heuristic value for a period of time, has the effect of stultifying or straitjacketing the analysis. This has been particularly true in the field of political leadership, not merely because personality types and background patterns are obviously numerous — even if no satisfactory classification has so far been achieved in this area — but perhaps even more because the determination of the diversity of the effects of leadership depends on a comparative assessment of the situations with which leaders have to cope. In order to know what rulers really achieve — whether they are effective or merely 'float' above the surface of events — we need to know what value to give to the 'denominator' of the equation, that is to say, to the type of situation with which the leaders are grappling. By describing the situations in a comprehensive manner, and specifically by analysing these situations in the framework of a number of dimensions, it will be possible to enrich the understanding of leadership and to obtain a subtler appreciation of the contributions of leaders.

Towards a general classification of political leadership
How, then, can we start to classify political leadership, and what aspects of leadership should we primarily take into consideration in the elaboration of the classification? Past studies offer limited guidance. The scheme of analysis must be general in order to cover all types of political leadership, but it must also be detailed in order to provide a basis for precise distinctions among political leaders. What criteria can be found that will make it possible to discover dimensions that are universally applicable?

The impact of leaders as the principal ground for classification
A preliminary step has to be taken before these dimensions are discovered. One cannot merely classify political leaders according to one, two or more dimensions unless one knows the 'problems' of leadership that these dimensions are expected to cover. These 'problems' are many; here I shall give only three examples. J.

McGregor Burns opposes 'transformational' leadership to 'transactional' leadership.[8] This is only a dichotomy, but it corresponds to an important distinction, namely, that between leaders who do 'great things' and those who effect compromises among groups and achieve results by combination rather than by new leaps. This is a distinction that refers therefore to the goals and policies of leaders. J.D. Barber, on the other hand, classifies leaders from a different standpoint: he divides them into 'active — positive', 'active — negative', 'passive — positive' and 'passive — negative' on the basis of their 'character'; the aim is to discover the differences in the personality types, not in the policies or the impact (Barber, 1977). There is, of course, a relationship between 'character' and goals, but the two problems are different. Meanwhile, R.H. Jackson and C.G. Rosberg, in their study of *Personal Rule in Black Africa* (1981), classify leaders into four types which are designated as 'princes', 'autocrats', 'prophets' and 'tyrants': the aim here is neither to describe 'character' nor to distinguish among policies or goals, but rather to present a number of 'regimes' of a personal type in which a number of 'styles' emerge and as a result of which leaders control the population and maintain themselves in office. Here too, of course, there are relationships to be established with other approaches: 'character' plays a part and policy goals are not unconnected with the regime styles that are described. But the specific purpose of the enquiry is different.

There are therefore different bases for the categorization and comparison of leaders; yet, at the same time, these different bases need to be related to each other by means of an overall conceptual framework, which will also help to include certain types of analyses and exclude others. For we are not interested in finding out *everything* about leaders; we do not want to know, for instance, about pastimes and hobbies, unless they are related to or have an influence on leaders' *political* activities. Similarly, we wish to know about the personality of these leaders, or indeed even about the character of the regime, if we sense that these aspects have an effect on the way in which the affairs of the state have been run. This is to say that the analysis of leadership is justified from a political point of view only to the extent that it is assumed that the leaders have an effect on the developments of the society. Were leaders to have no effect — were we to accept in full the leaders-do-not-matter thesis — the study of political leadership would have no justification. It is only because they have (or at least are presumed to have) some effect that leaders deserve to be examined; and, in turn, it is only to the extent that certain aspects of political leadership help to account for this effect that they deserve to be examined, at least in the context of a political enquiry.

A general classification of political leadership must thus start from the effect that leaders have (or may have) on their society. This is the cornerstone of the enquiry. Of course, the aim is to see whether this impact is due to some characteristics of leaders — personal characteristics, for instance — or to certain powers, normally institutional, that they hold. We want to know the *sources* of their impact. But it is the impact, as a dependent variable, that justifies our examination of the independent variables that personality and institutional instruments constitute. Thus, it is fair to state that the general framework that we were looking for is provided by the goal of the analysis — the analysis of the impact of leaders on society. This is why we must first examine what the impact may be; this is why, in this book, after having assessed in broad terms the role of political leaders and the changes in the perception of this role, I shall devote Chapter 3 to the elaboration of a general classification designed to determine, and if possible to measure, the impact of leaders.

The role of personal elements and of institutional structure
in the analysis of political leadership
The other aspects of political leadership will be investigated to the extent that they affect — or may affect — the impact of leaders on society. On the surface, it seems that these aspects constitute a discrete and almost infinite number. In his 1972 work, G.D. Paige lists several elements when he defines political leadership as consisting 'in the interaction of personality, role, organisation, task, values, and setting...' (Paige 1972: 69). The list is already long; it could even be longer; and there is no means of knowing whether it is exhaustive. If one examines these aspects, however, one finds that they come under two broad categories, personal attributes and 'regime' attributes, with the environment constituting a third, but differently related, set of variables. It is also clear that these characteristics relate to *political* leadership in that they help to account for the 'dependent' variable, that is to say, the impact that leaders make. Personality, for instance, is an important factor; but this factor acquires significance and meaning only because the leaders' goals and policy initiatives are felt to make a difference. Thus, the study of personality is important for the political analysis of leadership, not because personality is important in itself for such an analysis, but because personality appears to have (or is commonly believed to have) an impact on the goals and the policy initiatives of leaders. We are not, at any rate as political scientists, interested per se in the question of whether a given leader is 'active–positive', to use Barber's terminology: we are interested in whether the fact that a leader is 'active–positive'

accounts in part for the fact that this leader will engage in certain policies and will pursue them with greater or less zeal.

What has just been remarked about personality also applies to other aspects of political leadership. Paige, for instance, refers to 'role' and 'organization' as relevant elements in a comprehensive definition of leadership; indeed, both have traditionally been regarded as essential. In political analysis, 'role' and 'organization' are usually described in terms of 'regimes', which both 'organize' the leadership and specify the 'roles' to be played by the leaders. Thus, a parliamentary or cabinet system endows the prime minister with different powers and introduces different constraints from those with which a president is endowed in a separation-of-powers system. Leaders in absolutist systems have yet different powers and operate under different constraints; as Jackson and Rosberg (1981: 77 ff.) point out, one can distinguish a number of sub-categories among absolutist systems.

Here too, however, the reason why these different regimes are worth studying from a political point of view is because we believe (and there is apparent support for this belief) that consequences will follow for the goals and policy initiatives pursued by leaders. For instance, the 'regime' will set up institutional or procedural arrangements which will organize accession to power and duration in office in such a way that leaders endowed with certain types of goals are more likely to emerge than leaders with other goals, or that it will be easier or more difficult to carry out certain policy initiatives; moreover, the opposition will be more or less constrained in its means of preventing the leader from carrying out his or her wishes. Were it not for the fact that these institutional arrangements have some impact on goals and policy initiatives, they would not be studied, since they would not be felt to be significant. Indeed, it was because, in the 1960s and 1970s, many political scientists believed that the effect of institutions was rather limited that these tended to be less studied. This view was almost certainly mistaken, in that it was at least exaggerated; but, mistaken or not, it indicated that the institutional framework, like the personality characteristics, is worthy of investigation only if it is related to the impact of leaders.

The special position of the environment
The environment has a different impact. Its effect is not so much to account for policies, as an independent variable; it is more to introduce constraints and provide opportunities. It prevents some leaders from promoting policies that they might have wished to promote and which others may be able to promote elsewhere: the president of the Swiss Federal Council is unlikely to be able to embark on a vast operation of foreign policy; the president of a poor Third

World country is unlikely to be able to carry out large programmes of industrial development. There are thus structural constraints which stem, for instance, from the physical size or the economic base of the country; there are also temporary constraints which result from the specific conditions in which a nation finds itself at a particular moment. The pessimistic mood of the population, or the climate of crisis that may prevail as a result of internal or external difficulties, also constitute constraints on scope of activities of leaders: these are obliged to act in a particular direction and to concentrate on certain problems which may be more temporary in character than those they originally wanted to promote.

Conversely, the environment provides opportunities that are also structural or temporary. Leaders may be given a chance — including that resulting from a crisis — and they may be able to launch initiatives and to push forward some goals that might not be acceptable in other situations or when structural conditions are different. Some leaders are better able than others to make use of the opportunities the environment gives them; but these opportunities vary and enable some leaders to pursue policies that would not 'normally' be felt 'realistic'.

Thus the environment is not an 'aspect' of the study of political leadership as are personalities and institutional arrangements (though these are also part of the environment and thus partake, to some extent at least, of the same characteristics as the environment). While personality and institutional arrangements affect the character of leadership itself, the environment is the substance, the raw material, and also the framework for the goals and policy initiatives; it is, to use another image, the chessboard on which leaders play and have to play. Policy initiatives constitute the central basis for the classification of political leadership; but they are shaped, coloured and developed as a result of the type of environment, permanent or temporary, that confronts the leaders. Thus, while a classification of leadership should be essentially based on the categorization of these leaders' actions, a second and necessary step has to be the examination of the ways in which the environment modifies the dynamics of the actions of leaders and indeed sets the boundaries between what is possible and what is precluded.

Leadership and imposition

One problem remains, however: leadership is often viewed as the opposite of coercion; it is conceived as an ability to induce, rather than as a force compelling others to act in a certain way. The distinction is analytically valid, but the reality is more complex: in fact, there are subtle gradations between gentle pressure and full imposition. In this book we shall be concerned with leadership, rather than imposition. But it is worth remembering that leaders cannot be divided into those who rule through coercion and those who rule by consent: there is an infinity of steps between the two poles. On the one hand, there is imposition in every regime: some citizens disagree with some policies; some even disagree with the principles on which the policy is based. On the other hand, amounts of imposition vary markedly even among authoritarian states. It is difficult to be precise about these, however, as the measurement of coercion is imprecise, partly because it usually has to be done indirectly, since leaders of repressive regimes typically are not anxious to allow their citizens to express their views openly. One has therefore to rely on unsatisfactory indicators, and in particular on activities that are either the instruments or the consequences of coercion, rather than on the root cause: namely, the distance between the citizens and the leaders. One thus examines how far opposition is tolerated or harassed, how many political prisoners exist, whether citizens are allowed to travel abroad, and the extent to which demonstrations, riots and other disturbances occur in the country. Not only do these indicators not provide a direct measure of imposition, but they give a partial, even distorted, view of the phenomenon. Open disturbances may be a sign not of great coercion, but of relative tolerance. In any case, proportions of opponents are difficult to gauge in authoritarian regimes, especially since passivity is usually more widespread than outright dissent.

Thus, imposition is manifestly a badly known, and an even more badly measured, characteristic. What is clear is that it is both commonplace and rarely as massive as is often believed. What does need to be explored are the conditions that make imposition necessary as well as the point beyond which it becomes ineffective. Without attempting here to examine these conditions in general, a number of broad trends can be outlined.

Why and how imposition can be achieved

There is, of course, little need for imposition if the actions of leaders coincide with the desires of the population. Conversely, imposition *is* required if the actions of the leaders are at great variance from what the citizens want. A society in which there is much demand or need for change will be ruled by a conservative only with the help of substantial coercion; coercion will also have to be harsh if substantial change is pressed by a leader on a society in which there is basic contentment with the status quo. In between, when leaders' actions aim at a moderate extent of change, there will probably generally be less need for substantial coercion. Thus, the potential for strong imposition corresponds only to some types of situations; they are mainly those when leaders and population are at variance over major policy initiatives which leaders want to press for and to implement rapidly.

The need for imposition does vary markedly, however, as a result of three types of characteristics of society as a whole. First, coercion may remain light as long as the population is unclear about what the leaders are attempting to achieve. This often happens, as the policies proposed by the leaders may not be clearly perceived by the citizens. Indeed, the less clear the ideas of the population are about public policies, the less will leaders have to resort to imposition. Consequently, an ill-educated population, in a country where communications media are rudimentary, is less likely to have to be coerced into obeying.

The second reason why imposition may not need to be strong results from the isolation of the nation. Discontent tends to increase as a result of comparisons between life styles in the home country and life styles abroad. Where there is little knowledge of what takes place outside, pressure on the leadership will correspondingly be weaker; thus, rulers who wish to pursue policies that are at variance with those that might 'naturally' be accepted by the population will tend to prevent their citizens from being subjected to outside influences which might increase the discontent. This is true of conservative leaders, who might sense that the population would be even more anxious to see change occurring in the country if the borders were open, and of progressive leaders, who fear that their experiments may not appear successful or even valuable if the citizens could compare results with those of different policies pursued abroad. So long as leaders can credibly adopt a nationalistic line in closing their borders, and indeed in branding foreigners as potential enemies, isolation can be achieved without need for strong imposition; but even if feelings of nationalism diminish, leaders can stem the tide at least for a period by keeping their country as closed as possible.

Third, what is required of citizens is very rarely the active support of the policies of leaders: civil servants are obliged to display support, but most of the rest of the population is normally asked only to carry out its normal activities and merely to refrain from going beyond what is 'their own business'. Harsh imposition can thus be concentrated on those who have to implement the policies — and these people can be either threatened or lured into obeying. It is true that, the more modern a country is economically, the greater is the proportion of citizens who will be engaged in activities that stem directly from the leaders' actions; but it is also true that, at the end of the line of implementation, the distinction between active support of policies and ordinary activities becomes very blurred. Thus, many leaders can press on the nation certain goals without strong coercive measures affecting more than a relatively small proportion of the population.

The difficulties of imposition

The amount of imposition that is necessary for a leader to remain in power and to pursue policies to which the population may not agree can thus be relatively limited: the leaders' position will not be directly threatened, at least in many cases. In fact, what makes it difficult for leaders to persist in pursuing their policies results more often from the constraints stemming from the implementation of their policies than from the opposition of the population.

Probably the single most important factor is the physical inability of the leader to achieve the policies that he had set himself to pursue. This is indeed where revolutionary leaders typically face a more difficult task than conservatives; for revolutionaries want to change the society, but they cannot do so by pronouncements alone: they need economic results and socioeconomic transformation. Both are difficult to realize, and both have the effect of encroaching into the activities of citizens in such a way that the natural 'passivity' of the population, on which much imposition rests, comes to be shaken by the leaders' policies. Economic change cannot be obtained without major and costly undertakings: transformations in agriculture, industry and the social services require huge expenditures. They also require skilled manpower, which cannot be trained without further costs and over long periods. A major change in the economic and social basis of a nation tends to be beyond the capabilities of the country: the failure of the goals, as much as imposition per se, is likely to force leaders to abandon their aims and to cause discontent.

Some effects will also be felt because leaders may also want to change the values of the population in order to create a 'new man', or because economic achievements are felt to depend on the degree of 'mobilization' of workers. Leaders then can no longer rely on a passive lack of antagonism: they need active support, which may not be easily forthcoming. The dilemma of revolutionaries emerges at this point: so long as they can pursue their goals without markedly affecting the population, they can carry them out; but as they gradually realize that they need a mobilized citizenry or else face failure, they enter a cycle of activities that is likely to increase opposition rapidly and force through even harsher measures, which in turn further increase that opposition.

Meanwhile, it may not be possible for leaders to keep the country isolated. Outside pressures may occur because foreigners object to the goals, economic, social or cultural, that are being pursued; they may also occur because leaders need financial and manpower assistance to achieve the goals that they are pursuing. At this point, too, leaders are faced with a dilemma: the desire to keep the country closed may make it more difficult to realize the policies that are sought, but the need to obtain overseas aid will bring in its trail a series of consequences which will result in an increase of discontent arising from more comparisons being drawn with the outside world. Not surprisingly, revolutionary leaders zigzag between the two tactics, but some opening up of the polity is unavoidable: the regime then faces greater difficulties.

Thus, leaders find it difficult to impose their policies for very long periods, not so much because of a direct opposition of the population, but because of the consequences of their own policies. This is more likely to occur for revolutionaries than for conservatives, as the latter may not need as much active support in the population; but they, too, face problems: if the population wants changes to occur, costs have to be incurred to maintain the status quo, and these foster discontent, unless an exceptional bonanza, such as that provided by oil, enables leaders to bypass the citizens' purses altogether. The isolation of the country is also typically difficult to maintain. But there are enough examples of relatively longstanding — indeed, very longstanding — leaders who have opposed change and remained in office with the help of considerable imposition (Stroessner of Paraguay being perhaps the most obvious among a substantial number) for it to be unrealistic to claim that imposition inevitably leads to the collapse of coercive regimes.

Conclusion

Leadership is a complex concept which attempts to cover a complex reality: that of citizens prepared, to an extent at least, to follow a ruler in the direction s/he chooses. Not surprisingly, attempts have been made to simplify this concept, and in particular to distinguish sharply between cases in which 'true' leadership is exercised and cases in which it is not exercised at all — either because the ruler is too weak and is therefore fully dependent on the environment, or because he or she is so strong that followers are entirely coerced into achieving what they are ordered to do. The reality is different, because it is complex. There are many types and 'grades' of leadership, which need to be analysed in detail if one is to assess the contribution that leaders make to the society. A precise classification of leadership has to be undertaken, principally on the basis of the leaders' actions and the environment's response, as it is on the results of these actions and reactions that leaders have to be judged; although it is of course essential to understand how the personalities of rulers and the institutional arrangements from which these rulers benefit affect the overall outcome. We need therefore to turn to the examination of the actions of leaders; but in order to do so, we must first examine what part political leaders aim at playing, and are expected to be playing, in society. This means that we must analyse the role of political leadership as well as the changes that have affected this role.

Notes

1. The expression 'transforming leadership' is of Burns (1978: 141–254).

2. Lycurgus is often referred to as the prototype of the ideal statesman by the classical theorists. This is for instance the case with Montesquieu (*Spirit of Laws*, Book 4, Ch. 6) and Rousseau (*Social Contract*, Book 2, Ch. 7).

3. The position of President Mitterrand since the French election of 1986 has of course been markedly diminished, though it has remained stronger than under previous French republics.

4. But it is essential that a group should exist: leadership takes place within a group, however informal and even transient this group might be.

5. The views of leaders about leadership thus give leadership its character in a particular country or situation; hence the importance of the scope of leadership, to which we shall return at length in Chapter 3.

6. In his study *Leadership*, Burns (1978) opposes revolutionary leadership, which he considers to be transforming (pp. 201–40) to party leadership, which he considers to be transactional (pp. 308–43).

7. See Chapter 2 for a fuller discussion of Weber's ideal-types of leadership.

8. See above for a discussion of the two types of leadership that Burns opposes.

2

The role of political leadership past and present

Leadership is a recurrent topic of conversation among political observers. It is the subject of countless articles in newspapers and magazines; biographies and autobiographies of past and even current leaders appear to fascinate the public. But it does not, apparently, raise great interest among political scientists. A survey of over 2,500 articles that appeared in the *American Political Science Review* between 1906 and 1963, conducted by G.D. Paige (1977), showed that the words 'leader' and 'leadership' 'appeared in the titles only seventeen times' (p. 11). There has been some change in recent years, triggered among others by G.D. Paige himself, but leadership remains a Cinderella in political science. We know the background and views of electorates — indeed, of segments of electorates. We have now amassed this information over time; we can thus analyse changes in attitudes and voting patterns in great detail, and for many countries. But we do not know, in any systematic manner, who leaders are, where they come from or what they feel about a variety of problems; nor, indeed, do political scientists seem to want to know these characteristics: they do not appear to be markedly concerned with a rigorous examination of leaders' achievements.

This is clearly a strange state of affairs, so strange that it deserves examination in its own right. Why is it that, while leaders seem so powerful, or at least so pervasive, political scientists have neither collected information about them on a broad front nor decided to engage in theorizing about the subject? Is this a new development, resulting from a particular approach characterizing modern political science, or has it always been the case? To be sure, at least one famous classical political scientist, Machiavelli, was fascinated by leadership: but was he alone, or almost alone? On the surface, if one judges by the titles of the great works of the 'classics', leadership does not appear to have been the main focus of study. *The Republic, The Politics, The Leviathan, The Treatise on Civil Government, The Spirit of Laws, The Social Contract* — these are the key words: only *Leviathan* comes close to referring to leadership, although, of course, the book is not about leaders, or at least not primarily about them.

To a very large extent, the problem has to do with the changing role of political leadership. The classical theorists were unenthusiastic about leadership on the whole because they felt that most rulers acted improperly and encroached unduly on the affairs of citizens, though it tended to be recognized that leaders were often essential at the moment of the setting-up of a polity. Gradually, however, this view began to change. On the one hand, it became increasingly realized that leaders might have a crucial part to play when a major crisis affected society: this was in particular the view of Max Weber, whose contribution was, as a result, both considerable and somewhat limited. But it also became more widely recognized that leaders were essential not merely during crises, but at all times, in order to help 'development' and to preside over the progress of society, especially in the second half of the twentieth century, when the activities of the state markedly increased and indeed dominated social and economic life in many countries. Thus political science may have inherited a tradition of a limited role devoted to leadership, but, following the developments of the contemporary world, this tradition is being gradually superseded by a more positive approach.

The traditionally limited scope given to leadership in political science

So far, there have been relatively few studies of leadership in political science. The only aspect on which there is a large literature is the institutional study of national executives, and in particular of chief executives. Studies of the US presidency, of the British cabinet and, to a lesser extent, of similar organs in other countries are numerous.[1] Yet these studies have two types of limitations: they are normally country-specific or, at most, compare two or a few countries; and at least the traditional works in the field focus only to a limited extent on leaders and leadership as such, instead emphasizing the characteristics *surrounding* leadership. There is much discussion about powers, including limitations on these powers, and about relationships between the president, the prime minister and bodies such as legislatures or bureaucracies. But the aim is not to relate these institutions to the general phenomenon of leadership: it is to describe and at most compare these institutions. The emphasis was originally legalistic or constitutional: the advance consists only in considering more 'behaviourally' how the institutions work in practice.

Leadership has also been indirectly or obliquely studied in some other ways, and principally in three. Two of these approaches derive from sociology. First, elite studies have had a bearing on leadership, the characteristics of which have consequently come to be better known, although the field is still relatively underdeveloped. Since leaders (and potential leaders) belong to elite groups, the study of the background, careers and views of members of such groups and especially of political elites, has helped to circumscribe the milieu from which leaders of various countries tend to be drawn.[2] But these studies are still not sufficiently general to provide a clear picture:

we do not know, for instance, the composition of parliaments across the world in a systematic manner. In any case, the focus is on peripheral aspects of leadership, not on the phenomenon itself. The studies may point to some (likely) characteristics of leaders stemming from their origins; they do not help us to understand the activities of leaders, the moves that they make or the results that they achieve.

Sociology has contributed to the development of leadership studies in another way: it has helped to raise general questions about the nature of relationships at the top. One such question — admittedly, only indirectly related to leadership — is that of the 'inevitable' character of oligarchical structures within political parties. The late nineteenth- and early twentieth-century studies of Ostrogorski, Mosca and Michels had an echo in more recent analyses of decision-making within political parties, in particular in that of R.T. McKenzie (1955) on *British Political Parties*. But the main contribution of sociology to the analysis of leadership has been that of Max Weber, whose typology of authority and concept of charisma have been found to be particularly valuable for the understanding of leadership and indeed of political life in the Third World. (The specific contribution of the analysis of charisma is examined later in this chapter.) Some political scientists have been notably influenced by another discipline: psychology. One thus finds a number of biographies probing into the background and youth of leaders in order to account for why they succeeded — or failed — in their actions once they achieved national office. The best-known and probably most successful work in this vein is the study of A.L. and J.L. George on Woodrow Wilson, published in 1956. But the psychological approach had been pioneered before the second world war by H.D. Lasswell, whose *Psychopathology and Politics* was triggered by the development of modern dictatorships (Lasswell, 1960). Yet, while the field seemed promising when Lasswell opened it up, and while the work of the Georges was hailed as a model and a pathbreaker, followers have been few. Only a small number have attempted to relate psychology to politics in the leadership area despite the plea made by F.I. Greenstein (1969). J.D. Barber is probably the only political scientist who can be said to have attempted systematically to have a view of the *Presidential Character* (Barber, 1977). However promising the approach may have seemed to be, the achievements continue to be modest and the bandwagon never arrived.

Thus, the field of leadership has been little studied; since the 1970s, however, a change seems to have taken place and interest in leadership has begun to grow. Perhaps the greater realism in institutional analysis, as shown for instance by R. Neustadt's (1960) study of the US presidency, contributed to a growing emphasis on leadership as such. Although Neustadt found it difficult to go beyond rather general remarks on the characteristics of presidential leadership, J. McGregor Burns focused more specifically on the topic some years later — not surprisingly, since he was to be one of those who, in the 1970s and early 1980s, published the most substantial works so far on the subject (Burns 1973). The general studies of G.D. Paige (1972, 1977), the essay of R.C. Tucker (1981) and the efforts at systematic analysis of B. Kellerman (1984a) are perhaps the most important examples of the new interest in the field. They mark a conscious desire to look at leadership in a systematic manner, at a time when more numerous studies on charisma are fuelled by the desire to grasp better the nature of political life in the Third World.

A detour: the study of leadership outside political science
Despite this recent — and still rather limited — upsurge, the study of leadership is a minority pastime among political scientists; indeed, as we saw, much of the development seems to have been triggered by the impact of other disciplines, notably sociology and psychology. Curiously, perhaps, the influence of history has been relatively small, despite the fact that political scientists continuously raid history since they often have no other sources to draw their information from. But the phenomenon of leadership has played a rather peculiar part in historical studies. At one level, history is — or rather, traditionally, was — the study of great men; as B. Mazlich (1984: 2) puts it, 'Traditionally history . . . frequently "explained" a whole period or a major event in terms of some leading personality.' But this type of approach has in part been abandoned, and individual achievements have come to be gradually underplayed. More importantly, perhaps, the historians who concentrated on leaders have not on the whole been concerned systematically with leadership as a phenomenon. Great figures have been studied individually; they have been seen as representing moments in history and therefore as rooted in a particular situation. As Mazlich notes, 'Leadership in Tsarist Russia cum Soviet Union is obviously different from leadership in a representative democracy such as America' (1984: 3).

Some historians have attempted to generalize, admittedly, but those who have done so have been attracted by the study of social movements, leaving the study of individual leaders, either great or not so great, to the large mass of biographers who, on the contrary, by virtue of their own inclinations, were likely to focus on the specific characteristics of the men and women whom they studied. Thus, in the main, history provided a legacy of a large amount of descriptive material on masses of leaders and top politicians, but of material so geared to the uniqueness of those cases that it is difficult to use it as a basis for a study of leadership as such.

While history provided the material, but not the conceptual framework, for the study of leadership, the converse has been true of sociology. But these conceptual frameworks have tended to give a limited place to leadership. It is with Weber and Pareto that the concept occupies a central position. Most other sociologists, Marxist and non-Marxist alike, have given greater emphasis to structures. Moreover, as Pareto's analysis remained very abstract and Weber's classification too general to result in a precise categorization of types of leadership in various kinds of societies, the overall part played by sociology has been much greater in developing structural analyses than in helping to analyse the role of leadership. A discipline that had provided political science with an approach, a conceptual framework and even a typology seemed more recently to turn its back on the subject, as the survey of developments on leadership in the *International Encyclopaedia of the Social Sciences* indicates (Sills, 1968).

The contribution of social anthropology has perhaps been somewhat larger in recent years: the detailed descriptions of forms and powers of leaders in Africa and America give a complex picture in which leadership variations in primitive societies are substantial from one ethnic group to another. Anthropological studies have also provided a basis for a dynamic study of leadership out of which emerged general models of the likely relationship between type of leadership and type of society.[3]

Yet it is in the psychological field that the study of leadership has been conducted with the greatest rigour and determination, although even there progress has been limited, largely because problems of classification have not been overcome. Admittedly, as the brilliant survey of the field undertaken by C.A. Gibb in the *International Encyclopaedia of the Social Sciences* shows (Sills, 1968: 91–101), psychologists have undertaken many empirical studies. As we shall see in Chapter 5, the works of Gibb himself, and also of F.E. Fiedler, C.P. Hollander, R.M. Stogdill, B.M. Bass and M.G. Hermann, have helped our understanding of some of the key problems of leadership, and in particular the relationship between leaders and their environment; they have also begun to provide some elements of measurement of types of leadership.

There is still need for further progress in the field, largely because distinctions tend to be made among two or three types of leadership only. Moreover, psychological studies concentrate on leadership in small groups — not unnaturally perhaps, partly because experimentation is practicable only in this type of context, and partly in view of the traditional orientations of psychology. Consequently, these studies are not always very helpful for the analysis of the big, longstanding and also non-associational groups which are most prominent in political life. There even appears to be some wariness about future developments, as Gibb indicates in his survey when he wonders 'whether a more complete understanding of role will not supersede particular concern with leadership', despite the continuous flow of publications on the subject (in Sills, 1968: 94).

Whatever its limitations, the strong orientation towards studies of leadership in psychology is in sharp contrast with the more recent neglect of the subject in sociology and the lack of conceptualization of the problems posed by leadership in history; it is in even sharper contrast with the traditional 'peripherality' of the concept in political science. Political scientists even seem to display complete despair, as is indicated by the remark made by R.A. Dahl in an article on 'Power' published in Wildavsky's work, *The Presidency*: '[Political skill] is generally thought to be of critical importance in explaining differences in the power of different leaders... However, despite many attempts at analysis, from Machiavelli to the present day, political skill has remained among the more elusive aspects of power' (Wildavsky, 1969: 157) — not a very promising note, given that, despite the efforts of many and of R.A. Dahl in particular, the concept of power has remained elusive and its operationalization impossible. Is it the case, however, that the attempts at analysis have been 'many' among political scientists, whether before Machiavelli or after him?

The relatively limited interest in and the unease about leadership in classical political theory

The part played by leadership in classical political theory is peculiar and paradoxical. Of course, all political theorists mention leaders, give many examples of rulers in history, and analyse the way in which this rule has taken place in a variety of societies, in order to build a basis for the blueprint they wish to propose. But leadership is rarely central to the work; indeed, it seems as if it is never itself the object of study, except for Machiavelli — though even he, particularly in *The Prince* but also in The *Discourses*, conducted his analysis at the normative level of what a leader should try to achieve rather than at the analytical and empirical levels of the part played by leaders in the development of society.

Meanwhile, for Plato, Aristotle, Hobbes, Locke, Montesquieu and Rousseau, for instance, the central question is the organization of the good society (or at least, for a pessimist such as Hobbes, of the 'least bad' society). The examination of the defects, injustices and sheer failures of past and present societies is obviously one of the two reference points, the other being the presentation of the characteristics that the ideal society should have, if necessary through — and indeed, in most cases, on the basis of — an examination of human nature, of its limitations, and its automatic propensities when it is not guided by reason or principle. In order to redress ills, 'uplift curtains' or bring about at least some form of order, the solution proposed consists in elaborating institutional mechanisms which will ensure societal improvement. The aim is practical: the means are the structures. In this context, leadership as such plays a limited part; and, even if the part is occasionally expected to be large, attempts are not made to classify types of influence and types of leaders appropriate to various conditions.

Leaders and leadership are discussed in three main ways. First, past leaders are referred to, but usually in a negative manner. Often, in order to build a case for new institutions, classical political theorists stress the potential for despotism unless corrective mechanisms are introduced. Second, one type of leader is exalted: this is the wise man, the just, who rescues the country by giving it the guidance — constitution, laws — through which a good society will emerge. Such a leader is also temporary, returning to the privacy of ordinary life once he has accomplished the task he set for himself and which society needed. The archetype of this kind of leader is Rousseau's 'Legislator', who plays a crucial part in the process by which the polity comes to see where it should be going. He has a vision of what society needs — indeed, a better vision than the other members of the polity: such was Lycurgus of Sparta or Solon of Athens. So also were the leaders who, as the 'dictators' of ancient Rome, took power temporarily to solve a major crisis. But the classical theorists like to emphasize that such men, their task accomplished, leave the government. The best leaders — perhaps the only good ones — are thus those who view their task as that of a moment, although perhaps a major moment, in their country's history.

Third, with respect to the future, the classical theorists discuss rules rather than rulers and leadership. Typically, they wish to reorganize political institutions. Of course, leaders are expected to play a part in this context, but remarkably little is said about how they should behave in order to affect the development of the polity, Machiavelli being the outstanding exception. By and large, discussions are of powers, not of the type of rule to be exercised. The works of Locke and Montesquieu are specifically dedicated to this purpose. Rousseau displays more interest in the behavioural aspects of leadership, but only in a context that he does not support: that of the large nations which, according to him, fall inevitably under monarchical rule *(Social Contract,* Book 3, Ch. 1). Perhaps for this reason, he does not discuss various types of leadership among the monarchs of these larger nations, merely pointing to the unfortunate consequences in terms of large bureaucracies. Nor does Hobbes develop any model of types of leadership — surprisingly, perhaps, since his ideal (or least bad) blueprint is monarchical rule. Given that the monarch should rule, he offers only some advice — in ways not altogether different from those of Machiavelli — to suggest that rulers should not land themselves in situations in which the citizens might be drawn into rebellion, when pushed to this extremity by the sheer necessity of preserving their life (*Leviathan*, Part II, Chs 21, 30).

At first sight, admittedly, Plato seems to have a more elaborate notion of leadership, at least inasmuch as he really believes that any real-world society can be ruled by philosopher-kings. Yet even he does not expound a theory or present a model of types of 'good' leaders. He stresses the need for education — indeed, a lengthy education for potential or would-be leaders. But he does not state how philosopher-kings will behave, except that they will be perfect because they will follow justice; and he views leadership as a position or a state in which, after having been educated to see the light, rulers will be able to decide, to affirm, without any fear of sensible contradiction — rather like the Pope when he declares dogmas — what lines of conduct citizens should follow. Presumably the citizens, having also been educated during the same period and with the same guidelines, will follow the precepts (*Republic*, esp. Book 5 on Justice).

Thus, the bulk of the best-known classical political theorists do not have a model of leadership; at best, leaders are advised to show 'wisdom' in their actions. Machiavelli alone, in both *The Prince* and *The Discourses*, devoted the core of his analysis to the study of the way in which rulers should behave. Yet, precisely for the reason that leaders and leadership are the subject of his work, the analysis is conducted at a level that precludes any examination of what leaders are fundamentally about, that is to say, of the relationship between leaders and society. It is as if, by going to the opposite extreme, Machiavelli could not ask what leaders are for. The analysis is devoted to the elaboration of technical and tactical moves designed to ensure the success of rulers and, in the first instance, their maintenance in office. Leaders are not really viewed as contributing to the development of society in a particular way. The object of the study is almost the converse: namely, an analysis of the contribution of society to leaders. The environment is to be shaped by leaders, and Machiavelli suggests how this should be done. Not that rulers are viewed as able to fashion the environment at will: the extent to which they can change different environments does not interest Machiavelli as a general topic of enquiry. The question that is asked concerns the survival, or increased power, for a given leader who happens to be in office. To all intents and purposes, Machiavelli acts as an adviser of leaders, not as a detached observer of society. Perhaps his justification is that, at the time, the only sensible course was to try to achieve the best possible results with the leaders who existed: but this is not conducive to a general analysis of leadership, as we are not guided towards an understanding of what leadership truly is and of the forms and types of leadership that are most appropriate to a given task.

Why did political theorists, with the possible exception of Machiavelli, have such a limited concern for a detailed analysis of political leadership as a topic of enquiry, and why did their presentation of 'ideal' leadership, as in Plato or Hobbes, remain so simplified, so 'utopian', perhaps? If they had been truly concerned, they would have attempted systematically to assess how, when and under what conditions leaders are likely to be 'good' or 'bad'; they would have developed a model of right and wrong leadership, based on a thorough examination of the past, and such an examination would have no doubt resulted in the discovery of degrees and variations. This discovery did not occur; it did not occur because the classical theorists came to the subject with a different frame of mind.

The overriding factor is the pessimistic view that, without safeguards, leaders would be little concerned with the good of mankind: tyrants would proliferate, as the history of mankind seems to show. This pessimism was reinforced by the fact that many of the theorists had unsuccessfully tried to influence leaders. Machiavelli's political ambitions were frustrated; his personal liberty came to be at stake. Plato felt betrayed by the ruler of Syracuse in whom he had placed high hopes. Rousseau's work, too, reflects the fact that his dreams had proved unrealistic, both in France and in his native Geneva. This frustration was perhaps best summarized by Voltaire's bitter complaint against the King of Prussia who, having pressed the 'juice', felt no worries at dropping the 'orange'.

There has therefore been recurrent unease, among political theorists, about leaders: this unease has extended to leadership. Hence the desire to reduce the powers and the zones of influence of leaders, which only Hobbes does not share, because of his universal pessimism about human nature: for him, the best policy is to rely on the good sense of leaders — and on their fear of God — to obtain a result that is less unsatisfactory than might otherwise have been. Hence the emphasis on religion in the *Leviathan*, in which it plays a part not unlike that of education in Plato, creating within the leader himself the limitations to his or her innate malevolence or incompetence (*Leviathan*, Part 2, Ch. 31). Other classical theorists rely on more mundane constraints, generally provided by sets of institutions, procedures and arrangements that will simply make it impossible (at least in the opinion of the theorists) for rulers to overstep the boundaries of the reasonable. This is the message of Locke, of Montesquieu and of Rousseau (though education also plays a part for him), as it had been that of Aristotle. And Machiavelli himself, the most pessimistic of all perhaps, sees the advice he gives to rulers in terms of their own self-interest as also inducing these rulers to act a little better vis-à-vis their subjects. For the classical theorists, therefore, the one main question to be solved is the discovery of a realistic means of limiting the scope of rulers' actions; it is not essential to examine the potential role and effects of different types of leadership. One cannot rely on various personality characteristics to solve the problem, anymore than it would seem reasonable to explore whether various maniacs would be better suited to drive a motor car or pilot an aeroplane.

Thus, logically perhaps in this context, some theorists went even further and explored at least the possibility of organizing politics without rulers. These theorists are few, admittedly, as the pessimism — and 'realism' — of most political theorists extends to the whole of the citizens and is not confined to rulers, either because men's lives are felt to be innately 'nasty, brutish, and short' or because, as in Rousseau's case, only very small communities would ever be able to approximate the ideal situation of a world of angels in which all could govern. Thus, the Utopia of a wholly democratic, totally self-governing, polity has been dismissed by nearly all political theorists as being, indeed, a Utopia, with Marx perhaps the only one of the 'greats' to have come to believe that, if there were 'plenty', government could wither away. The Utopia of a polity without leaders and government is one that remains embedded in the feelings of many. 'If only it were possible' is a view that many classical political theorists shared. Thus, far from being a category of men whom they wished to study or improve, far from being a group that they felt was essential to mankind's development, leaders were viewed by classical political theorists as the object of a policy of 'containment' and, ideally, of 'rolling back'. The unease about leaders is thus truly at the centre of classical political theory; it had naturally considerable influence on modern political science.

The legacy concerning the unease about leadership in contemporary political science

The effect of the classical theorists' approach to leadership was widely felt throughout the nineteenth century. It is manifest in the prevailing idea that a 'government of laws, not of men' would be a government whose members would have less scope to influence events; but, as such a result could be obtained only by 'vigilance', it seemed logical to embark on the study of institutions and procedures rather than on the analysis of leaders. The events in America and France at the end of the eighteenth century seemed both to confirm the need and to show that the idea was, in part at least, realistic — in part only, since the coming to power of Napoleon demonstrated that ruthless leaders were able to break the constraints that institutions attempted to introduce. But nineteenth-century developments further seemed to indicate that it was indeed possible to contain leaders, by a patient effort and at the cost of many setbacks. Political science therefore embarked on a course in which the aim was to improve gradually the techniques by which limitations on rulers could be introduced, with the help and through the device, especially, of constitutional law. Political institutions would be the bodies that would realize these restraints, and the precise determination of the powers of these bodies would be the mechanism by which a tight grip would be kept on the Leviathan in general and on rulers in particular.

This tradition has lingered to the present day and has spread, of course, beyond political science to the broader public. The emergence of other political institutions beyond and around the constitutional arena — political parties in particular, and, to the extent that they engage in politics, interest groups, especially voluntary groups — created some problems for a while for those who held rigidly to a constitutional approach, but a broader view of the political system came to prevail. The result was that these 'informal' bodies came to be incorporated into a less narrowly constitutional, but yet fundamentally institutional, model of political life. This model, too, made it possible for leaders to be limited, even controlled, and at any rate somewhat accountable to the broader public. Although political science went through a behavioural phase in the 1960s, and although, as a result, the activities of political actors, including the people, came to be more closely monitored and were held to be essential to the understanding of politics, institutions have remained the stage on which, or the framework within which, political life is examined. Witness in particular the importance given to the institutionalization process in the analysis of developing countries. Part of the role of these institutions consists, in the eyes of political scientists, in constraining leaders and ensuring that, consequently, social life is more civilized and less arbitrary.

The unease about leadership thus continued to prevail within political science; it was indeed reinforced periodically, in the course of the twentieth century, by the occurrence of events that seemed to prove, beyond any shadow of doubt, that despotism and tyranny were always around the corner and could be avoided or limited only by continued vigilance. No sooner had the democracies won their victory in 1918 than new forms of dictatorship, based on a repressive personal rule, came to be installed. By the late 1930s it seemed that the progress that had slowly been made in the previous 150 years was completely wiped out, the single most important and most obvious factor being the overwhelming power of leaders.

Meanwhile, in the course of the previous several decades, and indeed since the early part of the nineteenth century, the growth of the other social sciences had led to a questioning of the importance of leaders. By gradual steps, economics and sociology, following views that were fashionable among philosophers and in particular among philosophers of history, had begun to stress the role of 'broad forces' which shaped the characteristics of society irrespective of the will of leaders. At the macro-level, the history of the world had come to be explained more and more in terms of successive stages of development; at a lower level, the analysis of the relationship between factors of production had helped to account for relationships that leaders and their governments could not control and, indeed, were merely 'embodying'. Thus Hegel, Ricardo, Comte and later Marx, among many others, had attempted to divest political leaders of their real decision-making capabilities and turn them increasingly into mere mouthpieces for the deeper developments that were transforming the social and economic fabric of the nations of the world. Whatever 'romantic' views some literary figures may have had about the role of Napoleon or other great 'heroes', the 'scientific' analysis of society seemed to suggest — and, indeed, in the eyes of some seemed to prove — that in reality leaders scarcely mattered and that they were replaceable or interchangeable: they were symbols of historical trends, not the engines of history.

Political science did receive some echoes from these themes; but the echoes were not all giving the same message. As we saw, the demise of political leadership from its traditional pedestal was not universally adopted in sociology: on the contrary, the general works of Weber and Pareto, as well as the more specialized studies of Michels or Mosca, emphasized, directly or indirectly, the apparently large role of elites and, within these, of rulers in both traditional and modern societies, though they stressed also that the role of leaders was related to the nature of the society and therefore could be viewed as constrained, as man is within the atmosphere, by the particular 'air' that different leaders breathed.

Although theories reducing the role of leaders to little significance could be viewed as fitting the 'unease' that they felt about leaders by enabling them to discard rulers or minimize their significance, political scientists, even the most behavioural contemporary political scientists, never adopted this approach. Perhaps this was in part because the 'leaders-do-not-matter' thesis, which some Marxist and non-Marxist sociologists had adopted, was extending beyond leaders and relating to the whole political arena, thus threatening in a fundamental sense the autonomy of political science. It was essentially because many sociologists considered that economic factors and their direct social consequences constituted the framework and introduced dynamics into society that they 'demystified' the role of leaders: but they also 'demystified' the role of all other political actors and of political institutions, which they judged to be superficial elements, mere epiphenomena, which could not provide 'real' explanations. Had political scientists adopted this standpoint, they would have been negating the profound significance of their own discipline. But the resistance they offered to the 'leaders-do-not-matter' view was not solely, or even primarily, due to the need to preserve the discipline or to a deep-seated tendency to give a major role to political phenomena. It was also, and more importantly, the consequence of the realistic examination of the world around them; it simply did not seem true to suggest that leaders did not matter in a context dominated by the deeds of Stalin or Hitler — or, indeed, by the actions of Roosevelt or Churchill. Leaders did seem to count, even if broad social and economic developments accounted in large part for the emergence of these leaders. Post-second-world-war developments seemed to confirm, indeed generalize, this characteristic, as 'personalized' leaders emerged in almost every new state, while in some of the older ones, both communist and non-communist, the phenomenon of leadership was glaring.

As a matter of fact, these developments were the continuation and the expansion of a movement by which leadership had transformed its character, slowly at first, and gradually more rapidly, in the course of the nineteenth and twentieth centuries. Two phenomena became increasingly apparent. One was that leadership was, or at least could be, a central element in the transformation of societies, and especially could provide the basis for the economic and social uplifting that newly independent states required; this meant that it was impossible not to look at leaders if one was concerned with development. The other phenomenon was that of 'personalization' or of 'charismatic' leadership, which seemed to play such a part in both the independence and post-independence periods. Political scientists had to become concerned with both these developments, which were indeed so intertwined as to appear to be part of a single problem. Fortunately, at least the phenomenon of charismatic leadership had been analysed by Max Weber, and it is Weber to whom we therefore need to turn before considering the extent to which, in the late twentieth century, leadership has markedly changed its character and acquired a new role.

Leaders and the crises of society: Weber's conception of charismatic authority and its limits

If an example was needed to show the spread of a social science concept among wide segments of the population, none could perhaps provide better evidence than charisma. Known almost exclusively to religious circles for nearly two thousand years because of references made in Saint Paul's writings, the word has come to be ordinary currency among journalists, politicians and the public at large: it has indeed been adopted beyond the confines of public affairs — in business or the media, for instance — to the extent that a dictionary states that it is 'often roughly equated with "sex appeal" and "glamour" '.[4]

The origin of this massive extension of the usage of 'charisma' is, of course, Max Weber. Contemporary political scientists and sociologists, D. Apter and S.P. Huntington among many others, have played a part in applying the concept widely to Third World countries, but they did so on the basis of, and by an extrapolation from, the writings of the German sociologist (Shils, 1968: 387). Thus, whatever limitations and difficulties may be found in Weber's typology, and whatever controversies may have arisen about the value or otherwise of extending the meaning given to 'charisma', the contribution of the German sociologist has been a major one: for it is he who first took the word out of the realm of religion and magic and placed it in the political field. This may have been misguided, as C.J. Friedrich (1961) seems to suggest; but, misguided or not, the move did occur, and it had the effect of opening up an approach to political leadership, and of introducing a social science concept which is clearly here to stay.

Granted that Weber's contribution has therefore been important historically, the problem today consists in assessing how far it is valuable to use not just the term 'charisma', but Weber's notion of the concept and the general classification of leadership of which charisma forms a part. In the words of a sympathetic commentator, R.C. Tucker, the question is 'to see if one can develop a theory of charisma into a more workable tool of understanding and research' (Tucker, 1968: 735). In order to achieve this goal, one might add, one needs to see whether Weber's scheme truly comprehends the various types and aspects of leadership that need to be covered if a systematic analysis of the phenomenon is to be undertaken on the basis of this model.

Weber's three types of authority

Max Weber's major contribution to the analysis of leadership relates to the discovery and elaboration of the concept of charisma. But the role of this concept in his scheme cannot be assessed fully unless we examine first the context in which, and the purpose for which, it was introduced into the social science vocabulary. The context is one of a tripartite classification in which charisma is one of three ideal-types, the other two being traditional and rational–legalistic rule: this, as we saw in the previous chapter, confirmed a tendency, widespread among social scientists, to divide leadership into a small number of types rather than on the basis of dimensions. Moreover, the purpose of Weber's classification is not specifically to describe and account for leadership: it is to determine the types of authority or legitimate rule that can exist in different societies. Many of the problems posed by the use of the Weberian scheme as a framework for the analysis of leadership stem from the constraints within which the concept of charisma has been developed.

An analysis of legitimate rule, not of leadership

Since Weber's purpose is to examine authority, and, in particular, the basis of authority, the characteristics of leadership and the behaviour of leaders are mentioned only to the extent that they contribute to an understanding of the emergence and development of legitimate authority. It is therefore not surprising that an all-embracing theory of leadership does not come out of Weber's work.

To begin with, Weber's analysis is concerned with legitimate rule only, not with just any kind of rule. For whatever reason, which need not be discussed here, coercion does not belong to his scheme. In the second place, even within the context of legitimate rule or authority, Weber is not concerned with the whole of the problems posed by leadership. In his elaboration of a conceptual framework for leadership, which was mentioned in the previous chapter, G.D. Paige lists six distinct components that need to be taken into account in analysing political leadership: these are personality, role, organization, task, values and setting (Paige, 1972: 69). Weber's typology addresses itself principally to the last of these matters, though it also covers indirectly, to some extent at least, the questions of role and organization, albeit in a very general manner. His is an effort to discuss the societal conditions under which various types of legitimate rule tend 'naturally' to occur — an important question, to be sure, but one that can be expected to cover only a part of the phenomenon of leadership.

The consequence is that Weber is not much concerned with the deeds of leaders and the impact of these deeds: he does not discuss whether, or under what circumstances, this impact may be large or small; and his model has little or nothing to say about such an impact. Nor is Weber much concerned with the specific way in which leaders achieve power, how long they rule or how they fall. Only to the extent that duration and fall may affect the legitimacy of the whole system are these problems examined — that is to say, in practice, only in the context of charismatic authority. His focus is on the bond between citizens and their rulers: where he believes that this bond is due essentially to societal characteristics and not to the rulers themselves, there is little or no reason for him to examine the origins, characteristics or role of leaders.

Thus, Weber's is a study of the environment of leadership. Consequently, his analysis — correct or not — can cover only a fraction of the phenomenon of leadership. Specifically, on the question of whether leaders 'make a difference', Weber's analysis can give only part of the answer, since the focus is exclusively on the origins of authority: there is no indication of the way in which leaders may modify this authority, except in the special context of charismatic rule. This makes the study of charismatic rule, in the Weberian scheme, particularly important for those who are concerned with the study of leadership; it is therefore essential to examine closely the nature of the special circumstances in which charismatic rule occurs.

Three ideal-types, two dimensions, or even 'one-and-a-half' dimensions?

Weber's main effort is to determine a relationship between types of social structure, in the broad sense, and types of 'leadership rule'. The answer is an ostensibly tripartite distinction which, also ostensibly, has the drawback of being based on clear-cut divisions and not lending itself to the determination of continuous dimensions. The rule can be traditional, rational–legalistic or charismatic. But this drawback is perhaps more apparent than real, as these 'ideal-types' might be converted into the polar ends of different continua: the scheme is not fundamentally altered if, instead of referring to traditional or rational–legalistic situations, one were to refer to societies that included both traditional and rational–legalistic components in varying proportions. The same would seem to be true, again ostensibly, for degrees of charismatic rule: it could be that a leader found himself drawing his authority from traditional forces and from his own charisma. Indeed, it does not seem inconceivable that a leader might partake from the three elements at the same time.

Thus Weber's scheme could be viewed as being based on a number of analytical components which, in the manner of the atoms that form a molecule, might be combined in varying degrees in concrete situations. The model seems more realistic as a result: many contemporary forms of rule have been characterized by a combination of two of the elements and, indeed, in some cases of all three. Some Western leaders appear to have had some charismatic pull while drawing much of their authority from 'rational–legalistic' structures; this has manifestly been the case of many communist rulers as well. Traditional rulers have often had some rational–legalistic support, while attempting, with varying degrees of success, to draw some charismatic support: the King of Morocco, the King of Jordan and the Shah of Iran are examples of the combination of all three elements. Thus the Weberian scheme could be diagrammatically presented in the form of a triangle, with individual leadership types located at various points within the triangle, depending on their proximity to and distance from each of the poles.

A substantial difficulty has to be overcome, however, if one wishes to turn these ideal-types into 'dimensions', as the scheme is asymmetrical. Two of the elements exclude leaders altogether: they determine a bond between citizens and society which is based purely on characteristics of the social structure. In both traditional and rational–legalistic rule (to the extent that the rule is purely traditional or rational–legalistic or, following the 're-elaboration' that we just proposed, to the extent that the rule is based on a mix of these two elements only), there is no place for the role of individual leaders. It is the institutional bond that supports the rule and, consequently, sustains the ability of leaders to claim obedience from the followers. On the other hand, in the charismatic context, leaders are the basis — indeed, the sole basis — of the link between the citizens and society. Thus Weber identified two poles — personal and societal, or personal and institutional — which help to categorize types of legitimate rule. In his presentation, these two poles are 'ideal-types'; but it would seem permissible, within the spirit of Weber's analysis, to view these ideal-types as extremes of dimensions and to imagine that there are intermediate cases. However, this is permissible only if charismatic authority is amenable to being 'watered down', if it is not so special or so self-contained that it has to remain within enclosed boundaries.

Let us assume that there is indeed a dimension ranging from a pure charismatic bond to a pure institutional bond: what is then the nature of the second dimension? To answer this question, one has to turn to the distinction that Weber makes between traditional and rational–legalistic rule. In both cases, the basis of support stems from the allegiance that the citizens have to the institutions, but this basis has a very different character as one moves from one ideal-type to the other.

In the context of traditional rule, the relationship between citizen and society rests on the 'natural' and automatic acceptance of a set of organizations and relationships that have been in existence from time immemorial. The citizens accept the system because it exists, because they have known no other, and because they 'feel' a part of it: the bond has an emotional or affective character. In the case of rational–legalistic rule, on the other hand, the link stems from the observation by the citizens that there are rules and arrangements that are regarded as being efficient and just. The citizens obey because the system appears to them to be correct. This is to say that the distinction parallels that made by F. Tonnies in the 1880s, when he contrasted the 'communal' basis to the 'associational' basis of groups in society (Tonnies, 1955). More deeply, the distinction corresponds to the division between 'affective' or 'emotional' linkages and instrumental or intellectual ties. In elaborating the two ideal-types of traditional and rational–legalistic rule, Weber thus refers to two distinct modes of relationship between followers and society, although, as was pointed out earlier, these two modes may be, and are indeed likely to be, mixed to a different extent in the situation of the specific allegiance of given citizens.

So far, therefore, we have discovered, on the one hand, a distinction between a 'personal' and an 'institutional' basis for authority and, on the other, a distinction between an 'emotional' and an 'intellectual' link between citizens and society in the context of the institutional basis of authority. We seem, therefore, on the way to transforming what appeared to be three ideal-types into a two-dimensional space. For this to be achieved, what would be needed would be to find, within the framework of the personal basis of authority, a distinction between an emotional and an intellectual link which would parallel the distinction that we found with respect to authority based on institutions. This is, however, where Weber's scheme is 'asymmetrical'. No distinction is made that would lead us to believe that the bond between citizens and leader can vary in character: it is always, so to speak, at the same end of the continuum. Thus we seem to have discovered not two dimensions, but two levels of distinctions: the first is that of the division between the institutional and the personal bond; the second, which relates to the institutional bond only, is between a form of allegiance that is emotional, as in a 'community', and a form of allegiance that is rational, as in an 'association'. The scheme does not lead to the determination of a true two-dimensional space.

Such a conclusion is uncomfortable, however. Before letting the matter rest, one needs to prod further and ask: is it impossible to construct a two-dimensional model on the basis of Weber's ideal-types, or did Weber not wish to do so (consciously or not) because of some other characteristic of the scheme that he elaborated? To answer this question, let us examine further the distinctions that have emerged from the analysis of Weber's model. A closer analysis quickly suggests that the distinctions between an institutional and a personal bond, on the one hand, and between a traditional and a rational–legalistic set of institutions, on the other, correspond to two complementary elements which enter into the definition of the bond itself. For the first opposition relates to the 'object' of the link between citizen and society while the second relates to the form or character that this link takes. In the first distinction, what is at stake is whether the citizen likes a person (the charismatic leader) or a set of arrangements (the institutions of the society); in the second, what is at stake is whether the citizen approves of the object (the institutions) on the basis of 'warm feelings', that is to say, emotions, or on the basis of some 'calculus', that is to say, an intellectual decision. Thus the distinction between the two aspects is a real one — indeed, one that needs to be made, if one is to explain fully the nature of the bond. There are therefore potentially two dimensions; in point of fact, the link between individual and society cannot be fully accounted for unless an answer is given with respect to both.

But if this bond has to be accounted for by reference to two dimensions, why then does Weber refer to two polar opposites with respect to the institutional link but not with respect to personal allegiance? Citizens who relate to society through the intermediary of institutions may do so for emotional or for rational reasons; but Weber does not allow for a similar distinction with respect to the attachment that citizens have towards leaders: in this case, his view of the bond is that it can be emotional. Since it is neither theoretically nor even intuitively obvious that this should be the case, it must be that it is important for Weber that the direct relationship between citizens and leaders be emotional only. We therefore need to turn to a closer examination of the place that Weber ascribes to this personal bond and to the nature of charismatic authority.

Weber's concept of charisma and its inherent limitations

If there is one element of certainty about charismatic authority, it is that it is based on the direct relationship between followers and leaders. 'Charismatic authority is lodged neither in office nor in status but derives from the capacity of a particular person to arouse and maintain belief in himself or herself as the source of legitimacy,' says A.R. Willner (1984: 4), a close follower of Max Weber. Unlike the two other types of authority, which, as we saw, develop through a link to institutions, the object of charisma is the person of the leader, directly and exclusively.

The conceptualizatoin of charisma. Here the certainty ends, however, because the scope — and, indeed, the very nature of charismatic authority — appears ambiguous and consequently somewhat vague. Rather than giving a precise definition, Weber provides us with impressions that are evocative, to be sure, but also confusing. He states that charisma is 'a certain quality of an individual personality by virtue of which he is considered extraordinary and treated as endowed with supernatural, superhuman, or exceptional forces or qualities (Weber, 1968:214); he says of charismatic authority that it rests on 'devotion to the specific sanctity, heroism, or exemplary character of an individual person and of the normative patterns or order revealed or ordained by him' (1968: 215).[5] Neither of these comments helps us markedly to be clear as to what precisely charisma is.

Nor is the matter clarified if one turns to examples given by Weber: he lays much emphasis on prophets and other religious leaders, but he also mentions a variety of other rulers, including some of his contemporaries such as Theodore Roosevelt or Kurt Eisner, the Bavarian revolutionary leader. Not surprisingly, C.J. Friedrich comments: 'The question must now be raised whether this term (charisma) is suitably generalized by broadening it to include secular and non-transcendent types of callings, more especially inspirational leadership of the demagogic type' (Friedrich, 1961: 15). Perhaps the question is not so much whether the term should be generalized to cover all these examples, but rather whether Weber does not, by doing so, change the emphasis and the characteristics of charismatic authority so much that a definition should have been given which is not so ostensibly loaded towards the religious examples.

Why, then, does Weber appear determined to maintain the emphasis on 'callings' and 'supernatural' elements? Is it that the German sociologist was genuinely uncertain about how far he wished to draw charisma out of the realm of religion? It was he who took the first step, as we saw, since before him charisma referred exclusively to a 'gift of grace' in a strictly religious context. Interestingly, and truly imaginatively, he decided that there were situations in the political realm (and, to begin with, at the frontier between politics and religion, as with prophets and other politico-religious leaders) in which what might be called a 'lay' gift of grace was 'bestowed' on an individual; but he never wished to divorce the concept completely from its origins, with the consequence that his analysis appears to be somewhat inconsistent or ambiguous and, perhaps more importantly, that the concept of charisma suffers from the vagueness that results from reasoning based on analogy. It is strictly superfluous to mention 'supernatural' and 'superhuman' qualities when it is also stated that these qualities have to be 'exceptional': someone viewed as being endowed with supernatural or superhuman qualities is *a fortiori* viewed as endowed with exceptional qualities. If Weber mentions the 'supernatural' alongside the 'exceptional', this must be because he wishes to retain the religious connotation as a symbol and even as the central core of the concept: the extensions that might occur in the non-religious fields will therefore be viewed as cases of charisma only if they come close to having at least outward manifestations of 'calling' and 'bestowal'. Weber's view of charisma is thus truly restrictive and narrow at the core; there may be a tail of political charisma which could be so large that it might wag the dog: but Weber endeavours to ensure, by repeated mentions of words stemming from religion, that the impression that prevails is one of an exceptional occurrence.

Why did Weber wish to adopt such a restricted definition of charisma and in particular to keep it so close to its religious origin, since it was he who took it out of the religious context? Clearly, this is because he viewed the concept, in its original religious sense, as having a special 'flavour' and a particular force which he was unwilling to trade off in order to incorporate in his model a much larger group of political situations and political leaders. The flavour and the force stem from the basically irrational bond which appeared to him to result from the total communion resulting from participation in a faith larger than those who belong to it. His conception of charismatic authority is therefore one that is entirely and absolutely emotional — more emotional, if possible, than the bond that exists between followers and society in a traditional context. Not surprisingly, therefore, Weber is unwilling to entertain the idea of a 'dimension' with respect to the link between followers and leaders in a charismatic context. Thus, it is not truly the case that the ideal-type of charismatic authority is the extreme pole of a continuum that might include many intermediate positions. While Weber does entertain the possibility of some 'move' from the pure charismatic pole towards the institutional end of the 'continuum', as the idea of 'routinization' of charisma suggests, he does not consider as 'possible' a situation in which charismatic authority could cease to be 'irrational' to become 'intellectual'. His total silence on this point must be interpreted as meaning that no legitimate rule can be based on a direct 'rational' linkage between followers and leaders, almost certainly both because he must have believed that such a bond would not be strong enough to sustain a whole society and because he also believed that 'rational' followers would 'naturally' turn to institutions if they wished to find a 'proper' basis for the organization of society.

This state of affairs has a tightrope character, however, because the definition must not be so strict that it eliminates all political leaders.

Given the apparently large descriptive and even explanatory potential of the concept in the political field, it is not surprising that there should have been many controversies and criticisms of Weber's concept. These are not merely the result of the efforts of purists wishing to discover what the author really meant; they stem from what has to be regarded as a genuine quandary which even the most fervent admirers, such as A.R. Willner or A. Schweitzer, cannot entirely conceal. Schweitzer in particular attempts to show that there is perhaps not much difference between the religious and the political situation. Having pointed out that Weber does not necessarily see, as C.J. Friedrich would like him to, 'the central charismatic act in the divine favour granted to a particular person by a supernatural being', but that 'the central point lies in the endowment of the selected person and in his belief to be called upon to perform a great and life-long task', Schweitzer concludes that 'in political charisma, however, the belief in a calling can take the place of a bestowal whenever the calling is not of divine origin but attributed to an unspecified destiny or fate' (Schweitzer, 1974: 152). For such a point to be convincing, one would need to be told more precisely what exactly such a 'calling' consists of and, for instance, what the difference is between a 'calling' and a mere ideological standpoint or an idea in which the leader strongly believes. The advantage of the religious 'calling' is that it is a well-defined concept (at any rate, for those who believe in the faith); a 'lay calling', which an individual receives and is 'attributed to fate', is naturally subjected to much greater controversies about its very existence. Nor is it more helpful to suggest that the followers believe in this lay calling, because, here too, there can be vast discrepancies between the types of 'belief'. Schweitzer does claim, admittedly, that 'the extraordinary quality of the person becomes identifiable in such a way that the followers can sense whether he acts out of conceit or an inner obligation' (1974: 153). But such an 'identifiable character' is doubtful: judging by the fact that there is very little agreement among scholars as to who the charismatic leaders have been in the past, it does not seem permissible to conclude as easily as Schweitzer does that the calling can be recognized by the followers.

The attempt to operationalize charisma

The desire to keep the notion of charisma as close as possible to its religious origins has resulted in an ambiguity in conceptualization. But difficulties have been even greater when attempts have been made to proceed to the operationalization of the concept. By and large, of course, the word has been used loosely in political science and sociology by those who have been concerned primarily to describe post-independence Third World developments. But at least one scholar, A.R. Willner, has attempted to remain close to Weber's thinking by retaining a narrow and restricted meaning. The result has been to indicate further difficulties and even to show the potentially very limited scope of the application of the notion.

In the early part of her work on the subject, *The Spellbinders*, Willner is concerned to discover characteristics that would show precisely what charismatic authority consists of. She goes further than anyone else in this endeavour by listing four dimensions of 'follower-recognition and response to the leader. These are (1) the leader-image dimension, (2) the idea-acceptance dimension, (3) the compliance dimension, and (4) the emotional dimension' (Willner, 1984: 5). She then proceeds to define these dimensions and to suggest the ways in which charismatic leaders have specific characteristics with respect to each of them. On the first dimension, she claims, 'followers believe leaders to have superhuman qualities or to possess to an extraordinary degree the qualities highly esteemed in their culture' (p. 6); on the second, 'followers believe statements made and ideas advanced by their leader simply because it is he who has made the statement or advanced the idea' (p. 6); on the third, followers 'comply because for them it is sufficient that their leader has given the command' (p. 7); and on the fourth, 'followers respond to their leader with devotion, awe, reverence, or blind faith, in short with emotions close to religious worship' (p. 7).

This elaboration goes some considerable way towards a clearer vision of what charismatic leadership is or might be. All four dimensions are, at least in principle, capable of operationalization, and they therefore provide potentially a more precise idea of who charismatic leaders may be than Weber ever suggested. But difficulties remain. First, to an extent, as with Weber himself, analogies are used and there is a slide from a higher to a lower level. It is rather vague to describe emotions as being 'close to religious worship'; like Weber, Willner apparently feels unable to cut the umbilical cord linking charisma to religion, with the consequential impression that there is an attempt at giving charisma a mystical character while having to recognize that political charisma is not truly religious. Similarly, the idea of 'superhuman' qualities is again mentioned, but, failing such qualities, the possession of 'qualities esteemed in the culture' to 'an extraordinary degree' does apparently suffice. As with Weber, the definitions would clearly have gained by not being encumbered with what are apparent, but not real, alternatives.

In the second place, there is no discussion of the reasons why these four dimensions have been chosen rather than others, or of the grounds for claiming that these dimensions emerge directly from

Weber's concept of charisma: only if these dimensions were shown to be logically deduced from Weber's idea of charisma could it be claimed that, by using them, a 'true' operationalization of Weber's scheme can be obtained. Of course, these dimensions appear to correspond broadly to what Weber had in mind; but the religious element is noticeably played down; and the notions of 'grace' 'bestowed' on the leaders, and even the sense of mission which enables the followers to 'see' who the charismatic leaders are, are not directly mentioned.

Thus, even Willner's attempt does not dispel the theoretical difficulties posed by the Weberian concept of charisma; and the four dimensions do not appear particularly helpful in practice in order to provide a clear-cut characterization of who the charismatic leaders have been in the twentieth century. Although the endeavour is by far the most rigorous, and indeed is apparently unique, the results are somewhat disappointing. First, the dimensions are not used systematically to discover charismatic leaders, although a determined effort is made in this direction: we are not guided as to why large numbers of leaders, who might have been thought to have been charismatic, are not mentioned and are presumably discarded. Furthermore, Willner's analysis results in a crop of only seven charismatic leaders since the end of the first world war. There is admittedly also a list of 'probables', which includes a further nine leaders, although it is not entirely clear why these do not belong to the group of the 'elect'. Even if they were included, this is a very small number by comparison with the number of leaders whom the world has known in over half a century.

The discovery that the group is so small raises serious questions about the concept of charisma as it was circumscribed by Weber. It is not, of course, a matter of indifference to know that only half a dozen to a dozen of the leaders of the last half-century or more deserve to be rated as charismatic. But if there is such a small number, one has to ask what the purpose is of the concept, especially if the concept is viewed not as the pole of a continuum, but as a self-contained category with closely guarded boundaries. This is especially so in view of the fact that there are other leaders who seem ostensibly to have played a major part in the development of their nations: concentrating on the Third World alone, if Castro and Sukarno are clear candidates for a major leadership role in the post-1945 world, it does not seem revident that their role has been superior to that of Nasser or Nkrumah, who are described as only 'possible charismatic leaders', or to that of Khaddafi, Nyerere or Kaunda, who are not mentioned at all. Of course, charismatic leadership is not deemed to measure the general impact of leaders, but 'merely' the extent to which these leaders 'support' the whole system through the 'faith' that followers have in them; but if charismatic leadership does not help to account for leaders of the importance of some of the best-known Third World state or regime 'founders', then it seems necessary to introduce further concepts to account for the part played by this last group. It even becomes questionable as to whether the concept of charismatic leadership, as defined in a 'restricted' manner, provides a tool for the understanding of the nature and characteristics not just of leadership, but even of authority (see Downton, 1973).

Charismatic leadership and the crisis of society. The importance of leaders, in terms of their impact, is not the only ground according to which the role of charismatic authority could be measured. Weber is concerned primarily with the analysis of the setting, as we saw, and it could therefore be that charismatic leadership would help to describe better the nature of some situations. He views charismatic authority as emerging when there is a major crisis in society, a crisis affecting the whole structure, since the institutions are no longer accepted and recognized by the citizens. From this follows a fundamental difference between charismatic authority and the other two forms of rule. Traditional and rational–legalistic rule are, so to speak, 'normal'; they occur when the situation is stable. Charismatic authority can be found only in the exceptional case of a breakdown (or when institutions have not yet had time to be solidified, for instance in a new country). Whether, in terms of effective duration, these exceptional situations are truly rare is a matter for empirical analyses; but they are exceptional in that, for Weber as well as probably for most social scientists, the breakdown of institutions is not viewed as capable of being prolonged without endangering the very existence of the state as an independent entity. Thus in a charismatic situation, as Willner points out, 'the leader has generally been seen as the least, if not the last, of the factors explaining charisma', at any rate in Weber's interpretation (Willner, 1984: 44).

But if this is the case, it is not immediately clear what part charismatic leadership can play in 'explaining' the situation in which crises occur. The sequence is indeed the opposite, especially since Weber does not suggest that a leader endowed with charismatic authority will always emerge in a time of crisis. The crisis is a necessary, but not a sufficient, condition. Thus, it could not even be claimed that the presence of a charismatic leader is a sign that the crisis has reached breaking point and that the distress of citizens has become complete; there is in fact no guidance as to what the conditions might be which might lead to the emergence of a charismatic leader, except for the fact that the institutions have to have reached breaking point. Leaders may or may not emerge who will be 'charismatic' and appear to the population to have a sense of mission and the capacity to save it from distress. But the evidence seems to indicate that cases are so rare that either it has to be concluded that such instances of distress are also so infrequent as not to warrant being treated as a special category, or else the relationship between crisis and the occurrence of charismatic leadership is very small indeed. Meanwhile, there appear to be many instances of crises that may not perhaps lead to a total collapse of institutions but yet are of major moment to the populations concerned, while there are many cases of leaders who may not qualify for 'full charismatic status' but appear none the less to play a large part in the development of their countries.

Thus the balance of evidence leads to the conclusion that charismatic authority, as a concept closely related to 'divine' powers or to 'superhuman' qualities, is not a manageable and practical tool with which to describe and account for political developments, even in polities that are undergoing a crisis. Yet, it is abundantly apparent that personal influence plays a part, evoking popularity if not, strictly speaking, charisma, in inducing citizens to follow leaders in large numbers of situations. It is because the role of leaders, in Weber's analysis of charisma, is exclusively related to crises that it is based on such exceptional, superhuman qualities. But this makes the framework too rigid and too narrow. Being concerned not at all with the general phenomenon of personalization, but concentrating entirely on the exceptional qualities 'required' in times of crisis, Weber provides no guidance to where the link is less strong and in particular to where it is intellectual or rational rather than emotional. Although he does allow for a decay of this personal link, gradually, if charisma becomes routinized, he does not offer much help as to what mixed forms of authority might be; nor can help be offered, since what is being studied is the role that leaders play in handling exceptional periods in the life of societies.

The idea of charismatic authority is very important: it helps to focus on the fact that regimes, and indeed societies, can markedly depend on the direct link between followers and leaders although there is only a slim probability that a system will depend entirely on this follower–leader relationship. But this is an effect of leadership that is distinct from another role of leaders, which Weber does not consider, and yet which is more widespread — indeed, probably plays a part in almost every country at almost every point in time — and is related to a broader policy-making role which Weber does not analyse, any more than the classical theorists did. Weber concentrates on crises, and considers the personal role of leaders in crises only. This is, in the last resort, why his scheme, which is in many ways so fruitful and which did advance the analysis of leadership well beyond that of the classical theorists has a fundamental limitation. Since Weber was adamant in confining the role of leaders to crisis situations, he refused to extend the notion of charisma to include many kinds and levels of popularity. Those who followed him did so: this accounts for the wide extension given to 'charisma' in the subsequent literature. What the importance of the popularity of rulers in general shows is that the role of leadership, while manifestly essential in crisis situations, extends well beyond these situations. It is to an examination of this general role that we now turn.

What are leaders for — foreign affairs, internal order or socioeconomic policy-making?

One extremely important change has taken place gradually over the last two or three centuries and has affected markedly the nature of leadership: this is the increasing importance of social and economic policy-making. By and large, in the past, leadership was exercised, and was regarded as having to be exercised, essentially in the fields of foreign affairs and defence; internally, the only proper area of intervention was law and order. This is obviously no longer the case. Social and economic matters have gained a high priority, while, almost everywhere and most of the time, foreign affairs have come to be viewed by the public as being of secondary importance and concern for law and order at home has become only spasmodic. Admittedly, especially in the 1980s, leaders occasionally have retreated from the view that social and economic problems should be at the top of agenda, yet these problems remain essential: there has to be a major pressure by the leader to discourage the intervention of the state in these areas.

This shift to social and economic preoccupations has profoundly affected the character of leadership. Social and economic policy-making entails a considerable involvement by large numbers of citizens, especially when it takes the form of 'development'. Mobilization is required, as in wartime; but war is not normally regarded as part of the daily routine of citizens: it has a beginning and an end. Social and economic development, on the contrary, is a daily affair, and one that has no end. Moreover, although a leader who engages the nation in large-scale war faces many dangers if victories are not forthcoming and even more dangers if he suffers defeat, a short war ending in victory can bring him or her considerable praise. Thus there may be major rewards as well as major losses, but in all situations there are clear criteria by which the leader's actions can be assessed. The situation is much less definite on the economic and social fronts: successes are often difficult to perceive, especially because short-term benefits may lead to long-term problems; and successes are often obtained at the expense of some members of the community, for instance through redistribution of wealth. The contentment of some is thus offset by the grievances of others.

It is therefore not surprising that, very often, the internal policy-making should appear burdensome. 'Let's drop the domestic stuff altogether,' John F. Kennedy is reported to have told Sorensen, his speechwriter, who was preparing the draft of the inaugural address; 'It's too long anyway' (Shogan, 1982: 67). Instead, Kennedy chose to talk about the gathering crises in the contemporary world and about the responsibility that he and his countrymen would have to share.

But can leaders choose to 'drop the domestic stuff' and concentrate on foreign affairs and vice-versa? Is the ruler the master of the terrain on which he wishes to concentrate attention? And are there no limits and no costs in exercising this discretion? We need to examine both traditional conceptions and modern conditions and see how far contemporary rulers have attempted to solve the dilemmas that confront them.

Classical political theory and the purpose of leadership
In the works of the classical theorists, by and large, the contours of the concept of leadership, like those of an emerging sculpture, are neither ornate nor delicate: broad categories are used. Thus, good leaders are described in terms of rather general concepts, such as wisdom or justice. Consequently, perhaps, it is not very clear what goals and purposes are assigned to leaders. On occasion, especially with Machiavelli but also with Hobbes, stability appears to be the overriding goal; but it is none the less possible to identify the two major columns of the sculpture: foreign affairs and internal peace, the latter being stretched sometimes to a vision of internal welfare and harmony.

Leadership and foreign affairs. Foreign affairs is the field that is the most neatly delineated, though only some of the classical theorists give it major emphasis. While Machiavelli's *Prince* is almost entirely devoted to this goal (to the extent that the reflections of the Florentine do not focus on suggestions relating to the maintenance of the leader in office), neither Plato nor Aristotle concentrates heavily on this function. This is due in part to the varied circumstances in which these theorists wrote; significantly, the only other great theorist who gave prominence to the foreign affairs function was Hobbes, who, like Machiavelli, lived at a time of upheaval in which states were continuously in danger of collapse from within or without. But circumstances are only part of the explanation, since Greek cities, too, were periodically if not continuously in a state of war with one another. Much of the difference in emphasis relates therefore to a difference in approach: while most of the classical theorists looked at the problem of leadership — or, perhaps more precisely, of rule — in the context of building up a case for a general organization of society, Machiavelli concentrates his attention on leaders, as well as potential leaders, and considers the ways in which they can remain in office or come to power, particularly in times of turmoil and war — both occasions for new rulers to emerge and the source of dangers resulting in eventual collapse.

Thus, while most other classical political theorists give some scope to problems of foreign affairs in their presentation of what leadership is for, Machiavelli is probably the only one among the very great to have discovered the essential value to rulers of exploiting the foreign affairs dimension. Given that his aim is to analyse how leaders can maintain themselves in power, he naturally directs his attention primarily to the means by which this goal can be achieved, with the result that the substantive purpose of leadership is (or at any rate appears to be) subordinated to the problems of the stability of rulers in office. There is thus a reversal of the 'normal' approach of classical political theorists for whom the object is to achieve good government while leaders are only a means; in Machiavelli's case, the fundamental object is the leader's success, and substantive policies or even 'good government' are the means to that end. But this reversal of the content of means and ends has the effect of enabling Machiavelli to discover and bring to the fore an extremely important element which, as we shall see later, continues to play a major part in the effective and concrete manifestations of what leaders are for. 'There is nothing [which] gains a prince such repute', he states in Chapter 21 of *The Prince*, 'as great exploits and rare trials of himself in heroic acts.'

The point is important, indeed fundamental, because it indicates the relationship between foreign affairs actions — and of course in particular actions in war — and heroism and greatness. Thus, if what is needed (for instance, in order to achieve power or, once in power, to consolidate the rule) is 'heroic actions', great lightning events which can strike the imagination of the population while probably also helping to get rid of some opponents, then the area that is particularly useful for the leader's purpose is foreign affairs and especially war. Thus, too, not only can and does foreign policy become subordinated to the 'larger' end of enabling the ruler to stay in office, but the focus of the ruler will be on foreign affairs rather than on other matters. It is not so much, as is often suggested, that foreign policy and wars provide a 'diversion' and take citizens' attention away from the problems of home affairs; it is, more positively, that foreign policy and war can constitute a way of providing legitimacy — of achieving charismatic or near-charismatic authority, so to speak — and, most importantly, of doing so quickly, almost instantaneously, at least if the war is short. Rather than having to earn his popularity in the course of a long career, on the basis of a regular job of a leader, one might say, the ruler who concentrates on foreign affairs can gamble; and, if fate is on his side, he can amass rapidly a large capital of legitimacy.

Classical theorists and 'good government'

Most classical theorists are either less cynical or less practically concerned with determining how a leader comes to power and stays in office. Their aim is to find the best way of achieving good government, usually by limiting the scope of the rulers' discretion. They are typically rather laconic about the nature of leadership; they are correspondingly equally laconic about what the purpose or aims of the activities of the rulers should be. They seem to wish leaders to be 'wise' in order that the results of government be 'good' and 'just'. Locke, for instance, in his *Second Treatise on Government*, states that the function of government is to rule 'for the common good' (Ch. 9); and laws (which of course are to be made by legislators, not by leaders) 'ought to be designed for no other end ultimately but the good of the people' (Ch. 11). The role of the executive power is 'to execute the laws', while the role of the 'federative' power, an office which, he points out, is unlikely to be, and indeed should not be, held by a person distinct from the holder of executive power, is 'the management of the security and interest of the public without' (Ch. 12).

Most other political theorists are not very specific as to what leadership is for in the realm of home affairs. Hobbes is perhaps the thinker who considers the matter in the greatest detail, specifying one major and general role and indicating a number of more concrete activities. The major role is that of the 'procuration of the peace of the people' — not unnaturally, since Hobbes's main preoccupation is to provide tranquillity, and since the achievement of such a goal is the fundamental justification of his social contract (*Leviathan*, Part II, Ch. 29). In this, he is perhaps in accord with the great majority, if not all the theorists, from Aristotle to Locke, Montesquieu and, indeed, Rousseau, who in his *Social Contract* declares that the objective must be to achieve 'public tranquillity' (Book III, Ch. 9). If there is a goal that leaders must achieve within the country, it must be the maintenance of order, which, indeed, can be linked to the external role by which leaders must ensure that citizens are protected from outside intervention.

Where Hobbes is more explicit than — though not necessarily at variance with — other political theorists is in the description of the types of activities that leaders must be engaged in. He states, for instance, that the sovereign must be involved in law-making, in making a variety of appointments, including those of teachers, and in supervising the administration of justice (*Leviathan*, Part II, Ch. 30). But this rather more explicit elaboration of the role or functions of the 'sovereign' is not a marked advance on the more general presentation, which states that rulers are asked to be wise or, as Aquinas puts it, 'to govern [the] subjects right' (d'Entreves, 1981: 23). It must be remembered that the 'sovereign', in Hobbes's interpretation, may be a person or an assembly; and, in the case of his own preferred solution of a monarchical sovereign, he probably feels obliged to enter into greater detail concerning the activities of the sovereign in order to ensure that this sovereign acts rightly: he thus states that 'the safety of the people requires further for him or them that have the sovereign power that justice be equally administered to all degrees of people' (*Leviathan*, Part II, Ch. 30).

Thus, the purpose of the 'sovereign', and of the leader if s/he is sovereign, is to ensure that the 'good' of the people be translated into laws or, if the leader merely executes the laws, to ensure that the laws be, as the US constitution was to state, 'faithfully executed'. It is indeed in relation to the making of good laws that several political theorists find some examples from antiquity appealing, particularly those of Lycurgus and Solon, and especially the former, since, after having, as Rousseau would have put it, 'legislated', Lycurgus chose to retire from public office.

The image of the leader who provides his country with the valuable laws and then disappears from the scene is not one that all classical theorists wish to convey as an ideal, however. Machiavelli finds himself somewhat cross-pressured between the two opposite types of heroes, the 'pure civilian' type and the 'pure military' or 'heroic' type, and it is not entirely clear which of the two models he prefers; other political theorists, especially Hobbes and Locke, project an image that is intermediate, with Hobbes's leader being rather more flamboyant, but also appreciably more dangerous, and Locke's being 'lower-key' and appearing contented with a position of less obvious influence.

The static or 'a-temporal' character of internal leadership in classical political theory. Whether the leader is to be flamboyant or somewhat withdrawn, whether his scope of action is vast or narrowly circumscribed, the role that is ascribed to him in internal matters is essentially static. It is static because it is viewed as 'a-temporal'. In the field of foreign affairs, activities and movements occur, of course, but they are in the nature of an ebb and flow of attack and defence, of incursion and repulse, not of a development occurring over a long period: Machiavelli's leader has to establish himself to force the incumbent out; he has therefore to ensure that he stays at the pinnacle that he has reached. But there is no grand design (except for what he views as a rather utopian hope that Italy might be united): the reality of the situation has more of the characteristics of a tactic than of a strategy.

While there is at least some movement in the Machiavellian scheme of foreign policy, a movement that Locke, for instance, would not deny since he sees the holder of the 'federative' power as having to cope with emergencies, albeit in the manner of a fireman who is always on call, there is no movement in the realm of internal policy; indeed, the ideal seems to be the total absence of movement, a situation that resembles the stillness of a very luminous summer day when the sun is at the zenith. This is precisely why classical political theorists are particularly impressed by the image of Lycurgus or other wise 'legislators'. Such men come to the fore, determine the best possible laws for their community, and then go into retirement when they have achieved a task which is to be expected to be valid for all times.

This static conception of the law has naturally affected the political systems which have been established, at least in part, on the basis of the models and theories of the classical theorists. Directly in the West, and indirectly in parts of the world that have been markedly influenced by ideas emanating from the West, constitutions and practices of government have been based, for many decades and continuing even to the present, on a model stressing the 'eternal', or at any rate 'a-temporal', character of the law. In this context, the purpose of leadership has typically been viewed in terms of one or more of three roles. One of these is rather modest: it is that of the Lockian executive who, like a good civil servant, ensures that laws are 'faithfully executed'. The other two roles are more exalted: one stems from the involvement in foreign affairs and very commonly in war; the other consists in determining the 'fundamental laws' which might, occasionally, be so important that they would reshape the character of the nation. But this is so occasional, so unlikely even, that it is perhaps not surprising that the more common purpose should have been foreign affairs and war only: leaders may be forgiven for wishing to win 'repute' and to undertake 'great exploits', as these may be the quickest means of achieving the desired result.

Social and economic policy-making and its effect on leadership

The emergence of economic and social development as a governmental function. Rulers have always had to be concerned with the state of their finances, partly in order to find money for their expenditures in foreign wars, partly in order to satisfy their needs and those of their entourage. Wars were, indeed, often occasioned by the desire to acquire some loot — expeditions overseas by Europeans being particularly motivated by this aim. But in the course of the sixteenth and seventeenth centuries, the cost of foreign adventures on the continent of Europe escalated; and little financial reward accrued to the exchequers. Thus, the need to obtain further revenues became increasingly pressing for some monarchs, in particular for the French kings, who began to undertake a policy of European domination. Because the tax base was insufficient, commerce and industry gradually came to be viewed as a means of obtaining revenue, both from nationals and by external trade. This was to be one of the main reasons for the early development of mercantilism under Louis XIV, whose chief minister for twenty years, Colbert, attempted with some success to set up modern industrial firms aimed at competing with the most advanced commercial countries of the time, Holland and England. The idea was to overcome economic backwardness as a result of a conscious policy of industrial intervention; in consequence, the French 'manufactures', especially in the field of luxury goods, did indeed acquire a considerable reputation across the world.

Colbert can thus be rightly regarded as one of the first in the history of the modern European nations who adopted a policy of state-led economic development. But, while the French state, through him, was involved in 'interventionism', the policy was that of the minister, rather than of the King himself. Indeed, Colbert had periodically to remind Louis XIV of the importance of industrial ventures for the purposes of the monarch, who was able to conduct wars on a larger scale because of the healthier state of the French economy. The leader was not directly involved; nor did he think that he had to be: the French king appointed his minister to handle the economic activities that were required. In such a philosophy, leaders are involved in economic problems to a very limited extent. Their prestige is not at stake. The engine of the policy is not the leader himself.

This attitude was gradually to change in the course of the eighteenth century. All over Europe, public bureaucracies began to expand and more and more ministers were concerned with the economic achievements of their countries; new ideas about progress became prevalent, as it became common to emphasize the need for public works, agricultural improvements and the development of manufactures. One of the very first monarchs who adopted these views was Peter the Great, who attempted to take Russia out of its backwardness by strongly 'dirigiste' means. Later in the century, the philosophy was adopted by large numbers of monarchs whose 'enlightened despotism' became a conscious and systematic endeavour, on the part of the leaders themselves, to achieve economic development by voluntaristic means. Admittedly, in some cases, and especially with Frederic of Prussia, the motives were mixed: 'imperialistic' hopes were an essential element in the drive towards economic progress; but other rulers, like Joseph II of Austria, were essentially concerned with economic change. The movement was thus truly the predecessor of the drive towards development in the Third World in the second half of the twentieth century: the aims were broadly similar in both cases, and the involvement of the leaders was of the same nature.

The idea was forgotten for many decades, however, as a result of the combined effect of the French Revolution and the industrial revolution in England. The French Revolution was essentially political in character, at least in its main manifestations; moreover, as it quickly led to a full-scale war across Europe, rulers naturally returned to their traditional preoccupation with foreign policy. The English industrial revolution undermined 'dirigisme' in a different way: the capitalist ideology that was associated with it resulted in the virtual domination of the ideas of laissez-faire: progress could be achieved not by governmental intervention, but only if the government was concerned merely with law and order. Admittedly, on the Continent, both during the Napoleonic wars in France and later in the century in central Europe, 'dirigiste' ideas lingered on: but the marked success of the British economy suggested that the liberal views were superior; of course, it came to be argued that 'infant industries' needed some help, but this help more often took the negative form of protection against foreign competition than the positive form of direct governmental action. The well-being of nations and citizens seemed to depend on the energy and inventiveness of unfettered entrepreneurs.

For a period at least, therefore, state intervention was to come from another preoccupation, one of a social rather than an economic character. The consequences of industrialization on large segments of society led increasingly to demands for action to prevent misery, these demands being triggered in part by altruistic motives and in part by the fear that exacerbated tensions would threaten the social order, especially in the rapidly expanding large cities. Thus, in England first, and throughout Europe gradually, governments came to be involved in forms of social welfare, education being also viewed as a means of achieving progress and uplifting the 'poorer classes'. To begin with, as in seventeenth-century France, policy intervention in this field was undertaken by members of the public bureaucracy or by individual ministers, rather than by the leaders themselves. Gradually, however, some leaders showed a substantial interest: in England, Peel and later

Disraeli had a social policy. These preoccupations then became increasingly common. Thus, in France Jules Ferry was associated with a policy of universal education, and in Germany Bismarck fostered a comprehensive social policy to prevent political disruption. By the turn of the century, the need for social policy-making had become recognized all over Europe, with socialist parties compelling the ruling conservatives and liberals to place these matters high on the agenda. By then, too, the leaders, and not merely the ministers, were directly involved in advocating (or opposing) ideas of social reform.

Economic intervention quickly became prominent again after the destructions of empires resulting from the first world war. It was to take two different forms, however. Russian communism in effect revived the old model of 'enlightened despotism', although the ideology was different and it was drastically modernized by the use of state planning and by total control of the economy; in a more diluted manner, the same model was to be adopted by large numbers of Third World countries after 1945 and even, to some extent, by some European countries, France in particular. Meanwhile, the consequences of the first world war and even more of the Great Depression resulted in another, less forceful, more 'liberal' form of economic interventionism in most countries of the West, by way of Keynesian macroeconomic techniques. While these were primarily handled by experts and specialized ministers, the manifest importance of the well-being of citizens and the felt need to avoid at all costs the recurrence of a major depression obliged most leaders to view themselves as doctors continuously concerned with the economic health of their countries.

Thus, by the 1960s the purpose of leadership had been transformed everywhere to include both economic and social policy-making. A 'revolution' in thinking had taken place which had to some extent dislodged the traditional functions of foreign policy and 'public tranquillity': high priority was given to social welfare and economic development, either in its very robust form of direct 'sectorial' intervention or in the more benign posture of economic management. Whatever may be claimed by some rulers anxious to reduce the extent of their involvement in economic and social matters, the new 'ideology' of leadership has been adopted so widely that the 'burden' cannot be shaken even by the most 'liberal'-minded leaders. Almost certainly, and almost everywhere, these rulers are judged by their successes and failures in the economic and social fields.

The impact of the ideology of development on the nature of leadership. The emphasis on social and economic preoccupation not only had the effect of shifting the attention of leaders away from foreign policy and even law and order: it also transformed the requirements of leadership because of the very nature of social and economic policy-making. In the first place, social and economic policy-making is inherently dynamic; it has an ongoing character. While law and order policies and the prescriptions for good government were static and a-temporal, social and economic policies have to be elaborated on the basis of the level of development of the country; plans in one field must be co-ordinated with plans in other fields. These policies have to be built brick by brick, so to speak. Thus, 'radical' or 'revolutionary' proposals have to be toned down because of failures in implementation; Western countries have had to borrow concepts (such as planning) from communist countries, while communist nations have had increasingly to rely on such 'capitalist' notions as individual incentives or the profit motive.

In the second place, social and economic policy-making transforms the role of the government and the relationship between leaders and other members of the national executive. Leaders have to work through their ministers in order to prepare plans, elaborate ongoing programmes and see them implemented. They depend therefore markedly, some might say entirely, on these ministers (and on civil servants) for the success or failure of their policies. Leaders have depended on diplomats and on generals in the past; but the number of policy fields in which governments are now involved transforms the nature of the problem of ministerial 'obedience' by multiplying the number of subordinates whose actions leaders have to supervise. Moreover, the size of the bureaucracies operating under the ministers, and the combination of technical and human skills required to ensure that policies are implemented, entail considerable, if not total, reliance on the ministers for the supervision of the direction of action and for the enthusiasm of the subordinates. Social and economic policy-making has, to all intents and purposes, created the concept of government, while resulting in a reciprocal dependence between leaders and ministers. Leaders may continue to be the most prestigious and popular members of the government, but they are hampered by the fact that their prestige and popularity are at stake even if the policies are largely outside their own control: they depend on the achievements of others whom they usually can dismiss but have often great difficulty in directing.

Third, social and economic policy-making is a source of conflicts among the population at large, especially since the very idea of social and economic development creates expectations (in part or even largely fostered by leaders and would-be leaders). These conflicts vary in intensity, but they result from both the introduction and the absence of new policies. This is in sharp contrast with past situations. Foreign affairs, and the conduct of wars, *may* lead to internal conflict if the choice of the occasion is wrong or if the conduct of diplomacy or military action proves ineffective. Social and economic policies, however, almost always result in conflict, as some sections of the community will be disadvantaged as a result of these policies, and, even if their fears turn out to be groundless, the belief that there will be drawbacks and losses is equally important. Therefore as leaders come to be increasingly involved in social and economic development, they find that their policies create divisions within the community: pains and tensions seem to be the inevitable consequences of efforts designed to 'uplift' society.

In the fourth place, these conflicts tend to occur often, and indeed principally, in the context of the financial demands that are being made of the citizens; the need for tax increases or declines in benefits sharpens antagonisms. But the general problem of the cost of social and economic development has become a major issue. Yet even the partial satisfaction of educational and welfare 'needs', and even a limited involvement in industrial or agricultural development, entail major and recurrent capital outlays which appear always to be smaller than what had been planned for, while always also being smaller than the expectations of the citizens and the hopes of the leaders. Thus, 'wars on poverty' entail large expenditures which are beyond the financial capacity of even the richest countries, with the dimensions of the problem seeming to become larger than preliminary analyses suggested. Leaders are not only confronted with large expenditures for which they must find resources; they live in an environment where uncertainty about expenditures is the norm and 'activism' appears to bring difficulties and no rewards.

Moreover, in the fifth place, leaders find themselves without clear guidance as to what 'proper' solutions should be. Successes and failures are hard to define and assess in the social and economic field. There seem to be no limits to what might be done: most leaders wish to achieve more (and are driven by their citizens to achieve more) than is possible. Meanwhile, the means of achieving success is remarkably obscure: the 'science' of military strategy may not have been without its flaws, but the 'science' of economic and social strategies is apparently even less advanced. What needs to be done to 'win' a 'war on poverty' or to achieve a bumper sugar harvest appears increasingly unclear. Even economic policy guidance seems beyond the reach of modern policy-makers: leaders of the 1930s were almost entirely powerless when confronted with the cataclysm of the Great Depression; but post-second-world-war leaders came quickly to discover that there were no clear guidelines to follow in order to uplift societies from basic underdevelopment, while even the steering of more advanced economies proved intractable. The rise and fall of economic advice, in the course of the second half of the twentieth century, has left leaders increasingly poorly armed to combat the difficulties posed by inflation, lack of growth and social injustices in the richer countries, let alone the major obstacles to development in the poorer states of the Southern Hemisphere.

Leaders are therefore rarely optimistic about social and economic policy-making. The strategies involved in waging a war are clear-cut and well defined. Leaders may be incompetent; they may overstretch their resources; the results may often be somewhat 'miraculous'; but they are, in the main, understandable. One may be over-cautious or over-sanguine, helped or let down by fate or the gods — but, on the whole, one knows what to expect. There are rules, so to speak, in the game of foreign affairs. But the rules in the game of social and economic policy-making are far from clear, and may grow increasingly obscure as leaders became more deeply engaged in the 'battle' for development.

Rulers are confronted with pressing new demands in the economic and social fields and yet appear increasingly unable to meet these demands. This is why social and economic policy-making has fundamentally altered both the purpose and the characteristics of political leadership in the world. Suggestions made by the classical theorists about what leadership should consist of have been superseded by new requirements in the contemporary world. It is no surprise that leadership should have come to be conceived differently by citizens and by politicians, and indeed that the leaders themselves should have acquired a different understanding of their role. It is not surprising either that, confronted with such difficulties, leaders should have tried to escape from the 'cornering' in which social and economic policy-making has tended to place them.

Contemporary leaders and the strategies designed to cope with social and economic problems
Most contemporary leaders believe that their role is to give high priority to social and economic policy-making. But the strategies that they follow differ. The most 'activist' among them embark on a road of comprehensive intervention, but the political costs are high. Thus some adopt, or are gradually obliged to adopt, a less 'aggressive' strategy — by concentrating on certain fields, for instance. Even this may appear too conflictual to those who are intent on remaining popular or whose views about change are less sanguine; they may therefore try to construct a consensus, which, however, may be difficult to maintain over time or may yield few results. Thus leaders may try to refurbish their strength and disentangle themselves from the difficulties engendered by their economic and social activities by

practising a partial or even total 'flight into foreign affairs'.

Ignoring social and economic policy-making altogether. Some leaders attempt to ignore social and economic problems by literally refusing to engage in development policies and by concentrating on maintaining themselves in office, an aim that is sometimes achieved at considerable human cost. In their analysis of personal rule in Africa, however, R. Jackson and C. Rosberg could find only two clear-cut cases of this type of regime: those of Amin in Uganda and Macias in Equatorial Guinea. Other examples, such as that of Bokassa in the Central African Republic, are more mixed, the truly tyrannical period having been only a phase in the rule of this leader (see Jackson and Rosberg, 1982: 244).

Purely personal rule is rare because leaders are able to avoid pressure for social and economic development only if the aspirations of their citizens are extremely low. This implies a pre-modern society which is also largely insulated from the beliefs that prevail widely across the world; it also implies that leaders are prepared to act ruthlessly and to see to it that any means is used to ensure that their power is not undermined. Indeed, this further implies that the leaders can succeed in preventing the infiltration of foreign ideas into the country and in defeating attempts to topple them from outside. Such a stance is rarely successful for very long: while Macias's rule was ended by an internal coup, Amin's was destroyed by foreign invasion, as was that of Pol Pot in Cambodia. To all intents and purposes, the strategy of ignoring social and economic policy-making altogether is simply no longer open to the overwhelming majority of contemporary rulers.

The 'head-on' strategy of assuming a full role in economic and social policy-making. Much more likely, and indeed ostensibly more natural, is the converse strategy, which induces leaders to assert emphatically that their role is to solve the economic and social problems of the country and to transform the situation that they inherited. Such a strategy corresponds closely to, and indeed to an extent anticipates, the demands of the population; it is therefore particularly appealing to leaders who have a positive conception of their role and who view themselves as having a mission to perform.

Many contemporary leaders have adopted such a strategy, for a while at least, in some cases because they were forced by circumstances and in others because it seemed to them imperative to do so. The first category includes some Western leaders, in particular those who came to power after a 'watershed' election which followed a long period of discontent. This was the case in the United States in 1933, in Britain in 1945 and in France in 1981; similar examples can be found elsewhere — in Latin America, for instance, in Chile in 1970. In the Third World, however, and especially in the newly independent countries, the anticipation of demands is often more pronounced, as it was in Russia in 1917 or China in 1949. Leaders who have come to power through a revolution, or military leaders who have espoused radical goals, have thus claimed that they would genuinely transform the conditions under which economic and social policy-making would take place in the country, seemingly beyond the demands of all but a small segment of their followers.

Yet the very radical manner in which the social and economic conditions are being transformed produces sharp conflicts. Popular dedication must be forthcoming, but it is often absent since only a small proportion of the population originally had any notion, even vaguely, of what the new social and economic order entailed. In Western countries, where the structure and culture of the political system make coercion very difficult to contemplate, let alone implement, a soft-pedalling becomes inevitable; but in authoritarian states, too, the strategy of 'head-on' attack on the social and economic structure becomes difficult to pursue after a period. If the leader himself does not introduce a 'pause', and if he is not toppled from office, his natural disappearance often provides the occasion for a rethinking which amounts to adopting a new strategy.

Lower-key involvement in social and economic policy-making. Those who once wanted radical change are thus often obliged to change their strategy; or a 'lower-key' approach is often adopted from the start, for instance by leaders whose desire for change is less marked. They may wish to bring about transformations in the industrial sector without attempting to modify conditions in the countryside or vice-versa; they may concentrate on social modernization and show a scant desire to achieve economic change. By restricting the domain of their intervention, such leaders can hope to reduce the level of conflict generated by their policies and therefore to increase the probability of implementation.

'Gradualist' strategies of this type have been pursued by many leaders, both in the West and in the Third World. They have occasionally been successful, as with Ataturk or Bourguiba, for instance, who substantially modified relationships among citizens. Policies of economic growth pursued in a number of Asian states, as well as in some Black African countries, such as Kenya, Gabon or the Ivory Coast, have had a marked impact on the living standards of at least a substantial segment of the population of these nations.

But difficulties often arise, even in those countries in which economic and social innovations appear, for a time, to be accepted without much opposition. Conflicts increase as the implementation of policies results in changes being demanded from sectors of the population. Thus, the social modernization policies of Ataturk or

Bourguiba have encountered opposition, especially in the countryside; this opposition has in turn contributed to the revival of 'fundamentalist' views which were also fostered by their concomitant re-emergence in neighbouring countries. It is the dynamic unfolding of the policies that is at the root of the increased discontent: policies of social modernization may appear in the first instance to be a-temporal, in that they 'declare' that the condition of a group — women for instance — will henceforth be different; but these a-temporal principles are implemented only through a gradual process of psychological changes, which requires continuous 'vigilance' on the part of administrators and therefore demands the dedication of the civil servants. Changes in economic relationships are, moreover, largely dependent on international markets, while they may result in considerable indirect costs, for instance in housing and education, if, as is usual, the policies lead to a rapid urbanization process. Over time, therefore, even a 'gradualist' policy of social and economic change will often result in marked pressures on the ruler and on the government, in a consequential increase in the strength of the opposition groups, and in rumblings among the supporters of the leader; the ministerial changes that may have to occur as a result may in turn foster further discontent. Only by careful steering — and much luck — can a 'gradualist' strategy be implemented and pursued without major political and social strife.

Attempts at a consensual strategy. Since the main problem encountered by leaders wishing to bring about social and economic change is that of increased conflict, attempts have naturally been made to devise a strategy that would obviate this result by giving highest priority to consensus-building. This is a difficult strategy to pursue: change requires some degree of redistribution. Yet leaders often hope to avoid the problem by means of economic growth, while a widespread belief in social justice or patriotic feelings may help to reduce the objections of some of the opponents.

Thus, 'gradualism' is often couched in 'consensual' terms. Lyndon Johnson, for instance, attempted to build a large coalition designed to eradicate poverty while sustaining economic growth. Nationalist leaders in the Middle East and in Africa — Senghor for example — have attempted to associate many groups in society — rural and urban, lay and religious — to their policies in order to achieve a (relatively modest) level of economic and social development. But the inherent contradictions between a 'consensus' strategy and the requirements of social and economic change typically become apparent after a short period. If 'sacrifices' are limited, the coalition may remain in existence; but also, the results are likely to be small. Consensus policies therefore will tend to remain in operation only if, by some happy accident, economic growth brings about benefits to all the partners — not a likely occurrence, in either the West or the Third World.

The flight into foreign affairs. The difficulties experienced by leaders in their attempts to bring about social and economic change often result from the part played by outside forces. Multinational companies may resist the policies that are put forward; commodity prices may move in directions that affect adversely the governmental strategy; ideological and social movements abroad may exercise considerable influence on the citizens and arouse conflicts; and governments of foreign countries may exert direct or indirect pressure. Seeing that their policies are affected in this way, many leaders, with some justice, blame these outside forces; naturally enough, too, the more radical among them will try to modify the operation of these forces by moving into the field of foreign affairs. In doing so, leaders often discover (or believe) that they can find a solution to their problems. The strategy of going into foreign affairs thus becomes perhaps the single most common answer given by contemporary leaders to the difficulties they face.

As we saw earlier, intervention in the field of foreign affairs can have rapid and high pay-offs. First, by blaming foreigners and external forces generally for the problems that they experience in the domestic field, leaders can hope to build a consensus for their policies, as the ground for support ceases to be the intrinsic merit of the case and comes to be its nationalistic symbolic importance. Thus, Nasser's revolution in Egypt or that of Boumédienne in Algeria becomes a revolution against colonialism. But intervention in foreign affairs can also bring prestige to the leader and consequently can result in popularity gains which are attached to the leader's person and therefore make it possible for him or her to embark, at less political cost, on social and economic policies. Moreover, as was pointed out earlier, foreign policy intervention may sometimes result in a clear-cut success. The enormous popularity gains won by Mrs Thatcher after the Falklands war and the (somewhat smaller) benefits accruing to President Reagan after the Grenada intervention are interesting examples, as is that of the King of Morocco, who gained ground internally by intervening in the Sahara.

Above all, the 'flight into foreign affairs' appears to have a somewhat 'cathartic' effect for leaders: they feel that they can engage in 'high politics' without being encumbered by the daily trivia of ensuring the gradual implementation of their economic or social policies; they depend markedly less on the goodwill and competence of members of the government, the civil service and, indeed, the population. They feel they are free agents operating in the field of international affairs.

Thus, the temptation to move to foreign affairs is common, almost universal, for leaders of the contemporary world, despite, but also in part because of, the importance of social and economic policy-making. But this 'flight' also leads to problems, since, while the gains may be rapid and large, the losses may be vast: miscalculations about easy victories have resulted in the loss of popularity and fall of many leaders, from Lyndon Johnson in the 1960s to the Argentinian military junta in the early 1980s; more insidiously, miscalculations about the possible part that leaders may play on the international scene have contributed to the decline in popularity of such 'grand' rulers as De Gaulle, Nasser, Nkrumah and Sukarno. For the need to be involved in social and economic policy-making does not disappear; the aspirations of the population may even be exacerbated, after a period, by what appears to be the limited concern of the leaders for the 'domestic stuff'. Whatever their hope of avoiding a confrontation with problems that appear insuperable and never-ending, leaders are reminded, and usually rather rapidly, that they may not ignore them with impunity.

Conclusion

The role of leadership has thus been markedly modified. It cannot any longer be viewed from the same standpoint as that of the classical theorists who, being concerned exclusively with foreign affairs and a static vision of 'good government', could attempt primarily to restrict the opportunities of leaders to have a negative effect on society. Nor is it realistic to confine the role of leaders to one exalted function: that of saving the polity. The role is permanent, continuous and deep: leaders have to deal with the social and economic development of their countries.

This places today's leaders in a serious, and, indeed, unhappy predicament, more unhappy than that which confronted their predecessors, when social and economic change was not the order of the day. Yet, because leaders have to deal with social and economic matters, it is often difficult for them to 'succeed', and especially to appear quickly to succeed, in the domestic field. The conflicts generated by new policies and the cost of these policies are such that the erosion of the capital of popularity is rapid and large. Yet only exceptionally do leaders have other means of regaining some of their lost popularity: the field of foreign affairs is attractive, but it is also dangerous and markedly dependent on good luck. As time passes, it is probably less and less likely to bring about quick successes, while it is also probable that citizens will become increasingly concerned with results in the domestic field. It is rarely up to the leaders to leave social and economic policies aside: in this manner, the contemporary world has placed on rulers a new and vast burden. Also, it is rarely up to these rulers to find a way, even a tortuous and complex way, of achieving, in the comparatively few years during which they are in office, the kind of 'success' that would establish their power and make them feel secure in their accomplishments.

Notes

· 1. There is no point in listing here large numbers of texts on this subject. A very valuable comparative work is that of Rose and Suleiman (1980).

2. See in particular Dogan (1975); see also Aberbach, Putnam and Rockman (1981).

3. See for instance Schapera (1956). Two of the great classical theorists in the field are Evans-Pritchard (1940) and Leach (1954).

4. Barnhart Dictionary. London: Longman, 1973.

5. See Willner (1984: 204ff.) for the problems of translation of the text.

3

A conceptual assessment of the impact of political leaders

In this chapter, we shall attempt to determine means by which to assess comparatively the impact that leaders have on the societies they rule. As we saw, this is the central question; there is little point in analysing leaders if we do not know how great their impact is or whether they have any impact at all. It is a difficult question to solve, however, as the contribution of leaders is closely tied to the environment in which they operate. In particular, the environment gives different opportunities and places different constraints. Some leaders come to power after a crisis that has destroyed the prestige of their predecessors and given them a chance to start afresh; others follow successful statesmen during whose regime the economy has progressed rapidly and social conflict has been markedly reduced. It is as if the first received five 'talents' and might be expected to amass another five, while the others received only two 'talents' and could not be reasonably expected to 'make' more than another two. The judgement on the 'worth' of leaders must therefore take into account the nature of the problems that have to be solved, and not merely changes that occurred in the state of the society between the moment the leaders took office and the moment they left.

To do this, we have to elaborate a model that will enable us to assess separately the contribution of leaders and the state of the society which they rule, and then to relate these two elements to each other. The object of this chapter is to describe the basis of such a model. We shall first examine the leaders and see whether they can be located in a general space which would help to assess the nature and extent of their contribution. We shall then turn to the characteristics of the society and examine whether these, too, can be located in a general space.

A general classification of leaders' goals

How can the leaders' contributions be assessed? Should we draw up a comprehensive list of their actions? Quite apart from the obvious empirical difficulties facing such an undertaking, there are theoretical problems as well. Actions of leaders cannot merely be added up: they have first to be ranked, as some are obviously more important than others. Yet there is no obvious criterion on which to base distinctions of importance. This is perhaps only an academic matter, as 'actions' may not be the crucial variable: leaders' deeds are rarely 'actions' in the physical sense; they are more often decisions, orders or requests which are implemented by others. They are also endeavours to convince and influence, by cajoling and manipulation, as well as coercion (though the coercive acts are probably in fact exercised by others). Thus, statements, speeches and conferences are as much part of the deeds of leaders as are the decisions they make; if, for instance, leaders are anxious to bring about a new 'climate' in social relations, or if they wish to 'mobilize' the population behind the policies they pursue, their 'deeds' might consist primarily of tours and visits, with conversations and speeches forming an essential part. In this leaders are rather special: other members of governments engage in speechmaking, but it is rarely as essential to their position as it is to the leaders', for, in the last analysis, ministers rely on the leaders' mobilizing ability for the success of their actions.

Indeed, as we have begun to note, the impact of leaders is normally not complete without the intervention of others — indeed, of many others. By and large, leaders give an impulsion, while the administration, including the members of the government, is concerned with its application. Of course, leaders have a part to play in the implementation process. Those who introduced new policies may have to set up new agencies; generally speaking, they have to be concerned with the loyalty of the administration. But it remains the case that we must distinguish between the contribution of leaders and the contributions of their subordinates.

Thus, the actions of leaders seem almost inextricably linked to the environment in which they occur. They are triggered by the problems that society faces; they depend markedly on the goodwill and competence of others. The distinction between leaders and environment seems to elude us; yet an assessment of the impact of leaders cannot be made unless that distinction can be operationalized.

If lists of separate actions of leaders do not provide the answer, because they are too concrete and too embedded in their context, could the solution be provided by moving to the opposite extreme, namely, to the examination of the broad intentions of leaders? These, too, are related to the environment, admittedly, but the link is not so close. Intentions are, so to speak, the dreams about the ideal society which the leader wishes to transform into reality. Yet for this very reason, while they may give a better idea of what the leader is and wants, they may not be satisfactory: they may be too vague and inchoate; they may even be rationalizations or excuses and may never be implemented at all.

We have therefore to find an intermediate concept between intentions and actions which will reflect the leaders' effective inputs in political life. Such a concept appears to be constituted by *goals*, provided that by goals we mean a set of intentions which leaders effectively attempt to put in practice, that is to say, that they summarize the *general orientation of leaders' actions* and are not mere expressions of hope or desires that remain unfulfilled. Goals must also encompass the cases of leaders who claim to have 'no' goals, that is to say, who wish to preserve the status quo and act on the basis of problems as they occur. This will be the basis we shall use to classify leaders in the course of this chapter.

The problems posed by the classification of the goals of political leaders

Even if goals are adopted as the basis for the classificatory scheme, many difficulties remain. First, goals are numerous, too numerous to be handled directly in a comparative analysis. They have therefore to be classified under broad rubrics. Second, because the goals of leaders may change, the classificatory scheme has to allow for movements. Third, it has to be decided whether normative considerations about the 'worth' of leaders should be part of the categorization: should 'bad' rulers be analysed alongside 'heroes'?

The two main fields within which leaders' goals can be organized. Leaders are involved in a very large number of fields of activity. For each of these fields, they have goals. Even if they ostensibly do not appear to have a general orientation, they are in fact following a line — that of maintaining the status quo. But since the activities of leaders relate to foreign affairs, defence, law and order, institutional arrangements, economic development, health, welfare, education and cultural affairs, there would seem to be as many goals as there are fields; and there might indeed be specific goals for several sub-fields within each area. As a matter of fact, leaders are likely to have somewhat different orientations with respect to each problem; these orientations will probably conflict with or contradict each other on some points. It is therefore unquestionably valuable, for the preparation of a detailed analysis of the orientations of a particular leader or a set of political leaders, to examine the goals that are pursued in each field and sub-field. But, for a first and general examination of types of political leadership, it is imperative that we should be able to elaborate a classificatory scheme that can also determine the broad manner in which leaders can be compared from the point of view of their general orientations. Some of the richness of the concrete details will be lost in the process; but there will be gains in that we shall be better able to obtain the overall view of the variations in the general orientations of leaders and, therefore, of the ways in which these differ in the impact that they may make on their respective societies.

The number of goals characterizing each leader must therefore be reduced to a minimum. Ideally, one would want to find one overarching principle on which all others would depend. This is not an unrealistic aim: to state that leaders have an overriding goal unifying their several orientations amounts to saying that leaders have an ideology. As a first approximation at least, it does not seem wrong to claim that there is an inherent unity in the overall purpose of each leader's actions. The ideology does not need to be elaborated in detail or highly intellectualized. What is suggested is that leaders' goals can be classified by reference to certain broad approaches to societal development. Does the leader wish to change the environment at all and, if so, to what extent? Leaders do not all have to have an explicit frame of reference, but, in practice, they must act in ways that suggest some basic unity in their approach. Indeed, even the leader who ostensibly has no ideology has in fact a status quo goal. The actions of this leader are directed towards the maintenance of society as it is; such a leader is truly conservative in the strict sense of the word. In most cases, however, leaders have 'goals' in the sense that they wish to see some developments occur which might modify the status quo to some extent. This suggests a modest departure from a pure conservative position — and also a general orientation organizing the actions and sets of actions of the leader.

It would therefore seem that we can elaborate a general classification of the goals — or general orientations — of political leaders without having to be concerned in detail with all the fields of government in which they may be involved. What we do need to be concerned with is the kind of 'vision', or at least the kind of 'view', that leaders have of their country, its past, present and future, and of their role in helping to realize this vision. The vision may be broad or narrow and, as in the case of the leader who has no goal besides staying in power, it may at the limit correspond to maintaining the status quo. But it is suggested that there is an underlying unity in the approach of every leader to action and that the categorization of leaders can be based on the elements that characterize this approach. The different approaches would thus constitute a space within which individual leaders would be located: they could then be related to each other by means of a comparison of the different global visions of society.

There is, however, a limit to this 'unifying' process: this arises not from the fact that some leaders lack a well-organized and conscious ideology, but from the fact that one area remains distinct from the others: the area of foreign affairs and defence. This distinction has a long history, as we saw in Chapter 2; it corresponds to different characteristics in the nature of leadership. The rules of the game and the dynamics of the process are profoundly at variance in the two cases; whereas, in the internal fields, leaders attempt to build a 'community', in the international field they are players in a game of several actors, each of which (in principle at least) is independent of the others. The international affairs game resembles poker or at best bridge; the internal political game has the characteristics of a team sport.

For this reason, one cannot expect more than a casual or episodic linkage between the ideology of the leader in the internal fields and the ideology on the basis of which he or she interacts with others on the international chessboard. It is true that a liberal or progressive leader at home will be more likely to be a liberal or progressive leader in the international field as well; but it may be that, precisely because a leader is liberal or progressive at home, he or she will wish to crush or at least render ineffective the countries that are pursuing policies that are neither liberal nor progressive. Indeed, this is not the only type of linkage between home and international goals or orientations towards action: we shall have occasion to see other examples of these relationships in this chapter. But, in principle at least, the plane of foreign affairs and the internal plane remain distinct: the overall purpose that characterizes leaders' actions on the home front does not directly help to characterize the same leaders' actions on the international plane. The linkage is casual, and may also be instrumental and related to a particular benefit that is being sought; it does not follow from the substance of the question at stake.

Within each of the two areas, however, it is permissible and realistic to consider the goals of leaders as being broadly united by a fundamental purpose. In the internal field, the unity of purpose stems from an overall vision that leaders have of the kind of society that they would like to see in their country — a vision that differs more or less from the existing situation and is more or less clear: it is likely to be clearer when it differs widely from the existing society. In the international sphere, the unity of purpose stems from the position which the leader holds in the circle of world leaders and which the country holds in the circle of nations. Leaders may need or wish to change this position to some extent: the vision that they have of the international situation may thus differ more or less from the current state of affairs and, in this respect too, may be more or less clear and precise. How these two visions intersect, reinforce or contradict each other is a matter of considerable importance for the impact of leadership; it is therefore a matter that we shall encounter at various points in the course of the subsequent analysis.

Changes of goals over time. While leaders have a certain view of the country's needs and of their role in satisfying these needs, it is unrealistic to believe that this view is unchanging. The reasons for changes in the general approach of leaders to goals are numerous and do not deserve to be examined here in detail, except to say that they stem in part from modifications in the personality characteristics of leaders; but we know little about the consequences of such modifications, and what we do know derives partly from alterations in the structure of the regime and partly from transformations in the environment. Not only do leaders often have to recognize that there are serious obstacles to the implementation of their goals, not only, conversely, do some opportunities emerge that give leaders the possibility of achieving goals that they previously felt to be unrealistic, but the goals themselves come to be altered. For instance, a leader may come to power believing that the country should be rapidly developed economically and socially; after a few years, this leader may no longer feel that such a development is so urgent but that, on the contrary, other goals are more essential, such as the defence of the nation against enemies without or within. An examination, even casual, of the contemporary world suggests that such changes in goals are a common phenomenon and that it would be absurd not to take them into consideration in a general classification of political leaders.

It therefore follows that such a classification must have a time dimension and must be inherently capable of allowing the position of leaders to be moved over time in any space that is being determined. Of course, little change may occur with respect to many leaders, either because these leaders have doggedly kept to the policy initiatives that they pursued on coming to power, or because they simply do not have the time to change the framework of goals they believed in on achieving office. As a very large proportion of leaders (about a third) stay at the head of their country for a year or even less and a substantial group remain in office for only about two years, the scope for significant change in goals is probably very limited for the majority of leaders (see Blondel, 1980: 163–92). For them, a single location in a classification of goals is not unrealistic.

But leaders whose goals change are among those who are the most important, since they are likely to be drawn primarily from the relatively small group who stay in office for substantial and even very long periods. The classificatory scheme must be sufficiently flexible to allow the changes in goals to be registered; this is essential not only to ensure the accuracy of the analysis, but also to provide an opportunity to discover the patterns of changes and the reasons for these patterns. We could examine, for instance, whether rulers become more conservative as time passes and they become older, a view that is often expressed but has never been systematically checked. Leaders may also alter their goals as a result of pressure from the environment: one should attempt to discover the extent to which 'circumstances' result in greater constraints or, alternatively, provide opportunities, and the extent to which leaders adjust to these changing situations. Thus, a dynamic categorization of leaders' goals is likely to provide important insights into the understanding of the effects of governmental office on the behaviour of leaders.

'Good' and 'bad' leaders. Some leaders are unanimously applauded for their vision and their actions; others are viewed as tyrants, almost as beasts, and are felt not to deserve to be recorded in the annals of mankind. Many rulers, indeed the majority, are between these two extremes, with judgements about them oscillating at times, for instance as a result of the reappraisals of historians. Should a general classification take into account these normative standpoints? Or should it, on the contrary, remain neutral and place on the same level the 'bad' and the 'good', the tyrants and the 'real' heroes?

Although the classification of political leaders has still not advanced markedly, there have been striking controversies about the advisability of including tyrants among the leaders. No doubt this standpoint is due in part to the legacy of suspicion about leaders which modern political science has inherited from classical theorists; but it appears to have been strengthened somewhat as a result of the numerous cases of tyrants who have characterized the contemporary world. It seems shocking to include Hitler among the leaders, especially because his influence cannot be realistically described as minute and because, as a result, he should be compared not with ordinary and moderately effective rulers, but with the 'great heroes' who seem to have shaped the history of mankind. Thus the dilemma seems to be that either one simply does not consider as 'real' leaders those men and women whose excesses have made the world significantly more barbaric than it would otherwise have been, or else one is constrained to place such tyrants alongside and very close to the great leaders who, on the contrary, have markedly contributed to the elevation of the human condition.

Whatever distaste one may have in including such rulers in a general classification, it seems unjustifiable, unrealistic and indeed practically impossible not to consider them alongside other leaders. The aim of the enquiry is to examine the effect that individuals may have on society in different circumstances; it may be that, ultimately, we will wish also to assess whether the effect is 'positive' or 'negative'. But such a judgement cannot be passed unless we have examined all types of rulers, including tyrants. 'Bad' rulers have therefore to be examined alongside heroes.

It is also unrealistic to exclude 'bad' rulers, as there are no clear criteria by which to establish such a distinction. It may seem obvious that Hitler was awful, but it is less clear whether Robespierre or

Napoleon was; nor is it entirely evident that Stalin or Mao belong to the same group. If the criterion for exclusion has to be the unanimous distaste or rejection expressed about these tyrants, very few rulers indeed would come to be excluded; and these would be drawn mainly from the recent period, as one tends to forget the misdeeds of past rulers. It is therefore unrealistic to attempt the division: if a category is so small that only a few recent leaders would be placed within it, it is better to abandon it and recognize that the aim of the classification is to compare the goals and policy initiatives of all rulers.

Indeed, a further difficulty would have to be faced since, in this as in other respects, a dichotomy opposing tyrants to 'heroes' is a manifest oversimplification. Some rulers have been awful, while others may have been 'saints'; but the large majority should be located somewhere between these two extremes. This is why it is difficult to state whether Robespierre, Napoleon, Stalin or Mao should be placed in one or the other of the categories. They have had a 'positive' legacy in terms of institutions or modes of behaviour, even though they were also directly responsible for huge numbers of deaths and for immense sufferings. Thus, a realistic division into 'good' and 'bad' leaders would have to be based on a detailed weighting of achievements (presumably determined by the value of their actions for subsequent generations) and of hideous acts (presumably defined essentially in terms of violations of human rights). Such a weighting would be extremely difficult to undertake in view of the limited data at our disposal (in large part because tyrants, or even ordinary 'bad' leaders, are naturally anxious to conceal the extent of their misdeeds); it would also be wholly subjective. The purpose of the classification is not to apportion blame or exclude leaders from the analysis on the basis of a judgement, however general, passed on their worth: it is to discover how far these had an effect on society. It is surely only after the magnitude of such an effect has begun to be determined that it will become possible to examine how far leaders who achieve much tend to do so by means that are repugnant to civilized mankind, as classical political theorists seem often to have believed.

A two-dimensional framework for the classification of leaders' goals [1]

Leaders should therefore be classified according to their goals if their impact is to be related to the societal conditions in which they operate. These goals can be brought together, in the internal and international fields respectively, under the umbrella of the general view or 'vision' that they have of the future of the society which they attempt to bring about, since the definition we adopted for goals is that of an orientation towards action. We can thus now embark on an endeavour to classify these general 'visions', on the understanding that each leader may change the vision over time and that we are not proposing to state whether we believe these visions to be good or bad.

Two problems need to be overcome in the elaboration of such a classification of goals: first, the classification must be broad enough to encompass all the types of 'visions' that leaders may have; second, it must be sufficiently precise to lead to eventual operationalization. This means that we cannot resort to a typology based merely on dichotomies or trichotomies: we have to discover dimensions along which leaders can be located at many — indeed, theoretically at an infinity of — points. It means, too, that the distinguishing criteria which will serve as bases for the dimensions should be comparatively simple in order to correspond relatively easily to the reality of leaders' 'visions'.

How can such criteria be discovered? We know that we shall eventually be obliged to elaborate two sets of spaces corresponding, respectively, to internal and international affairs; but, in the first instance, the best move is to be guided by the kinds of differences that seem intuitively to exist among leaders, particularly (to begin with) among leaders who are commonly regarded as being 'great'. As a matter of fact, these intuitive distinctions appear as soon as one concentrates on the broad goals that these leaders had for their countries. A first group to emerge is that of the 'saviours', that is to say, of those who appear to be able to solve a major problem facing the nation or the state — in many cases, the threat of total annihilation. Before the saviour appears, the nation is on the verge of collapse; afterwards, the danger is avoided and peace and calm return to the community. It seems that Moses, the archetype often mentioned since Weber, falls into this category; but Churchill, as well as Adenauer and arguably de Gaulle, would also seem to belong to this group, though in a somewhat different manner in each case. Churchill was a saviour in the face of outside attack. Adenauer was a saviour in that he was able to solve contradictions that had previously existed within the political system of Germany: he was able to bring about a consensus with respect to the overall operation of political life. De Gaulle was a saviour in both senses. The main characteristic of these leaders is that they strengthened a polity or nation that was collapsing or had collapsed. They did not so much transform the polity as boost its resolve or eliminate difficulties that had emerged in the past and had made political life hectic or unmanageable. This is why they can legitimately be called 'saviours'.

We already see some difficulties and indeed distinctions at this point, since someone like de Gaulle, for instance, is both a saviour and more than a saviour, in that he brought about a new political system which markedly modified the character of French life. Perhaps he can be deemed to be a saviour in this respect as well, but in a different way from that which characterized Churchill between 1940 and 1945. Here we begin to see some of the differences that emerge as a result of the distinction between an internal 'vision' and an international 'vision', although we also have to note some interrelationships between the two aspects.

Yet is is worthwhile to proceed, and to contrast those whom we have just described as 'saviours' with another group of leaders: leaders who are normally considered great, but who played a very different part. They can probably be labelled 'transformers', in the sense that they sharply modify the basis on which society is organized;[2] they usually do so through a revolution, since it seems that only by a revolution can a 'radical' change in the norms and modes of behaviour be achieved. But, while they are revolutionary in terms of the way in which they achieve power, the substantive distinction between transformers and saviours lies in the fact that the former propose to implement a complete ideology, one that extends to all facets of society. Perhaps the clearest example of such an 'ideology' is Mao, since he wished, through the Cultural Revolution, to alter in a spectacular manner the modes of thought of the Chinese population. But Lenin and Castro clearly also belong to this group, as their apparent contribution to social, economic, cultural and political change has been massive.

One major difference between saviours and those who might be labelled as revolutionary transformers is that the former appear to be concerned primarily with preserving while the latter are involved in bringing about change, indeed major change, in society. At this point we seem to come to what appears to be a major distinction in the posture of leaders. It is manifest that some leaders 'maintain' the political and social system as it is, while others want to alter it dramatically. But if change is the *raison d'être* for the difference, there is no basis for seeing the distinction in terms of a dichotomy: the revolutionaries may wish to change society 'radically', but it seems reasonable to assume that other leaders may wish to stand half-way, or at some other intermediate position between the saviours who do not wish to change and those who want to create a wholly new society. This appears indeed to be the case with many leaders, either because they are anxious to buttress certain aspects of the existing 'system' or because they wish to preside over the introduction of some changes in a variety of other aspects. Some kings or other 'paternalistic' leaders fall in this category, for example the enlightened despots of the late eighteenth century in central Europe, or Bismarck, especially with respect to his introduction of national suffrage and aspects of social security; in the postwar world, the Shah of Iran attempted to maintain many aspects of traditional society while dismantling various elements of the social structure. Similarly, though from a different standpoint, many 'populist' leaders of the Third World fall into the same category, as they wish to introduce some changes but do not want to upset the whole society, and they seek to accomplish this end either by 'integrating', rather than destroying, the tribal underpinnings of the social structure, or by committing themselves to a 'middle way' in the introduction of socialism. Ataturk and Cardenas, Nasser and many African leaders belong to this group.

It seems therefore realistic to conclude that leaders can be located at different points — in practice, at an infinity of different points — depending on the extent of change which they bring about in the society. Indeed, it is more satisfactory to view the distinction in this manner, since the extreme positions are unlikely ever to be held — even the 'purest' of saviours modifies somewhat the structures of the society in order to preserve it or to make it function better. Adenauer and de Gaulle introduced substantial institutional changes at the political level in order to ensure that the democratic system of government should operate efficiently; Churchill allowed himself to support a substantial rethinking of at least some aspects of social relations in Britain in order to bring about greater consensus in the country. Conversely, those who wish to introduce 'radical' change always stop short of what would be a 'total' transformation of the society, in part of course because of resistances, which we shall have occasion to discuss further. Thus, by plotting leaders along a dimension, it is possible to be more realistic and to introduce finer distinctions. What is significant is the relative extent of change which they are instrumental in bringing about.

Change has to be viewed here in a 'neutral' manner, moreover, and to include both movements towards a 'new', hitherto unknown, type of society and movements that consist of a return to the past. For leaders who want to take society backwards — the 'reactionaries' — are equally concerned with change as those who want to achieve 'progress'. Hitler was a 'revolutionary ideologue' in that he wanted Germany to have the 'pure' characteristics which, he believed, it had in the distant past. While supporters of African socialism want to see their society change in a 'progressive' direction, Bismarck or the Shah of Iran introduced changes that manifested both a return to the past and a movement towards the future. In general, populists and paternalists are characterized by an attempt to introduce relatively gradual changes; but sometimes they are concerned simultaneously with bringing about changes in a 'progressive' direction and changes in a 'reactionary' direction.

Thus, a further distinction has to be made between 'right' and 'left', or between 'reactionaries' and 'progressives'. But, especially with respect to 'paternalistic' leaders, the mix of reactionary and progressive policies is often such that it is difficult to disentangle them from the overall 'package'. In a preliminary stage of the analysis, therefore, it is more prudent to view the dimension as one ranging from almost no change (as characterized by saviours) to very large change (as characterized by revolutionary transformers of both right and left), while noting that the 'direction' of the change, in ideological terms and with respect to each particular state, can be positive or negative.

It is at this point that we must begin to introduce the distinction between the internal and international planes, a distinction which, as we shall increasingly see, plays a considerable part in the determination of the characteristics of leaders. We have contrasted saviours with transformers: this is because these two types of leaders are the best-known and also the most 'heroic', though we noted that there were many well-known leaders also among those who occupied intermediate positions, such as some of the populists. But, of course, in a strict sense, the contrast between saviours and transformers occurs on two different planes: saviours are saviours because they want to preserve their country from encroachments from outside, while transformers are determined, in the first instance, to alter only their own country. Yet there are those who want to preserve society and direct their attention to internal matters alone, while, on the other hand, there are those who want to transform the external order but do not wish to modify the internal order. The preservation of society that a saviour such as Churchill wished to bring about is very different from the preservation of society that a leader such as Pinochet in Chile or Pétain in France wanted to achieve. Similarly, the transformation of the world that Alexander the Great or the Emperor Charles V, or indeed Hitler, wished to bring about is different from the transformation of the society internally with which Lenin or Mao was primarily concerned.

Thus we discover that there are, in effect, two different and parallel planes, the internal and the international, on which it is possible to locate leaders with respect to the contrast between preservation and transformation. Indeed, the discovery of those two different planes helps to solve some of the problems that we encountered earlier in classifying some saviours. De Gaulle may have been a saviour, a preserver, at least in 1940, but he was instrumental in introducing major changes in the structure of politics in the late 1950s: in the first case he operated on the international plane, in the second he operated principally (at least for a while) on the national plane. Some leaders of course aim at introducing change on both planes — Hitler for example, though he was more of a revolutionary on the international plane than internally — while others, following perhaps the precept of Machiavelli that the internal structure of the country should be modified as little as possible, wish only to bring about changes on the international plane and have a conservative vision as far as the future of their own society is concerned.

We have so far considered only those leaders who are usually described as 'great'. It was pointed out in the previous chapters that a major difficulty arises from the fact that there is a seemingly unbridgeable gap between them and the 'ordinary' heads of governments. The dichotomy seemed to arise from, and possibly to replicate, the distinction between leaders who are held to alter society directly and those who are 'mere' managers or policy-makers. On the surface, this distinction, while being ostensibly essential, seemed to be the major obstacle towards the building of a general model of leadership.

What we have considered so far in this chapter has shown, however, that, if there is to be a fundamental distinction, it cannot be between transformers and mere policy-makers: only in the sense that saviours re-establish or increase the strength of the structures of a society could they be said to be transformers; this is manifestly stretching the meaning of the word unduly. In truth, the distinction between the 'great' and 'ordinary' leaders cannot be based on the extent of change that they bring about in their nations: the difference must be found elsewhere. It begins to emerge when we consider more precisely what we mean by policy-making or policy development, by contrast with the goals of leaders which we have discussed so far. What de Gaulle was concerned with, in 1940 or in 1958, was the *whole* life and structure of the nation: he had a 'vision' of France which he was anxious to maintain. What policy-makers are concerned with, on the contrary, is the introduction or maintenance of sets of arrangements relating to an *aspect* of the life of the country. For them, the nation, country or political system is a given: what is of importance is, for instance, an educational system, an economic structure, a particular relationship between the centre and the periphery. Of course, if they are leaders, rather than departmental ministers in charge of a sector of government only, they are potentially concerned (and indeed actually concerned, at least nominally) with other aspects of the 'system'; but, first, they tend to concentrate their activities on one aspect or at most a few aspects of this system; and, second, they see the whole as a number of discrete sectors, not as an overall problem in need of a comprehensive solution.

Such leaders are obviously different from saviours and from those who might be called protectors, from revolutionary transformers or even from paternalists or populists. They seem to be different in stature or 'prominence', to be sure; they may indeed be different in that they do not have such a large popular following. But these characteristics do not relate directly to their impact on society as such; specifically, they do not relate to what they view their impact to be. What distinguishes them from the leaders we have discussed so far is the fact that their activity, and probably also their field of interest, is more limited. They are de facto specialized in an area, and consequently the impact they may have, in the first instance at least, can be related only to one or a number of fields. They are policy-makers because it is by their achievements in a specific policy area that they can make a difference.

It is indeed because of this greater specialization that they are usually or intuitively felt to have a smaller impact. Leaders (and ministers) who make their mark essentially in one domain are unlikely to be rated as being the 'great leaders' of history. If some of them become political 'heroes', this seems to be only when they succeed in moving up to a broader area of activity. But the question of the size of their impact, so to speak, has to be viewed as distinct from the scope of their activity; arguably, they may even have a greater impact, because of what they achieve in their sphere, than 'global' leaders who do not achieve much or who fail in what they (and the nation) feel to be their mission. This matter can be put aside at present: what is important at this point is to notice that the scope of involvement is very wide in the case of the 'great leaders' whom we examined earlier and, on the contrary, narrow in the case of the 'policy-makers'.

The fundamental underlying distinction between the policy-makers and the others relates therefore to the *scope* of the area of intervention, and to the range of problems or aspects of the polity that is being covered. But when it is conceived in this way, the distinction ceases to appear as a dichotomy. In the first instance, one is inclined to contrast the great leaders, who seem to affect the 'whole' system, with the policy-makers, who appear concerned with a limited area only. But further examination suggests that only very rarely do great leaders concern themselves, in fact, with the whole system. For the 'system' may mean the political or institutional sector; it may mean also the social structure or the economic arrangements; it may even mean the overall culture, the norms of the society. Some leaders may be concerned with the whole system, admittedly; but many, even among the 'great', are concerned with only some aspects of the system. At the other end of the scale, some policy-makers may be concerned with a rather narrow sector within a policy field, while others may be concerned with a very broad area, covering for instance all aspects of economic policy or social welfare. Thus the scope of action of leaders must be described not in the form of a dichotomy, but in terms of a range: this action can vary from a very wide to a very limited front.

Indeed, it soon appears that there are large numbers of intermediate cases. Many policy-making leaders — indeed, perhaps the majority of them — are involved in a number of policies; or they are involved in a number of related matters (matters which at least they view as being related) which they want to solve in a co-ordinated fashion: these may concern the economy, or wide aspects of the sphere of intervention of the government in social affairs, for instance. On the other hand, the 'great' leaders who appear at first sight to be concerned with the 'whole' system deal in fact with a segment of the system only: they may be concerned with the norms underlying economic relations, but not with political institutions. This happened frequently in the West after 1945: some leaders tried to 'comfort' a population worried by the speed of change; without being 'protectors' in the strong sense, because the system was not about to collapse, these leaders were concerned essentially with 'curing', with 'calming' the citizenry. Others wished to 'redefine' the agenda, for instance in terms of the relationship between the population and the state, in order to 'make people stand on their own two feet' (Thatcher) or to 'take the government off the backs of the people' (Reagan). This type of approach has a global element, to be sure; but it is not *fully* global as it does not affect the whole system. Thus, between those who maintain, reconstruct or otherwise concern themselves with the 'whole' system and whose who devote their activities to one or a very limited number of policies, there is a large number — indeed, an infinity of — positions which leaders may and, indeed, do take. The *scope* of intervention thus truly constitutes a dimension along which leaders can be, and must be, located.

We have thus discussed two dimensions of analysis: one distinguishes the 'great' leaders among themselves, depending on the extent to which they are concerned with maintenance or change in the society; the other helps to differentiate between 'great' leaders and policy-makers by assessing the scope and range of intervention. But the dimension of change also concerns policy-makers. Not all leaders dealing with educational problems, with housing or with agriculture want to bring about change, and, if they do want to bring about change, not all of them wish to effect the same extent of change. Although the evidence is circumstantial, it seems overwhelming: there are substantial variations between those who introduce and implement major reforms and those who do not. It is therefore clear that one cannot lump into one simple category all the 'specialist' policy-makers; on the contrary, it seems necessary to distinguish sharply between a number of types, ranging from those who introduce large changes to those who do not.

At one end of the scale are those who are concerned with taking the decisions as they arise and with ensuring that there are few frictions either in the administration or among the groups in society; at the other end are those who initiate a number of entirely new policies and who are therefore potentially able to change the nature of the social 'landscape' within the area of government with which they are mostly concerned. The first type of leaders should be described as 'managers', while the second consists of 'innovators'. What distinguishes them is the extent to which they achieve — indeed, intend to achieve — an element of change. In between, there are policy-makers who modify the policies they inherit only to a limited extent; at a lower level, these 'adjusters' correspond to the populists who were described when we examined the 'great' leaders. They are agents of moderate change within the context of a more specialized area.

The distinction between managers, adjusters and innovators suggests that there is, among the 'policy-makers', a parallel distinction to the one that was made between protectors and transformers: in both cases, the basis for the distinction is the amount of change. It therefore follows that, while there is a dimension helping to distinguish between leaders who relate to the 'whole' system and those who relate to parts of the system or a limited area, there tends to be another dimension, also applicable to all leaders, which helps to distinguish between the amount of change that these leaders wish to introduce (Figure 1).

We have thus elaborated two dimensions, and have done so by considering primarily the internal developments within the country; but it is quickly apparent that the same dimensions are also applicable to the international field. We noticed the important contrast between saviours and those who wish to modify 'completely' the world order — a Napoleon or a Hitler, for example; but there are also many leaders whose involvement in foreign affairs is more limited and concerns either a small region of the globe or some specific aspects of international development. Those who were concerned primarily with the build-up of a united Europe after the second world war, for instance, can be deemed to have been 'reformists' on the international plane, while many other leaders have merely been innovators or even managers.

An examination of the goals and broad policy initiatives of leaders, therefore, shows that there is appreciably more than the distinction between 'great' and 'ordinary' leaders, or between transformers and 'mere' policy-makers. The nature of the impact can be varied and leaders can be distinguished in a complex manner. There are in fact two dimensions according to which, theoretically at least, leaders can be located and therefore be related to each other. Moreover, it seems that the position of a given leader can, and often will, vary over time in such a two-dimensional space: de Gaulle's position in the 1940s was not the same as the one he occupied in the 1960s. Whether it is as yet possible, in practice, to locate precisely large numbers of leaders in this space, and to locate them differently at different points in time, is a matter that needs further investigation; but there does not seem to be any theoretical reason why such an operation could not be conducted. If it can be conducted, some substantial advance will have been made in the analysis of leadership; if it cannot yet be undertaken, or if it can be undertaken only to a limited extent, there is clearly a need to improve our empirical knowledge of the goals of leaders. But the two-dimensional categorization of goals can at least guide the empirical enquiries and thus help to bring closer the moment when leaders' goals can be precisely assessed in practice and, consequently, when the impact of leaders on society will become better known and understood.

The broad framework of environmental influence on leadership

Leaders' goals are obviously related in some manner to the environment: the question is, how close is the relationship? For some it is viewed as one of complete dependence; but, assuming that this is not the case, the role of the environment can be thought to vary markedly. One can imagine two extreme possibilities: that of near-total freedom enjoyed by the leaders, who would be able to handle any situation by pursuing their own pre-determined goals, and that of near-complete impotence, when leaders may not make more than a trivial mark on the societies which they rule. Between these two extremes, what are the positions in which leaders are most likely to be found?

In a fully-fledged analysis of this problem, one should of course be able to specify exactly the point at which each leader can be located on this continuum. But this is clearly a distant aim. In moving towards a partial answer, however, one step at least can be taken. This consists in distinguishing among 'classes' of situations with which different leaders are confronted. Not every ruler can save his nation, whether or not he wishes to do so: this is because not every nation 'needs' to be saved. If it were possible to discover in a similar manner a number of broad types of environmental 'stages' on which leaders have to play, one might be able to begin to circumscribe the broad characteristics of the problem of the impact of leadership.

In all probability, leaders have some freedom to act; in all probability, too, leaders exercise this freedom to a greater or lesser

FIGURE 1
A two-dimensional typology of potential leadership impact

DIMENSION I	Maintenance	Moderate change	Large change
DIMENSION II			
WIDE SCOPE	SAVIOURS (Moses, Churchill, De Gaulle)	PATERNALISTS/ POPULISTS (Bismarck, Stalin, Shah, many Third World)	IDEOLOGUES (Mao, Lenin, Hitler)
MODERATE SCOPE (aspect of a system)	COMFORTERS (Eisenhower)	'REDEFINERS' (JFK, Reagan, Thatcher)	REFORMISTS (FDR)
SPECIALIZED SCOPE (policy area)	MANAGERS (ministers who administer day-to-day problems)	ADJUSTERS/ TINKERERS (ministers who modify an aspect of a policy)	INNOVATORS (new policy: i.e. land reform)

Notes:
1. In each category there are those who succeed and those who fail and make no impact, or very little: e.g. someone who maintains by no action because the system is strong or the policy viable is a 'do nothing'.
2. Change may mean 'progressive' or 'regressive' or a combination of both.

extent. The overall purpose of the analysis of leadership must be to determine how large the freedom is and how far leaders use it. While, on the one hand, this freedom is manifested by the goals that leaders choose to adopt as their orientation towards action, it is also circumscribed by the fact that the environment makes, so to speak, some types of goals easier to implement than others. It is less difficult to mobilize a nation against another nation if the population already has aggressive sentiments *vis-à-vis* that nation; it is less difficult to bring about reforms in the economic or social field if much of the population is discontented with the current economic and social structure.

The purpose of the analysis of environmental conditions is thus to determine the ways in which leaders are likely to be helped or hindered in the implementation of their goals by the characteristics of the society that they rule. The point is not to establish that leaders *must* pursue certain goals because the society commands that these should be pursued: on the contrary, the overall aim is to assess the leeway that leaders appear to have, in the contemporary world at least, by confronting the goals that are being pursued with the underlying conditions of the society. It is also to see, consequently, how likely leaders are to depart markedly from the underlying conditions of society and to assess by what means such a strategy can be achieved. The aim is, further, to examine these matters as precisely as possible, that is to say, to discover the *extent* to which leaders are able to depart from underlying societal conditions, rather than merely to suggest that leaders are either 'strong' or 'ineffective'.

The distinction between the internal and the external environment
In order to proceed, we need to be able to differentiate between various kinds of general situations with which leaders may be confronted. This means attempting, again, a classification. The first distinction that comes to mind is that between internal and external matters which we found to be essential with respect to leaders' goals. Clearly, leaders' goals with respect to foreign affairs differ from leaders' goals with respect to internal problems because the subject-matter, so to speak, is so vastly different. Thus, if it is essential to distinguish between two planes of leaders' goals, external and internal, it is equally essential to distinguish between internal and external environmental pressures. On the one hand, leaders are faced with forces outside the nation with which they have to cope and which might at the limit threaten the very existence of the nation; on the other, there are pressures within the polity which, if they are not dealt with, might lead to situations that can be dangerous for the persistence of the regime (and, of course, for the maintenance of the leader in

office). These pressures are clearly different in origin, therefore, from the pressures that originate from outside the polity.

These pressures would also seem to be different in a number of other ways. The intensity and immediacy of the external threat is sometimes more obvious: internal pressures may result in the ending of a regime, but external pressures may go further: they may destroy entirely the fabric of the nation, and result in an annexation of the territory and subjugation of the citizens, involving mass destruction and mass killings. The threat to internal order may, in extreme cases, end up in civil war, but the danger of external war is more common and more widely feared. Moreover, external problems often appear to be more 'contingent', more 'accidental', than internal problems. Not all internal difficulties are predictable, of course, while many external situations may be foreseen; but, to a degree at least, actions of foreign governments seem to confront leaders with surprising moves and pressures which often result from developments within the country of origin over which these other leaders have no or almost no control.

The distinction between external and internal pressure is far from neat, however, in many if not most situations: there are many and complex interrelationships. This is in part because pressure for action on the leader of a country arises both from outside events and from internal demands for external action: a foreign government may threaten a country but, conversely, the population of that country may pressure its government to intervene in the affairs of another state. Moreover, external pressures may take many forms, ranging from sudden, almost accidental, events, which may result from a foreign leader's actions, to diffuse and almost subterranean influences which may affect markedly the demands of the citizens. For example, US influence on a country results not merely from the pressure of US leaders and government officials; it also results from the fact that the American way of life may induce citizens of other countries to want to acquire different goals, achieve different results and so forth. Some have even claimed that there is, as a result, full 'dependency'. This is true not only of US influence: a similar impact may result from other nations. Of course, large and powerful countries are more likely to influence smaller ones; but neighbouring nations exercise pressure on each other in many ways. Thus, while it is important to distinguish between external and internal environmental pressures on leaders, one must look specifically at the many ways in which external forces exercise pressure indirectly on a nation, as well as the many ways in which internal demands within a nation may force action on the external front.

Furthermore, the external environment is often used by the leaders of a country to counteract pressures to which they are subjected internally. Leaders take initiatives in foreign affairs for many reasons: the need to respond to a perceived threat is one of them; but leaders may also provoke external activities because they believe that they might reap some benefits on the home front. Many wars seem to have been started, at least in part, because of considerations of this kind. Interventions by national leaders on the external front thus have to be viewed as means aimed at indirectly influencing the internal situation, although such interventions are likely in turn to result in countermoves by foreign governments which may have further consequences, unforeseen by the leaders who originated the process.

The framework within which leaders operate is thus a complex web of relationships linking the internal and external planes of action. Yet, as internal and external activities are ostensibly largely autonomous, and may follow different paths for long periods, it is best first to examine separately the general conditions under which internal and external pressures emerge and to see how these are likely to induce leaders to adopt a given type of goal — and, indeed, to facilitate the successful implementation of this goal. We will then have to return to the interrelationship between the two planes.

The direct pressure of the environment on leaders

There are thus pressures on leaders relating to international affairs and pressures relating to internal matters, which, for the moment, we should examine separately. On each of these planes, leaders pursue goals that may have a broader or more limited scope and may aim at maintaining or changing the policies previously adopted. What, then, are the pressures by which leaders may be 'induced' by environmental forces to adopt a particular stance at a particular point in time?

'Normalcy' and the 'need' for managers. Let us start from the situation in which these pressures are essentially directed at maintaining the status quo. If there is complete satisfaction within a polity about the way in which the distribution of goods and services occurs and the political life is conducted; if, moreover, there is a stable equilibrium in the relationship between the country and other nations — if other nations make no demands, and if the citizens of the country have no aggressive tendencies towards their neighbours — then the situation is one of total peace at home and abroad. This state of affairs is very rare, of course, but contemporary Switzerland may be felt to provide a good approximation.

Major consequences for the characteristics of leadership follow from such a situation, as leaders appear to be constrained in their movements. Internally, the 'happiness' of the population results in an intense desire to maintain the status quo; externally, the lack of aggressive inclinations of the population makes it very difficult for leaders to hope to obtain support, were they to wish to engage in 'adventures'. Nor are they triggered to act in response to foreign action, since it is assumed that foreign countries have no quarrel with the nation. Thus there are vast pressures on the leaders not to make any moves at all; the potential scope for leaders' initiatives is greatly reduced and, at the limit, non-existent. The type of leaders who can be expected 'naturally' to emerge in this case will therefore be managers, since these are men and women whose goals consist of the discovery, piecemeal, of compromises between the various actors in the society. The suggestions are promoted by those actors, and the function of leaders is primarily processual: they smooth the path of demands rather than initiate them.

'Normalcy' thus 'naturally' results in leaders being managers. Conversely, only when the situation is 'normal' is there an environmental pressure for leaders to be managers; when the society is under threat, on the contrary, there are demands for 'comforters' or 'protectors'. Management is not enough: if a vessel is about to sink, there is only a limited need for a purser, however effectively he organizes the arrangements for meals and entertainment; the purser will therefore be called upon to perform different functions. Similarly, within the state, managerial leaders are not sufficient. Thus the French leaders of the 1950s were unable to cope with the problems the country faced: indeed, their basic inability to meet the challenges of the time led to tension and increased the call for a saviour.

But managers are also ineffective even when the demand for change is limited. Management is concerned with the solution of problems as they arise, on the understanding that no innovation or reform is required. When there is dissatisfaction with some of the institutions or some of the policy directions, leaders who are 'mere' managers are likely not to provide satisfactory solutions. Discontent will grow. Thus, leaders will have to become adjusters or innovators; otherwise, they are likely to be replaced or the tension in the society will increase.

Pressures on the internal plane and their potential effect on the goals of leaders. A society in which dissatisfaction is high is one in which conflicts are strong. The focus of the conflicts may be the state, or more specifically the government, when there is a long tradition of centralization and authoritarianism; or it may be communal groups, in countries where divisions on tribal, ethnic, religious or class lines are very pronounced; or it may be a combination of the two. In all these cases, leaders will be confronted with demands for change, from one part of the population at least; in fact, they will probably be confronted with contradictory demands on the part of those who want to see change take place and those who wish to preserve the status quo.

This state of affairs has four types of consequences. First, and quite obviously, leaders who wish to be or can only be managers will soon be overtaken as wholly inadequate. Second, existing leaders will have often to modify their goals and steer a difficult path between preservation and reform or even transformation. Third, as this is indeed a difficult path, alternative leaders will emerge, who will claim to embody better the demands of at least a fraction of the electorate. Fourth, if such a situation persists, tension may well increase, the demands of both sides may escalate, and calls for the preservation of the status quo may be matched with equally strong calls for revolutionary transformation.

Hence a number of scenarios, which may all correspond to the situation in a particular country at different points in time. At first, there could be demands for change in a limited number of fields, such as education, housing or an aspect of the economy; alternatively, these demands may relate to the procedures of the administration or result from conflicts between policies rather than from the policies themselves.

The level of discontent may be higher, however, if for instance specific demands have not been met during the preceding period. Leaders may then be pressed for more global alterations; they may have to engage in a 'redefinition' of the political agenda, or present a programme for reform. If they do not, alternative leaders may come to the fore and declare themselves able to provide the solutions that current rulers are unable to bring about. Sometimes, however, leaders who are in office sense the need for change and introduce reforms themselves. Thus, the decision to press for land reform was initiated by the Shah of Iran in the early 1960s in order to regain the political initiative; Bismarck's social security proposals in the 1880s are an even clearer case of a move towards a somewhat paternalistic form of populism designed to counter the increase in discontent from which socialism might otherwise have benefited markedly. Many long-serving leaders of the contemporary world have altered their goals in a similar fashion: Franco did so in the 1950s and 1960s; and Third World founders of states have had to do the same after some years in power, Bourguiba of Tunisia being an outstanding example.

In practice, however, the situation may be even more complex, as there will be pressures in various directions. There would not be pressures to maintain the system unless there was also some pressure for change in society. Conflicts will therefore emerge which will have to be resolved by the leader in favour of a number of different positions, but the result may be a tightrope operation from which the leader may not be able to emerge victorious. There may be gradual escalation of tension, and the demands may be not just for a comforter or a reformer, but for a ruler able to preserve the status quo at all costs, on the one hand, and for a proponent of revolutionary change, on the other. This is the type of evolution that has resulted in the coming to power of authoritarian leaders of the right, as in Chile in 1973, or of the left, as in Ethiopia in the following year.

The level of conflict that is required for a call for revolutionary transformers to be widespread has to be very high. This is why the probability of such situations arising is relatively low. Internal conflict has to be very high; but very high conflict does not normally arise in an instant, or even very quickly. It arises either out of enduring social cleavages or out of new social conditions which often, in turn, stem from economic change. If the cleavages are old and enduring, presumably they are old and enduring because the level of conflict that is generated is tolerable; otherwise there would have been a societal break-up. If the conflicts are relatively new and arise in particular from economic change, they will increase gradually and are likely to result in a demand for innovators or at most reformists, during an early period at least. Thus, internal conflicts will become very high only after a substantial period and provided no attention has been given to these conflicts during that period, that is to say, if the leaders of the time maintained society as it was, an outcome that is unlikely to happen unless extraordinary pressures were used deliberately in order to prevent change. This is so rare that, in most cases, events external to the polity need to have played a part.

Moreover, even if they occasionally emerge as a result of 'natural' internal pressures, for instance if, by an extraordinary coincidence, enduring social cleavages are juxtaposed to social conflicts stemming from rapid economic change, these revolutionary situations are unlikely to last for long and leaders are likely to have quickly retreated to a more 'conservative' standpoint. The new system that has been introduced needs to be preserved; but less rapid change is also likely to be demanded by the society. This is why Stalin should be described as a (hard) paternalist leader rather than a revolutionary ideologue, for instance. Those who have preached 'permanent revolution' have found it impossible to carry out in practice for more than a few years at most, and they have done so at the expense of their own leadership. Mao is perhaps the clearest example of a leader who succeeded in being 'revolutionary' over a long period, though even he failed to meet the 'standard' during many years, and re-established the pre-eminence of the revolutionary ideal only at great cost; interestingly, he was quickly succeeded by manifestly reformist leaders (in the conservative direction).

Pressures on the external plane and the goals of leaders. In most countries, concern with foreign affairs is by and large less intense than the concern with home affairs; but citizens do have prejudices, and indeed aggressive tendencies, towards other nations, which are fuelled by the behaviour of these nations. Meanwhile, the pressures exercised by foreign governments are often strong, and in a few cases paramount, and override all other considerations. This is naturally the occasion when there is a call for a 'saviour' to come to the rescue of the nation, for instance in cases of imminent or actual invasion. Moses was such a saviour: he could, by his inspiration, protect the Jews against their enemies and move them towards the promised land — not by changing the characteristics of the nation, but, on the contrary, by maintaining existing ties, by boosting morale, and by finding a solution to the problem posed by the outside threat.

Saviours can also emerge when internal difficulties combine with environmental pressures originating outside the nation. If the country's institutions need some strengthening in order to be able to meet outside pressures, the saviour may have to repair the edifice; the nation will then be able to offer greater resistance against the elements. But the main call for the saviour must result from external troubles, since, as we saw, 'protectors' are unlikely to emerge without there being also a demand for change on the part of some segments of the population. Pure saviours will be required by society only if society 'wishes' to be saved. To put it differently, a saviour is likely to arise only if there is some will on the part of the nation's citizens to maintain their society. The citizens, like the King of France at the time of Joan of Arc, may despair of the chances of maintaining the society in being; they may have given up hope or be on the verge of doing so. But they must be profoundly oriented in a positive manner towards that society or the regime that is breaking up; they must be lamenting its possible disappearance — while feeling impotent, by themselves, in the face of the major threat. By and large, the internal problems that may exist will provide an opportunity for a saviour if these problems are viewed broadly as the cause of the external weakness of the country. Such was the situation in France in 1940 or 1958; what was wanted by the population was a stable (or more stable) arrangement along the lines of a liberal–democratic system, in part in order to be able to meet the external challenge.

Two conditions thus have to be fulfilled for saviours to emerge; these conditions are strict, and therefore will occur rarely. Only certain societies, at certain times, are likely to be both under imminent threat of break-up and populated by citizens who are anxious to maintain the system, if at all possible. This, of course, does not mean that saviours will always emerge in these circumstances, or that leaders who wish to be saviours will always succeed in their task. The impact may be varied; saviours may not achieve their goals. But these conditions are prerequisites; to put it differently, they constitute the framework within which saviours emerge.

A somewhat similar, though watered-down, situation occurs with respect to the type of leadership that was described in the previous section as that of the 'comforters'. These fulfil a somewhat analogous function to that of saviours, but at a somewhat lower level of threat to the overall system, or at a level at which only part of the system is threatened. Comforters are needed when there is a general and diffuse feeling that the society is under some stress. There may not be clear and immediate dangers, but there is the belief, for instance, that the country may be less secure or that enemies may gradually be gaining in strength — if not in military terms, at least in economic terms. This relative economic improvement of other nations may appear threatening if it is viewed as a decline of the country's own position. The population therefore needs to be 'comforted', because, as when it looks for a saviour, it wants the status quo to be maintained. There is support, even if it is diffuse and rather passive: the worry comes precisely from the feeling that the society which is supported and 'liked' may be passing. Thus, in the case of both the saviour and the comforter, there has to be an external threat and internal support, although the levels at which both conditions need to exist are not the same in the two situations.

Not all external pressures 'require' comforters, saviours or indeed managers, however. Some, on the contrary, provide opportunities for leaders to modify the status quo among nations. What are considered here, of course, are only those instances in which the situation induces leaders to promote change in the world order, and not cases, which we shall examine later, in which the leader himself initiates action or even cases in which there is a complex interrelationship between external and internal pressures. But there are instances when the desire to modify the status quo arises from pressures within the population and/or are triggered by actions of foreign governments. If the population, or an important part of it, feels aggrieved by happenings at the border of the state; if it feels that a neighbouring territory should be annexed because that territory is inhabited by a group with which it is closely associated; if, more generally, the population views other parts of the world — usually, but not necessarily, parts that are relatively close geographically — as being the 'legitimate' prey of its imperialism, then leaders are manifestly pressurized or induced to engage in aggressive actions. Such was the situation, to some extent, in Japan in the 1930s; similar points can be made for various countries of central Europe from the second half of the nineteenth century. In these cases leaders may be incited to act as 'transformers' (in effect, 'aggressors'), or at least as 'reformers' or 'innovators' in the international sphere, in the same way as they may be asked to act as

transformers, reformers or innovators on the internal plane in order
to bring about political, social or economic change.

By and large, however, the pressure for change in the international
field is rarer than the pressure for change in the internal field. Thus the
most frequent observations are, on the one hand, those in which
external pressures are relatively high and comforters or even saviours
are 'required' to maintain the country in existence or in a state of
'well-being' vis-à-vis other nations, and, on the other, those in which
internal pressure for change is strong and the polity naturally looks
for redefiners, reformists or populists to solve problems; there may
even be an opportunity for revolutionary ideologues to become
leaders; but environmental conditions, internally, are unlikely to be
'ripe' naturally, and they will certainly not be 'ripe' for long.

On the external plane, most other types of leadership goals are
unlikely to result naturally from the pressures of the environment, as
they are viewed with suspicion and even in some cases with horror.
Internally, transformers tend to be preferred to protectors and even
comforters, as these appear to prevent progress from occurring —
which, indeed, they do. Especially in the contemporary world, they
are associated with repression, more even than are the revolutionaries:
'progress' is associated with change, and those who achieve some
internal change are judged positively, even if the means that they used
are disliked. On the external plane, however, transformers are in fact
aggressors and are judged negatively for this reason, while those who
wish to maintain the status quo, such as the saviours and the
comforters, are considered positively. By and large, leaders are
regarded as 'good' if they are saviours externally and reformists or
revolutionaries internally (although there is regret that revolution
appears to be associated with repression). This may not explain why
transformers on the external plane — aggressors — and protectors of
the society internally are relatively rare; indeed, saviours and
revolutionaries, even reformists, can rarely be found, either. But the
pressure, to the extent that it exists, is for external saviours and
internal reformists and revolutionaries, a situation that must, to an
extent at least, increase the numbers of those who strive to play this
part.

The 'call' for managers, too, is limited, since, as we saw, only
countries living in harmony internally and with the rest of the world
are likely to require managers. Managers may exist in other situations,
admittedly, but this is probably why they are usually regarded as
leaders of a lesser kind: they are associated with small achievements
and, at the limit, with a 'do-nothing' posture in cases where there is a
demand for some external action, if only relatively limited. While
'aggression' is typically disliked, a posture of total disengagement

from foreign affairs is viewed generally as unsatisfactory. This may explain in part why, as a matter of fact, 'pure' management on the external plane is rarer than might perhaps have been expected, and is indeed rarer than on the internal plane.

Indirect external pressure and the goals of leaders

The direction of leaders' goals can therefore be 'expected' to be different depending on whether they are related to the country internally or to the world position of the nation. Yet, in the concrete reality of the life of states, external and internal aspects of the environment interact frequently. Internal environmental pressures colour to a substantial extent the ways in which some leaders intervene in foreign policy matters; even more importantly, external elements both modify the characteristics of the internal environment with which leaders are confronted and give leaders opportunities to have an indirect, but often strong, effect on this internal environment. One of the most renowned examples of such an impact occurred in 1914. Both Germany and Austria were confronted at the time with substantial internal opposition and with marked discontent on the part of substantial segments of their populations, including, in Austria, many of the nationalities that composed the Austro-Hungarian Empire. Yet these apparently large conflicts were suddenly reduced — indeed, seemed to vanish — as the two countries entered the war. An external threat had silenced internal discontent.

This example, like that of many others that come readily to mind — including the advent of the Russian Revolution in the aftermath of defeat in 1917–18 — indicate the potential strength of the impact of external events on the internal situation. It is therefore essential to examine the forms that this indirect role of external events takes in confronting leaders with constraints as well as opportunities. The converse effect — that of the internal situation on the external predicament faced by leaders — may also be important; we have indeed already noticed that possible 'aggressive' postures of the population may have an effect.

How external pressures indirectly affect internal conditions. What, then, are the ways in which the world scene may indirectly affect internal societal conditions and thus 'induce' leaders to adopt certain goals? The change in conditions if any, must take the form of a modification of the dynamics that we examined in the previous section. Leaders, as we saw, are confronted with 'demands' for the maintenance of the status quo and with 'demands' for change, both of which are of varying intensity. The insertion of a (new) external problem will have an effect only if this balance is transformed, that is to say, if some of the pressure for maintenance and for change are modified.

Such a modification can occur only if external events alter markedly the prevailing 'mood' in the country: those who want to bring about change then feel obliged to reduce their demands, or those who want to maintain the system become less inclined to do so. The external pressure must thus be strong enough to modify the extent and amount of conflict in the polity. This, of course, will happen if there is an armed conflict; but a change in conflict levels can also occur in less dramatic circumstances. Indeed, one can locate the ways in which external circumstances or activities may affect the polity internally along a dimension ranging from 'covert' to 'overt'. At one extreme, there are the basic influences that result from the general and pervasive influence that a country or group of countries may have on others and which may make others dependent as a result, for instance because they are larger, or richer, or better organized politically, socially or economically, or have an appealing ideology, or indeed are felt to have a more developed culture. At the other extreme are the more 'contingent' happenings, of which war is an extreme case. This dimension is important because the effect is likely to be different, both in intensity and in duration: the continuous but somewhat covert influence may not appear to affect markedly the conditions under which leaders are able to rule, though, in the long run, the consequences may be large and indeed deeper than when there is a brutal shock, which may result in a sudden break-up, but may not have more than temporary consequences.

External factors, subdued or not, have an impact on levels of tension in the polity because they affect sentiments of national pride. For instance, when the citizens of a nation prefer the way of life of a foreign country to their own, their behaviour amounts to a display of a low level of national pride: their esteem for their own country is reduced while their esteem for other countries is increased. When the population reacts vigorously to attacks made against its country by a foreign power, or when that population embraces the decisions of its leaders to threaten or even to go to war against another country, the feelings of national pride are, on the contrary, very high: the esteem for one's own country is much greater than that felt for other nations.

When feelings of national self-esteem are low, citizens are likely either to wish to 'exit' or, more commonly, to look for improvements in their own country; they will therefore turn to their leaders and impress upon them that goals must be changed in order to achieve a better way of life. Thus, in a situation in which the national feelings of the citizens are made to suffer, internal tension (and not merely external conflict) will be higher, while, in a situation in which the national pride is boosted, internal tension will be decreased. This is why, in 1914, Germans and Austrians could silence their 'differences' and all be Germans or Austrians; this is why, on the other hand, faced with the feeling that the country is less successful economically than, say, the United States, citizens in many nations have a sense of frustration which increases the conflicts within the society.

The type of indirect impact of external conditions on the internal situation will therefore depend on the extent to which the action has the effect of depressing or, on the contrary, inflating feelings of national pride in the country. To be sure, absolute feelings of national pride vary from country to country as well as within each country; but what is more relevant is the relative increase or decrease in feelings of national pride. Thus, where an action or, indeed, a generally diffuse condition contributes to a depression of national pride, the level of conflict in the society will tend to increase and pressures on leaders will hence increase for them to modify their stance; when, on the contrary, the sense of national pride rises, pressures on leaders will decrease and the leaders will be better able to maintain their policy initiatives.

National pride and changes in levels of internal tension. It therefore becomes possible to explain why leaders — both those who have been in office and new ones — find themselves confronted with changes in internal tension as a result of external pressure. First, leaders will be subjected to greater pressure if citizens come to admire the way of life of another country, or if there is a reaction against a feeling of 'dependency'; these leaders will cease to be able to act as managers and will have to become innovators or even reformists. This happened to a substantial extent in Western Europe after the second world war, as a result of the 'Americanization' of the societies (the Soviet Union also, for a while, exercised an attraction in some quarters). The same occurred to a substantial extent in Japan until the 1970s, while in the subsequent period the situation has partly been reversed between the United States and Japan. Conversely, if nationalism becomes stronger as a result of external pressure, the level of internal 'crisis' will decline and leaders may no longer need (or be able) to introduce large reforms. This often occurs when leaders who came to power as reformists become national heroes. It happened to an extent with F.D. Roosevelt; it might even be said to have happened with Stalin during the second world war.

There are indeed many examples of the effects of increased or decreased tension resulting from wars or other forms of international pressure. I have already mentioned the case of Western Europe after the second world war, when the loss of prestige of the countries of that area resulted in a 'demand' for actions designed to achieve better economic and social standards. Similarly, much of the pressure for 'development' in the Third World results from increased tension within these polities as the gap between the countries of the South and the West has become recognized. Conversely, the victory achieved rapidly by Mrs Thatcher in the Falkland Islands is an example of a limited armed conflict that had a manifest — indeed, measureable — impact on the popularity of the British leader in reducing tension resulting from internal conflicts, and thus in making it possible (or easier) to carry out policies that ignored some of the demands for change that had hitherto been prevalent.

Failures in the diplomatic field — and, even more, defeat at war — result in internal tensions being markedly increased, as feelings of national pride are deeply hurt. Wounded nationalism reverberates on the leaders, whose tenure of office may be shortened and in some cases abruptly brought to an end as a result of these failures. But the collapse of a regime in circumstances in which external factors play a substantial part correspondingly results in the coming to power of different men and women who are thus helped significantly by the combination of tensions resulting from a loss of national self-esteem and of severe internal conflicts.

These new leaders not only achieve power; they also thereby obtain an opportunity to pursue goals which neither they nor anyone else might have been able to pursue in ordinary circumstances. They are in a position to implement goals that depart significantly, radically even, from policies previously followed. There is thus a close relationship between the *seriousness* of the failure of the previous leadership and the ability of new leaders to push for rapid change: it is typically when an international catastrophe has occurred that revolutionary leaders are able to pursue their goals. The Russian Revolution was born out of the trauma of the first world war, while the Chinese Revolution occurred after a long war with Japan combined with a civil war. Indeed, the 'radicalization' of the French Revolution which occurred after 1792 was at least in part the consequence of an international conflict.

External pressures thus modify in a number of important ways the conditions under which leaders are able to rule. If national pride is boosted, internal conflicts will be lessened and the leader will be able to continue with policies that are moderate or conservative. If national pride is affected, internal tension will increase; and if there has been a massive failure externally, the loss of national pride will often result in the fall of the leader (and of the regime). When this failure is coupled with an already high level of internal tension, a new leadership may be able to introduce radical policies, as these can be regarded as a means of resolving the country's difficulties. 'Revolutionary transformers', who usually cannot achieve power as a result of internal tension alone, have a chance to try out their policies when external disaster is added to internal conflict.

The combined effect of internal and external pressures does not stop at this point, however. Further consequences follow, which can be viewed as ordered along a continuous dimension. At one extreme, the polity may be entirely recast: this occurred in 1918 in Russia and in 1945 in Germany. At the other extreme, the durable, though subdued, influence of some nations on others may provoke a gradual increase in nationalism, which may, as currently throughout the Third World, create a profound and persistent sense of discontent against the 'imperialistic' powers. In between, there are the often violent but largely temporary effects of sudden shocks. Limited wars or instances in which a nation has to give in to threats — as well as limited victories and short-term gains — may be forgotten rapidly; with time, the population may gradually return to its traditional patterns of conflict. As the sense of national self-esteem ceases to be boosted, earlier internal cleavages may once more become prominent, unless transformations have occurred in the intermediate period within the society, for instance if the relationships among groups have been altered. If this has not happened, the support for the goals pursued by the leader may be eroded. Thus, a conservative leader who can use bolstered feelings of national pride to his or her benefit may find that pressures for internal change are once again strong; thus, the standing of the revolutionary leader emerging after a defeat may be reduced, not only because many old cleavages come back to the fore, but because the new policies pursued create further problems.

The role of leaders in manipulating external influences on society. Leaders often have the desire to 'escape' into foreign affairs. By doing so, they want to avoid the drudgery of domestic policy-making; but they also hope to increase their standing internally. Thus there is often the temptation to win a 'quick' war; but there is also the desire to be involved in conferences and in visits abroad, as well as to make statements that are viewed as resulting in points being scored on the international chessboard. Although these activities may not result in substantial changes in levels of national pride, there appear to be at least some occasions in which leaders can for a time diminish tension somewhat through the use of these tactics. Moreover, as large numbers of leaders engage in these activities, those who might not do so might lose popularity; tension will increase as citizens begin to think that their country is absent from the international scene.

The environment thus places before leaders constraints and opportunities which are of a very different character and which suggest that leaders will have to adopt very different postures. Although the characteristics of each situation are distinct, since they result from a different combination of internal and external pressures, it is possible to circumscribe, in a broad and somewhat cursory manner, five main types.

There is, first, the situation of harmony at home and abroad, where the leaders required are managers or, at most, and occasionally, adjusters. In such a situation, which is obviously highly exceptional, leaders will find it difficult to be other than managers, although they may be more or less successful in the managerial art that they display.

Second, there are the situations of intense external pressure combined with internal harmony, either predating the external pressure or, as we saw, resulting from external pressure: these situations are not very common, but they occur occasionally. If the external pressure takes the form of armed aggression, a saviour may be needed; if the external pressure is weaker, there will be a need for a comforter. Indeed, as we know, the need to restore the country can take many forms, ranging from the defence of the whole society to a state of affairs in which the need is only to reassure citizens who might feel disturbed by pressure from abroad or even by the sheer military or economic superiority of other nations. An analogous case is that of the new nation which emerges after a struggle for independence (violent or not, quick or protracted): there, too, citizens need to be reassured that there is no longer any extensive outside threat. Such situations are of relatively short duration: the nation that is under attack may be subjugated, and, temporarily perhaps, there may be no possibility for a saviour to accomplish his task; or the nation may overcome the threat and the need for the saviour may gradually diminish. Indeed, there may finally no longer be a need even for a comforter.

Third, there are situations in which there is widespread demand for limited changes in the social, economic or political fields. These demands can be handled by leaders who are adjusters or innovators. These are cases in which the bulk of the population agrees about the ills of some aspect of the structure, for instance because citizens feel that solutions adopted in other countries are more appropriate than in their own, but do not, on the whole, prefer the life styles of these countries. If innovations occur to 'solve' the problems at hand — indeed, if, in the course of time, leaders anticipate problems by proposing new solutions — the situation may be stable. Both leaders and society may be in harmony, though in a dynamic manner, in the sense that only by introducing some change do leaders succeed in keeping abreast of the requirements of society.

The fourth and fifth types correspond to situations where, on the contrary, such 'harmony' does not prevail. Fourth, if there is conflict, arising for instance from divisions among the population as to whether the present structure should be maintained or altered (whether these divisions arise from ancestral, for instance tribal, antagonisms or from more recent conflicts over development, fuelled in particular by the desire to imitate or shake the influence of other countries), leaders will be confronted with conflicting demands; they may also be confronted with strong demands if they or their predecessors have failed to introduce adjustments or innovations in earlier periods. In such cases, the centre of gravity of the environmental pressure will be close to the point in the two-dimensional space of leaders' goals where the society 'needs' redefiners: but the variance may be large, indeed very large, as some will press for preservation and others for reform. This places leaders in a difficult predicament. If they introduce major changes, they antagonize those who wish to maintain the system; if they do not introduce change, they are attacked by those who want profound alterations to society. They thus have to try to lower the tension, which they are unlikely to achieve by their actions on the internal plane only. This is why external pressure, often contrived, may be a means of 'pulling the country together' by reducing the pressure of those who wish to bring about change.

If, however, this is not achieved, the country may move to a fifth position, in which there is very high conflict and a widespread call for reformists, indeed revolutionaries, on the one hand, and for protectors on the other. Such a situation is of course very unstable, unless external pressure, there too, enables the leader gradually to reduce the call for revolution and brings the country nearer to 'normalcy'.

Conclusion

Leaders are subjected to the environment, which creates conditions that they cannot disregard; but, while constraints are strong, there is also room for manoeuvre. As pressure often comes from many directions within the polity, leaders appear forced to exercise some choices, for instance between conservatism and change. As pressures from outside the polity have to be taken into account alongside internal pressures, leaders can also acquire some leeway, unless they are here, too, forced to make difficult choices between what are often contradictory forces. Whether because they are forced to choose or because they are able to choose, leaders seem prima facie to be able to make an impact on the complex network of the environment. Clearly, there is an interplay between the will of leaders, their aims and ambitions, and the reality around them. It is by gradually analysing the conditions of this interplay that we shall be better able to assess the precise impact of leadership under various types of circumstances and discover the ways leadership can serve nations in the manner most profitable to their populations.

Notes

1. This classification originates in part from a model developed by Cartwright (1983). See also Hoffmann (1967: 109–12).

2. To use Burns's terminology in *Leadership* (1978).

4

The influence of personal characteristics on political leadership

If leaders make an impact on their societies, common sense concludes that this must be due, in very large part, to their personal qualities. This is the subject to which countless biographies and autobiographies are devoted; indeed, negatively and indirectly, it is the subject to which works aiming at reducing the power of leaders are devoted, since these naturally assume that, unless rulers are constrained, they will act arbitrarily. The interest and belief in the personal role of leaders is widespread; it extends well beyond academic and even political circles.

Yet the link between personal qualities and impact remains vague and obscure. Biographies and autobiographies may provide detailed descriptions suggesting — asserting, often — that the personal attributes of leaders have a large effect; indeed, more recently, studies of a psychological and a psychoanalytical character have tended to relate this large influence to deeper elements of the personality or to events that occurred in childhood. But in spite of these developments, the part played by individual attributes has still not been demonstrated.

Of course, part of the difficulty stems from disagreements about the extent to which leaders make any impact at all; but part also comes from problems relating to the assessment of the personal components of the leaders' influence. It is not easy to distinguish these from institutional facilitation, which is clearly also important, and to which we shall devote the next chapter. To understand the role of the persona itself, we need to be able to see how it is able to modify the course of events; this means that we must be able to decompose these personal characteristics into elements and show how they combine differently in different cases. Of course, we do this all the time at a more casual level — we talk about the courage, the tenacity, the intelligence of some leaders. But a systematic analysis must do more: it must provide means of assessing precisely the origin of this personal influence; it must, therefore, identify the components of the personality; it must then link these personal characteristics to each other as well as to the impact of leaders.

This goal is still rather distant. In the context of political leadership, systematic enquiries have been relatively recent, despite the centuries-old tradition of individual ruler assessment; as a matter of fact, the limited number of general studies contrasts with the many efforts undertaken in the field of psychology; as was pointed out in Chapter 1, the study of political leadership remains a Cinderella by comparison with the study of other types of leadership. But even in the general psychological field, there is still no overall framework that might be indirectly applicable to politics; also, findings are often controversial or imprecise, and the types of leadership that are analysed are usually rather simple.

The purpose of this chapter therefore has to remain rather modest. First, I shall summarize findings relating to personality, both in the political context and outside; I shall then outline the directions in which the study of personal characteristics of political leaders might proceed; and shall assess the extent to which it is permissible to believe, at this early point in the development of analyses, that personal characteristics have a substantial influence on the impact of political leadership.

The analysis of personal factors in political leadership

There has long been a general interest in the personal characteristics of political leaders, not just in political science proper, but also in history and in literature. This may indeed be why much of the work has been based on individual analyses, with actions and events being 'explained' by the specific circumstances of the person most involved rather than by general factors applicable to a class of leaders.

Alongside this 'individualistic' tradition, political science and empirical sociology have been interested primarily in the recruitment of political elites. Attempts have been made to examine the background of leaders over time and cross-nationally, often in order to assess the role of factors such as social origin, education, occupation and ideology in the selection of leaders. But, as the concern of these studies is sociological rather than psychological, there has been little cross-fertilization between individual studies and elite studies. In particular, elite studies have been little concerned with decision-making; on the other hand, as psychological studies have been devoted to the behaviour of individuals, they have had little cumulative explanatory value. More recently, however, some change has occurred. Psychological analyses have become more general; there is, for instance, a concern for the determination of dimensions applicable to all types of political leaders. Although psychological studies are still a long way from having developed a general theory of the role of personality variables, there is now a discernable movement in that direction.

Demographic characteristics and the impact of political leadership
Even in this age of the common man, national political leaders are not
drawn proportionately from the various groups that form the
populations they rule. Both single-country studies and cross-national
analyses have shown without any shadow of doubt that distortions are
considerable (Blondel, 1980: 115–34). These national leaders may no
longer come from an extremely narrow segment — in effect, from one
or a few families whose members succeed each other on the throne or
at the head of the government — but there are still considerable
restrictions. To begin with, even outside monarchies, the hereditary or
family principle still plays a substantial part. Perhaps the most
extreme example is that of India, which has been ruled during 35 of its
40 post-independence years by three members of the same family —
grandfather, mother and son — while the other two prime ministers
lasted in office for only very short periods; similar developments have
occurred in other countries, such as North Korea, Taiwan, Sri Lanka
and Argentina.

Moreover, even if succession by heredity or through marriage has
become the exception, leaders come from rather exclusive
backgrounds. They are overwhelmingly male; they are relatively old,
a majority being over 50 when they come to power; they are
comparatively well-educated, over two-thirds having been to a higher
education institution; and they are middle or upper-middle class by
virtue of their occupation. There are some variations from country to
country, from region to region and from regime to regime — there
have been more men with a working-class background among
communist states, for instance. But, by and large, professional men
(and especially lawyers), civil servants, teachers and members of the
armed forces have usually had a strikingly greater than average chance
of becoming leaders. These distortions are large everywhere and often
very large. Opportunities to come to the top are thus limited: it is
simply not the case, for instance, that everyone has the same chance of
becoming president of the United States, despite the claim that has
repeatedly been made about the nature of politics in that society.

It is not immediately clear, however, what the consequences of this
distortion are from the point of view of the goals that are pursued or
the impact of these leaders. No systematic analysis has been
conducted to explore the direct effect of demographic characteristics
on political leadership effectiveness, in large part, if not essentially,
because the assessment of this effectiveness has so far been largely
impressionistic. But the impression that emerges is that there is no
very strong and manifest impact of age or occupational background
on the effectiveness of leaders.

It may therefore be that social background variables do not have a marked influence on the impact of leadership, a conclusion that is confirmed, indirectly at least, by the findings of Rejai and Phillips on revolutionary leaders (Rejai and Phillips, 1979, 1983). Numbers are too small to allow for a clear-cut conclusion, but, although revolutionaries do include a number of leaders issued from the 'lower class', they have been drawn predominantly from the middle class — indeed, largely from the same occupational strata as other leaders. They include lawyers as well as military men; a large majority have had a higher education; they are not particularly young; they come in general from mainstream ethnic and religious groups; they have had mainly a 'normal' family background. Prima facie, therefore, it would seem that it makes no systematic difference in terms of the goals of leaders whether they happen to be drawn from one of those (narrow) segments of the population from which they are currently mostly drawn.

This does not mean that leadership would not have different goals and a different impact if national rulers originated from social groups that are at present excluded from the competition to the top: since the empirical evidence is by definition not available, this question cannot be answered, although it has often been claimed indirectly that this is the case. Theories of the 'ruling class' are based on the assumption that the social background of leaders plays a major part in the determination of policy goals and the general orientation of political life in a country.

Before exploring further the possible impact of these demographic characteristics, it is worth examining one rather peculiar indicator which does seem to show some clear influence on leadership goals and effectiveness: that of the 'birth order' of the leader within his family. Although the effect of this variable has not been tested generally, a study undertaken by Louis Stewart in the case of US presidents and extended to British prime ministers suggests that there are intriguing differences between the part played by leaders depending on whether they are only sons, first sons or younger sons (Stewart, 1977). The major findings are two-fold. First, it appears that first and only sons are appreciably more likely to have been successful in situations of crisis than in more ordinary situations. The most intriguing aspect of this matter is that the population seems to recognize this fact: if US elections are divided into 'crisis' and 'non-crisis', a first or only son was elected in 8 out of 9 cases of crisis while in non-crisis elections younger sons were elected in 12 out of 21 cases.

Second, it appears that only sons, first sons and younger sons are particularly suited to three different types of situations, as they seem to have three distinct 'styles' of leadership. First sons seem to be most at ease in situations of expansion, often leading to external conflict;

younger sons aim at adjustment and are concerned to solve problems by compromise; only sons devote their energies to dealing with societal breakdowns (Stewart, 1977: 226). Parallel conclusions are drawn about British prime ministers: Asquith and Chamberlain, who were both younger sons, were ill-equipped for the war situation and gave way respectively to Lloyd George and Churchill, who were both first sons.

The argument is based on the type of socialization that these leaders received during childhood and adolescence. Different kinds of leadership are thus fostered within the family: 'Take for instance the only child,' Stewart argues:

> If we assume that from the child's eye view of the family the parents represent past society and the children represent present society, it follows that of all the birth order positions the only child, being the sole heir of past society and the sole member of present society, would on both counts be best able to identify with society as a totality. (Stewart, 1977: 211)

He then states that a first child 'would be uniquely in touch with the demands of an expanding society while also inheriting responsibility for weaker members' (p. 211). Similarly, younger children find themselves in a position 'which appears to maximise opportunities for diverse relationships while at the same time demanding adeptness at mediation and accommodation' (p. 212). Stewart suggests that the last-born may be the natural champion of the oppressed.

These findings are intriguing in themselves, as there does seem to be enough evidence to suggest that the birth order in the family has an impact on the type of leadership that emerges, and that the population, or at least other politicians, become aware of these differences in their approach to leadership. They thus plump for leaders who have the characteristics appropriate to the situation — and these leaders happen to be found at particular points in the birth order of the family. The conclusion that seems to follow is that the 'systemic' relationship between leader and environment becomes very close in the process; but it also seems to follow that the leadership characteristics required are moulded to an appreciable extent by the socialization process that goes on in the family, a conclusion that coincides with findings of psychologists and psychoanalysts which we shall examine later in this chapter. Leadership therefore appears to be fostered or fashioned by the surrounding forces; and if this is the case in relation to the way in which children are treated when they are alone, come first or come later in the family, it seems at least permissible to suggest that other environmental forces, many of which are mediated through the family, may play a considerable part.

Thus, while it has so far not been possible to prove — and, as was

suggested earlier, may indeed be impossible to prove in the future —
that demographic variables play a major part in determining the goals
and effectiveness of leaders, there do seem to be at least some general
grounds for believing that the leaders of the world are shaped in some
significant manner by their background. Education and occupation,
as well as (probably) religion, ethnicity or even geographical origin,
are likely to have some effect, although we may never be sure of this
point, since those who come to be leaders are relatively homogeneous
in their origins, especially within each region and within each country.
The weight to be given to the role of demographic variables must
surely be considered greater than would seem ostensibly to be the case,
at any rate as long as national political leaders continue to be drawn
primarily from the relatively narrow groups from which they have so
far been chosen in what might be viewed in future as a transition
period following the collapse of the monarchical and aristocratic
order.

The psychological characteristics of national political leaders
    Biographical analysis. The study of demographic variables of
national political leaders is still not very advanced. There is much to
explore in order to become better aware of the many aspects of the
background of current leaders, let alone to attempt to understand how
their background affects, consciously or otherwise, their goals and
their impact on society. But at least these studies are comparative and
potentially general: they aim at establishing the characteristics of
leaders by considering them as a group. When one turns to the
examination of psychological variables, in the political field at least, a
major difficulty in coming to any definite conclusion stems from the
traditional focus, as I pointed out in the Introduction, on individual
cases. The result has been an almost exclusive concentration on each
case at the expense of attempts to generalize. There is indeed even
some suspicion of generalizations.

In their traditional form, moreover, biographical studies have been
based only on cases; they have also tended to be descriptive rather
than analytical. In the process, admittedly, certain psychological
'elements' have typically been presented as important, and these are
often used as they help to give some continuity to the narrative. Thus
the leader is presented as courageous, or cunning, or as having a deep
sense of the long-term national interest. These characteristics, or
traits, are occasionally compared between leaders, but this is rarely
done in the systematic manner of Plutarch in his *Parallel Lives*. The
comparison, or more often the contrast, is typically made between the
hero who is the central character of the story and his colleagues or
other politicians who may, for instance, have less foresight or less

intelligence. The result is that these traits are rarely examined systematically, let alone precisely defined and carefully operationalized: they are lighthouses guiding us during the journey, not components carefully brought together to build an edifice.

These characteristics are not presented systematically in the sense that the qualities of the hero are set against all other possible qualities that the leader might have possessed. Thus one cannot infer from the analysis what characteristics would be required for a general model of leadership to be developed: it is the subject of the biography who is delineated, not the problem of leadership that is analysed. Traditional biographies may thus provide a kind of raw material, but they do not help to build a series of personality 'types'.

Biographies have a further limitation: in the main, they concentrate their attention on exceptional leaders rather than on ordinary or even average ones. Autobiographies may be undertaken rather more 'generously'; but biographies are rarely written unless it is believed that the leader has moulded the polity in a distinctive manner. They therefore reinforce the penchant for dichotomies which has been endemic in the analysis of political leadership, instead of giving the sense of a range in the impact of different leaders.

Thus, a psychological analysis of national political leadership has not emerged from traditional biographies. We have not learned whether leaders needed to be 'intelligent', 'imaginative', 'stubborn' or 'extroverted' in order to be successful; nor have we learned whether these or other components particularly suited some types of situations rather than others. We might infer from the examination of one case that stubbornness could be advantageous, while another case might suggest that this quality can result in disaster.

'Conventional' biographies have tended to be superseded by more sophisticated analyses, however, as interest in leadership has grown in political science. Although the life history remains the essential framework, emphasis has come to be placed in recent decades on less descriptive and more analytical case-studies. Lasswell's call for an examination of the 'psychopathology' of rulers resulted in a number of 'psychobiographies', which placed much emphasis on events having occurred in the distant past and in particular during childhood.[1]

These deeper biographies thus aim not merely to narrate a story, extol a leader or set the record straight: they aim to provide an understanding of the personality. Yet in many respects they share the same broad characteristics as other biographies. They too focus on exceptional rulers, either because the role of these leaders has been vast (for good or evil) or because they have engaged in activities that appear different from what might have been expected. It is natural that one should explore in depth the motivations and mental states of Hitler or Stalin, Luther or Gandhi;[2] it is also interesting to understand puzzles such as the manifest inability of Woodrow Wilson to handle the US Senate over the Versailles Treaty,[3] or the strange modes of behaviour of Richard Nixon. But the analysis of these cases leads, even more than conventional biographies, towards the highly exceptional leaders, and thus provides few insights on the mental processes of even moderately effective ones.

Moreover, it is not clear that the 'explanations' that are provided by these studies do give answers to questions of motivation, let alone to questions about leaders' effectiveness. The reference to the formation of the personality in adolescence or even early childhood helps to explain why a given leader may have acted in a certain way; but it does not suggest why a given element of the personality contributed significantly to the rise of that leader to power and, once in power, to the impact of the leader.

Psychoanalytical studies also have so often concentrated on 'unbalanced' leaders that it seems that abnormality is at times the only element that is being examined. Admittedly, leaders affected by a manifest 'mental health' problem need to be investigated; it is also surely right to point to the number of these cases. Enquiries into the madnesses or eccentricities of rulers were undertaken long before the 1930s, when the power of irrational dictators was at its height — for instance by T.F. Thiselton in 1903 and A.S. Rappoport in 1910. It was claimed by a psychologist in the 1960s that 'at least 75 chiefs of state have led their country, actually or symbolically, for a total of several centuries, while suffering from severe mental disturbances'.[4] But, naturally enough, the rise of the 'great dictators' of the 1920s and 1930s led to an increased interest in understanding the mechanisms — including personality mechanisms — that might result in the coming to power, and the behaviour patterns once in power, of individuals who are clearly abnormal.

Such an emphasis obviously restricts the scope of the analysis, however; indeed, it biases the approach. It is clearly not possible to concentrate on such 'abnormal' cases and hope to build a general theory of leadership. As a matter of fact, although the cases of Hitler, Stalin and some others are truly out of the range of even the moderately peculiar, it has come to be recognized that an objective definition of madness or of abnormality is difficult to provide, as the concept is closely linked to culture and the environment; at a minimum, it might not be worthwhile to draw conclusions based on a large historical fresco. Consequently, in the 1970s and 1980s political scientists have become more cautious about the value of using the criterion of mental illness as a major indicator, thus perhaps helping to bring the analysis closer to an examination of all types of leaders — abnormality being only one element of the analysis alongside many others that needs to be investigated.[5]

While these psychoanalytic studies are therefore important and indeed path-breaking, since they direct our thinking towards a deeper examination of what constitutes the personality, they have the disadvantage of inducing political scientists to jump too quickly to what might be regarded as the most fundamental plane of explanation before a general mapping of the personality has been undertaken. For a systematic analysis of the influence of the personality on the effectiveness of leadership must surely go through a number of stages. First, it must be established that leaders do make a difference, a matter which, as we saw, is fraught with considerable difficulties; second, one must attempt to see to what extent that 'difference' is due to the personal characteristics of leaders rather than to the structural conditions of the offices that they hold or the institutional arrangements within which they operate. Only where personal characteristics have been found to be a significant factor in themselves in accounting for at least part of the variation is it permissible to move to the next plane and ask, if personal qualities are important, what, in turn, accounts for the existence of a given set of personal qualities in a particular leader? Since political science has so far not given more than very limited answers to the second question — whether personal characteristics do account for the rise of leaders and their effectiveness — it is premature to engage in a major enquiry designed to answer the third question, namely, what accounts for given personal characteristics of specific leaders? It is worthwhile, to be sure, to begin to explore this matter; but it is not very productive to attempt to look for general explanations of the particular set of personal characteristics, since it may be that these are of little overall significance, and in any case it is not clear which of these characteristics is of the greatest relevance.

There is therefore little that one can conclude from the consideration of biographical studies, whether conventional or psychoanalytic. One can say that there are many types of leaders, that some have shown more foresight than others, that some have shown more intelligence than others, or more imagination, or more cunning. It is clear that these different leaders have had some impact; what is not clear is whether any one of the 'qualities' that they possessed was particularly instrumental in their achievements. Psychobiographies may show that events in childhood fix the personality in a certain way; they also make us aware of the extraordinary cases of unbalanced rulers and throw some light on the reasons why their minds have been unbalanced. But these studies have to be viewed as limit-cases, which it is important to examine in order to be able to see how far — and how far wrong — leadership may go. They do not, and cannot, give a general panoramic description of what the psychological qualities of exceptional leaders might be, let alone of all types of leaders.

The beginnings of a general conceptualization. Admittedly, it is perhaps not surprising that the literature should have been devoted to the in-depth study of a few exceptional cases, since political science and political discourse generally tend to focus on the great heroes rather than on ordinary leaders. It is therefore not surprising either that the move that has been made in the direction of a more general analysis of personal characteristics should have focused on the one class of leaders that is the most exceptional: namely, revolutionary leaders. Meanwhile, however, studies of revolutionaries have gone beyond psychopathology, both because of the desire to show or account for the 'positive' accomplishment of those leaders and because qualities other than madness had to be emphasized.

By far the most comprehensive studies that have been undertaken in this field in recent years have been the two works on revolutionary leaders by Rejai and Phillips (1979, 1983). Theirs are systematic efforts, within the realm of the special type of rulers that revolutionaries constitute, to break away from a case-analysis and to provide a general description of the characteristics of these leaders as a class. The aim is to combine a psychological and a sociological analysis in order to show the extent to which personal and situational factors account for the emergence of these leaders. The studies admittedly concentrate on revolutionaries as leaders, rather than focusing on the specific impact that these leaders have had, it being assumed that they did, indeed, have an impact. However, given that an impact can probably be assumed in the context of this particular group, these studies constitute a genuine advance in the analysis of at least one class — an exceptional but clearly important class — of political rulers.

The Rejai–Phillips studies are based on an empirical analysis of over one hundred rulers from all parts of the world and across history. The starting point is the recognition that revolutionaries are embedded in a situation but that this situation alone does not account for their emergence: 'For a revolutionary leader to emerge, it is imperative that the situation coincide with the presence of a certain kind of person or personality' (Rejai and Phillips, 1983: 36). And the authors continue: 'This person or personality has two essential characteristics: (1) a mental set or a psychology that propels him towards revolutionary actions and (2) a set of skills — particularly verbal and organisational — that enables him to perform his tasks' (p. 36). The authors then go on to describe the psychological characteristics of these leaders, which include 'vanity, egotism, narcissism' but also nationalism, a sense of justice and a sense of mission; there is, moreover, relative deprivation and status inconsistency (p. 37). The skills of revolutionary leaders are then described; these are, for instance, an alternative vision of society or a great concern for grievances and injustices (p. 38); these leaders also need verbal skills and organizational skills to put their views across. The authors conclude: 'It is clear that the theoretical posture advanced here combines trait theories of leadership with situational theories' (p. 40).

There are some problems with this presentation. Despite the fact that these points constitute a more sophisticated and more precise presentation of the elements that have to be taken into account, it is not stated why these are privileged by contrast with other factors. It may seem intuitively justifiable to claim that revolutionary leaders need to have organizational skills and a strong ideology, and that this ideology is based on such feelings as a sense of injustice and/or the desire to bring about a new political and social order; but it is not clear whether all these leaders display these characteristics to the same degree. Indeed, Rejai and Phillips acknowledge the point when they state: 'any number of dynamics may play roles in sharpening the mental set of revolutionary elites. We hazard the proposition, however, that no single motivation or dynamic is sufficient to explain the formation of all revolutionary personalities. Nor do we anticipate an invariant mix...' (Rejai and Phillips, 1983: 38). If this is the case, it must be that the categorizations are presented more for purposes of illustration than because they are exhaustive. But there is no reason, then, not to assess the extent to which other traits, such as various aspects of intelligence, sociability or 'personality' in general, are not also very important. Since the endeavour aims at discovering the relevant qualities alongside the 'situation', to be sure, it is difficult to understand why all the different aspects of personality are not examined, or at least discussed.

The empirical analysis does at least attempt to consider some of the personal characteristics of these leaders, however. Six traits are identified as elements of what constitute the psychological dynamics of revolutionary leaders: vanity, puritanism, relative deprivation, marginality, oedipal conflict and romanticism. Puritanism and marginality are the two elements that appear the most important, while others, except for oedipal conflict, also play a significant part. The difficulty is, of course, that there is no control group, either of other leaders or of followers, among whom it might be possible to assess the incidence of these characteristics. But puritanism, especially in the postwar period, and marginality seem so important in these cases that it seems unlikely that they would be as widespread in the whole population or among all leaders. To this extent at least, the study does provide evidence suggesting that revolutionary leaders have some specific personal characteristics. The points that are made in case-studies of individual revolutionary leaders are thus broadly confirmed; but they are now confirmed generally, although the enquiry clearly does not exhaust the personal characteristics of leaders. Not only is it a limited window open on the personality of leaders, but parts of the personality of revolutionary leaders remain unexamined.

General studies of the personality of national political leaders are not confined to revolutionaries, however: the combination of conventional biography and psychobiography on the one hand, and of the apparently greater interest devoted to leadership on the other, has led to the emergence of some enquiries into the psychological characteristics of all leaders. This is especially the case of J.D. Barber's work on the *Presidential Character* (1977) which builds on an earlier analysis of Connecticut legislators, *The Lawmakers* (Barber, 1968). The aim is to elaborate a psychological classification which is universally applicable. At about the same period, B. Heady's (1974) study of *British Cabinet Ministers*, though not devoted exclusively to top national political leaders, had the same overall purpose and arrived at comparable sets of categories.

Barber's two dimensions are based on energy ('activity' v. 'passivity') and on satisfaction with the job (a 'positive' v. a 'negative' approach). The model is then applied to US presidents who are located in one of four positions. The basis for the classification is psychological. The concepts that enable Barber to determine whether a president is, for instance, 'active–positive' are 'activity and the enjoyment of it, indicating relatively high self-esteem and relative success in relating to the environment' (Barber, 1977: 11). 'Active–negatives', on the other hand, show a 'contradiction between relatively intense effort and relatively low emotional reward for that effort' (p. 11). While 'passive–positives' are other-directed and search for affection, 'passive–negatives' have an orientation towards dutiful service and 'are in politics because they think they ought to be' (p. 13).

These distinctions are conceived as universal. Barber applies them to presidents of the United States, both past and contemporary, but they could be applied to any leader. Thus, the first four presidents are viewed as corresponding to the four categories, Washington being described as 'passive–negative', Adams as 'active–negative', Jefferson as 'active–positive' and Madison as 'passive–positive'. F.D. Roosevelt was also 'active–positive', as were Truman and

Kennedy, while Eisenhower was 'passive–negative' and Nixon 'active–negative'. The model is even viewed as being predictive since, on the basis of the character defined in this manner, it is possible to foresee the results (good or ill) that a given holder of an office will achieve, or at least the directions in which he or she will go.

These characteristics are thus expected to account, at least in part, for the impact of leaders and for the nature of this impact. The detailed description of the behaviour of presidents given in Barber's work aims at demonstrating that actions follow 'character' and that there is therefore evidence that character matters. By providing a universally applicable categorization, Barber has unquestionably opened a new line of general enquiry. The work is thus both valuable substantively and seminal methodologically, since it could be extended to leaders of other countries.

There are difficulties, however, which stem in large part from the somewhat vague nature of the distinctions that have been adopted. As a first attempt at categorization, the dimensions of 'active' v. 'passive' and of 'positive' v. 'negative' begin to help to circumscribe the problem; but the limits of the categorization emerge in the detailed analysis, where the author has to recognize that the complexities of the personality appear to go beyond the rather simple divisions that have been put forward. Thus, Kennedy was an 'active–positive' who, none the less, was characterized by much uncertainty (Barber, 1977: 343); thus, predictions regarding Carter, who was viewed as an 'active–positive' as well, do not seem to have corresponded to reality, perhaps because Carter was not classified correctly and was more of an 'active-negative' than an 'active-positive'; perhaps, too, because a precise analysis requires more than the two distinctions that have been suggested.

Part of the problem might have been alleviated if the dimensions had been fully used: presidents might then have been located at a larger number of positions within a space; even though it is difficult to assess precisely where a given 'character' should be placed, it seems at least possible to go beyond a categorization that allows for four cells only. But even such an improvement would not meet all the difficulties: the categorization of 'active' or 'passive', 'positive' or 'negative', entails bringing together a number of psychological elements, such as self-esteem, other-directedness, ambition, assertiveness and so on. Why these components of character succeed in being compressed into four categories is not clear; nor is there even an attempt to provide clarification. Thus, each of the positions is a 'compound' resulting from the combination of 'atoms'; it is assumed that these form, so to speak, a stable molecule, but this assumption would need the backing of substantial evidence. If 'active–positives', for instance, have a high self-esteem, a desire to develop goals and an emphasis on rational mastery, the link between these elements should be shown; we should be made to see that there is, so to speak, a factor, and that a number of elements are clustered in the concrete reality of the character of existing leaders. The model provided by Barber does constitute an advance. It indicates that one can discover some personality characteristics by which to compare leaders, and that these characteristics can be related to the impact they may make; but the characteristics need to be further explored, and it remains to be shown that these, and not others, are the critical variables.

The study of the personal aspects of national political leadership has thus progressed. The instruments needed to assess the precise extent to which personal characteristics affect the achievements of leaders are being elaborated, but the progress is slow. Too much effort, perhaps, is still devoted to detailed individual analyses, while too little is done to develop general criteria. Is it that these criteria do not exist, or merely that political scientists have failed to use for national leaders the tools applied by psychologists to other types of leaders? We need to turn to the analysis of leadership and of its personal components in the general psychological area to assess how far further advances could be made by a wider borrowing from the tools of psychologists than has been done so far.

Psychology and the general analysis of the personal components of leadership

Studies undertaken by psychologists provide substantial evidence suggesting that personal factors play a part in the development of leadership; but unfortunately this evidence is in most respects rather vague, despite the considerable interest in the field and the many studies that have been undertaken. There have been attempts to determine a number of components that jointly or separately have an influence on the effectiveness of leadership. So far, however, these have not been analysed systematically and listed comprehensively; little effort has been made to relate them to each other in order to determine the precise extent to which the character and the role of leadership are affected as a result. Above all, there is as yet no general model or theory that would help to provide an accepted definition of what constitutes personal characteristics; nor is there a readily acceptable doctrine about the links between personal elements and situational factors.

To a very large extent, the difficulties raised by the analysis of the impact of political leadership stem from the fact that the central concept in the analysis, that of personality, is itself rather unclear. There is disagreement as to what personality consists of. As

Greenstein pointed out in his *Personality and Politics*, 'There are differences within psychology over what is meant by "personality" and, furthermore, the term tends to have different connotations to political scientists than it has to psychologists' (Greenstein, 1969: 2); he further notes that Allport lists 'no less than fifty *types* of definitions' (p. 3). The personality of an individual has to be defined in terms of the stable elements that underlie and appear to give some consistency to the many discrete actions and reactions (emotional as well as intellectual) of this individual over time; but there is no proof that personality 'exists' in any real sense. As Greenstein also notes, it is an 'inferred reality' rather than an observable phenomenon; it is a construct which enables us to understand and predict the actions and reactions of others. Thus, though the 'discovery' of the personality of an individual is the result of an empirical examination of the attitudes and behaviour of this individual, it is also based on the assumption that individuals do have some basic consistency, a point that is at best based on the general 'impressions' that we have of individuals. While there is evidence for a large degree of consistency, there is also considerable evidence suggesting substantial degrees of inconsistency. It seems, moreover, that the personality of an individual is modified over time, although psychologists have shown that many characteristics of individuals are formed in early youth, and although many studies have aimed at demonstrating that the formative years of childhood could markedly fashion the political behaviour of political leaders.

A structured personality is not a prerequisite for the existence of an influence of personal characteristics on political leadership. Even inconsistent or unpredictable leaders could make an impact or exercise influence; it might even be argued that these leaders exercise more influence as a result. But if these personal characteristics cannot be subsumed within the context of a general personality, they can scarcely be examined and analysed. Wholly unstructured modes of action of leaders not only defy predictability: they defy *post hoc* analysis, as they cannot be related, since they are unstructured, to some describable personal characteristic of the leader. In consequence, we cannot expect to discover fully the role of personal characteristics unless they are encapsulated within a broader framework which we might label 'personality'. Admittedly, as our understanding of human psychological processes develops, we shall be better able to understand some of the inconsistencies that are at present unexplained and unpredictable. But there will almost certainly be a residuum. Thus, the influence of personal factors will almost certainly also be underestimated, and the process once criticized by Greenstein, whereby personal characteristics tend to be brought in when every other explanatory factor has been used, will continue to prevail and, to some extent, will have to prevail (Greenstein, 1969: Ch. 2).

The personal elements that appear to play a part in the emergence of leadership
Assuming, therefore, that there is a 'personality', the first problem is to identify its components. The variations in personality from one individual to another cannot be perceived unless we can identify different configurations of components between these individuals; these components, too, must be stable and enduring, since if they were not it would of course be impossible to 'define' individuals through their intermediary. Hence the idea of determining personality traits, which would constitute the basic elements of the analysis.

The study of traits has a long history in psychological analysis; but after an early period, when it seemed obvious that individuals (and leaders in particular) had traits that distinguished them from others, there has been disillusionment with the approach, partly because so many traits were identified, partly because they were rather vague or at best imprecise, and partly because a heavy emphasis on traits seemed to break the unity of the personality and lead to a dissociation of individuals from the environment in which they acted. Yet it is difficult to see how one can avoid using a number of rather specific elements: as a matter of fact, the psychological analysis of leadership over the last decades has consisted of an endeavour to discover to what extent some personal characteristics are more prevalent than others. Whether these characteristics are 'traits' or not, they do constitute elements that help to build a comprehensive picture by being combined together in different ways.

Indeed, the main problem is perhaps not the emphasis on traits, but the fact that there are too many to choose from. In his *Handbook on Leadership*, Bass (1981: 43–96) reproduces articles by Stogdill, published in 1948 and 1970, which summarize findings from 1904 to the end of the 1960s: over 160 articles are referred to, covering a large variety of physical and psychological characteristics of leaders. The findings of this literature are classified under more than 40 elements which have been found by scholars to be, to a varying extent, associated with leadership. These 40 characteristics are in turn grouped by Stogdill under 6 main headings: physical appearance (such as age, but also energy), social background, intelligence, 'personality' (which includes such diverse matters as adaptability, enthusiasm, resourcefulness and self-confidence), task-related characteristics, and social characteristics (which include such resources as administrative ability, popularity and tact). The characteristics listed by Stogdill thus cover the entire range of elements that can be associated with a person and, in particular, 'objective' social and demographic elements as well as 'pure' psychological traits.

The elements that are mentioned here are those that have been found to be 'relevant' to leadership in at least one and, in most cases, many of the detailed studies that Stogdill analysed in his 1948 and 1970 surveys; that is to say, a substantial number of 'traits' have been shown to account for the development of leadership. The first conclusion must therefore be that, without a shadow of doubt, many components of the personality are at the origin of leadership. In this context, of course, we mean any kind of leadership, and indeed usually not political leadership; but if some components account generally for leadership, it seems permissible to conclude that they also contribute to an explanation of national political leadership.

These elements have all been found to be related to leadership in some of the studies; however, the weighting to be given to each of these relationships cannot be deduced from the examination of these enquiries. This large but disparate set of studies does not provide clues as to which of the components is more powerfully linked to leadership, let alone what is the relative ranking to be given to each of them. The closest one can come to a weighting is by adding up the number of studies that reported a relationship between a given component and leadership, as this number provides at least an impression of the strength of the relationship. For studies reported in the 1948 Bass survey, one can also discover the number of cases in which no relationship was found to exist between leadership and a given component. Thus, for instance, over 20 of the studies that have taken place since the late 1940s suggest that intelligence, dominance, self-confidence, achievement drive, sociability and energy (classified, as we said, under physical characteristics) are positively correlated with leadership (Bass, 1981: 75–6). On the other hand, very few studies have shown extroversion, enthusiasm, the ability to enlist co-operation, attractiveness, nurturance, popularity, tact or appearance to be positively correlated to leadership. This may not signify that these qualities are not indeed related it, since the number of studies devoted to these matters may have been small; but psychologists have found evidence to support the view that intelligence, dominance, self-confidence, achievement drive, sociability and energy have a high relevance for leadership.

Yet the evidence is usually not overwhelming, and it does not always go in only one direction. It is in the 1950s and 1960s, in particular, that an 'abundant reserve of energy' or 'stamina' appears to have been found particularly significant (p. 77); the survey undertaken by Stogdill in the 1940s did not find so much evidence, possibly because the matter had not been investigated by so many scholars. There is even more controversy with respect to intelligence: both the 1948 and 1970 surveys indicated that many investigations had found a correlation between intelligence and leadership (the overall correlation between intelligence and leadership (the overall correlation being 0.28); but other studies stressed that 'extreme discrepancies between the intelligence of potential leaders and that of their followers militate[d] against the exercise of leadership' (p. 79). One work suggested that the relationship was curvilinear, 'with those individuals earning both low and very high scores [on intelligence] with scores at intermediate levels' (p. 79). There were also some discrepancies in relation to the two elements of 'personality' that scored high in the 1970 survey, ascendance and self-confidence (p. 80): while self-confidence was very high in the 1970 survey, it scored lower than other variables (for instance intelligence) in the 1948 survey. Admittedly, this may have been because fewer studies had been concerned with the problem, but ascendance or dominance had a very high score in the 1970 survey, while the results were mixed in the 1948 survey. Not only was the number of studies that stressed the role of ascendance relatively small (ll), but a substantial number (6) showed that there were many negative findings. There were also differences in the results of the two surveys with respect to the one task-related characteristic (achievement drive) and the social characteristic (sociability), which scored very high in the 1970 survey (p. 81).

Putting it differently, leadership seems associated with psychological characteristics covering many, if not all, of the aspects of the human personality. Leaders are likely to be drawn from among the more intelligent; they are likely to be drawn from among those who have more energy; they are likely to be drawn from among those who want to achieve more results, who have a clear orientation towards their task; and they are likely to be drawn from among those who are able to socialize with others, who have, to quote Stogdill, the 'capability to structure social interaction systems to the purpose at hand' (p. 81).

On these points, Bass and Stogdill have no doubt. Bass feels that he can go even further and thus come closer to the question of the impact of leadership; for he states that, as a result of the wealth of the evidence, these characteristics make it possible to 'differentiate leaders from followers, effective from ineffective leaders, and higher-echelon from lower-echelon leaders' (p. 81). These last two conclusions are of course of considerable importance in determining the role of personal components on the impact of national political leadership. If they are valid, they suggest, when taken jointly, that effective national leaders are particularly likely to be drawn from the intelligent, the energetic, the achievement-oriented and those who wish to be and can be popular. But some doubt has to remain, as these conclusions are not as firmly supported by the data as they are presented in the *Handbook* (Stogdill, 1974).

The problem of a general framework and the question of the demographic components

Although the evidence may show a relationship between some personal elements and the emergence and perhaps even the impact of leadership, there is still no clear general framework within which to relate these findings to each other. The efforts that have been made so far to group the components into broader categories are highly idiosyncratic. Perhaps this is because the concept of personality is itself elusive and lacks 'objectivity'; what is apparent in any case is that different groupings are made by different authors. Thus, Borgatta (1964: 10) suggests the existence of five clusters which together describe personality: assertiveness, likeability, emotionality, intelligence, and task interest. Hermann, on the other hand, lists only four elements: beliefs, motives, decision style, and modes of personal interaction. Intelligence is not mentioned; nor is emotionality, at any rate in a direct manner (Hermann, 1977: 21). Meanwhile, Bass follows Stogdill and adopts, as we saw, a different grouping: for him, the categories are energy, background, intelligence, 'personality', task-related characteristics, and social characteristics. There is therefore no widely accepted framework.

Nor is it clear what the relationship is between the elements of the characterization. Intercorrelations have not been calculated; the problem of intercorrelation is not even raised in theory. Thus we do not know whether we are faced with factors that are independent of each other. Moreover, it seems ill-advised to treat psychological and demographic elements in the same manner. Psychologists note, for instance, the part played by age, career or background; but they do not examine the possible relationship between these elements and psychological variables. Yet it would seem reasonable to suggest that energy diminishes with age and that, as energy is required for leadership, older rulers are less likely, on balance, to be effective leaders (though a number of important exceptions immediately come to mind). One might also say that a good education is likely to be correlated positively with intelligence, that it might in turn result in fostering a sense of superiority which will result in a desire to dominate, and that, on these grounds, leaders are more likely to emerge among persons with a good education and effective leaders are even more likely to be found among them. Corresponding hypotheses may be advanced for the other demographic characteristics; indeed, the same demographic characteristics may be found to foster more than one of the elements or traits that have appeared to be particularly prevalent among leaders. Since the correlation between demographic and personality variables is still unclear, it is impossible at this point to know what part is played specifically by demographic variables and what part by psychological characteristics in the development of leadership.

Leadership characteristics and the situation with which leaders are confronted

We have seen that personal characteristics still need to be analysed and assessed; but the link between these characteristics and the particular situations that leaders face needs even more to be examined and assessed. The problem has long been recognized, to be sure. Stogdill, for instance, in the conclusion of his 1904–47 survey of studies on the subject, lists among the factors 'which have been found to be associated with leadership', alongside capacity, achievement, responsibility, participation and status, the role of the *situation*. This includes the characteristics of the followers; he adds, as is now generally accepted by psychologists, that 'leadership is a relation that exists between persons in a social situation and that persons who are leaders in one situation may not necessarily be leaders in other situations' (Bass, 1981: 67).

The matter of the 'adequacy' of leaders to particular environments has to be considered in two ways. First, there is the *general* question of the 'sociability' of leaders. As Bass points out, 'the leader must be able to know what followers want, when they want it, and what prevents them from getting what they want' (p. 111). Leaders are circumscribed by the environment to the extent that what the followers want has a critical importance. Thus, those who have the ability to perceive what followers want are more likely to be leaders, and, presumably, effective leaders. Second, and perhaps more important, different types of leaders are appropriate to different kinds of situations. Churchill or de Gaulle had to wait for situations in which saviours were required before they could be truly recognized and make a major impact on their societies. However endowed an individual may be with 'leadership qualities', he may be able to cope with only some types of situations and not with all.

If this is the case, however, it becomes more difficult to believe that there are *general* characteristics of leadership, such as those described earlier. Indeed, this conclusion may be drawn from the work of some psychologists. Fiedler, for instance, has attempted to show empirically the association between personal characteristics and the type of situations that the leaders face. According to him, when the problem to be solved is simple, the most appropriate leaders are those who are 'task-oriented'; while in complex situations the best leaders are those who are concerned more with establishing a relationship with their followers, and with having considerable empathy for them (Fiedler, 1967). If one can generalize from Fiedler's analyses, it would seem that it is not permissible to state in general what leadership qualities are, but that one would have to discriminate among these qualities according to the circumstances. In some cases, but not in others, leaders may have to be task-oriented in order to be effective; in some cases, but not in others, leaders may have to seek popularity and indeed to be popular.

This conclusion may not entirely contradict points made earlier, which suggested that leaders tend to be drawn from among both the task-oriented and the 'sociable': it may be that, in contrast with followers, leaders do have to have these qualities. But an analysis that takes into account the characteristics of the situation facing the leader has to be more sophisticated, in that it has to introduce a further form of categorization. Indeed, the distinctions made by Fiedler are probably not the only ones in which differences in the 'situation' suggest differences in the most effective form of leadership; they do constitute an important starting point and, while they have been made with respect to types of leadership that are less exalted and general than political leadership, and in particular national political leadership, they seem to have considerable potential value.

It is true that national political leadership is so comprehensive that it appears on the surface to require both task-orientation and popularity; but the two elements do not seem to be needed to the same extent in all circumstances. As a matter of fact, Fiedler's analyses echo to an extent Weber's ideal-types of bureaucratic and charismatic leadership or, in more ordinary situations, the distinction between those who are concerned with administrative implementation and those whose main aim is to appeal to the people and rally the citizens to their cause.

The difficulty, however, is that Fiedler's model has been tested not only outside the political context, but in relatively simple situations of a laboratory character. The experiments have been conducted either with relatively small groups of college students or with managers, often at a lower level, in organizations such as businesses or the army. The problems faced by national political leaders are vastly different, both because they are appreciably more complex and because the conditions under which this leadership is exercised makes it more bureaucratic and hierarchical. National political leadership is never face-to-face, as is often the type of leadership that is examined by psychologists. Thus, the distinction may not be fully applicable to the political realm. Fiedler himself suggests indirectly that this might be the case when he states that task-oriented leadership is particularly suited to simple situations: since political leadership, and national political leadership in particular, is always concerned with complex situations, the model may not be directly transferable. At a minimum, it seems prudent to view the distinction in terms of a tendency rather than in the form of a clear-cut division when it is applied to political life.

The analyses undertaken by psychologists have thus to make further advances before it becomes possible to state precisely what the relationship is between personal characteristics and the ability of individuals to become effective leaders. They have also probably to be modified in order to be applicable to national political leadership. But some of the basic exploration has been done. One begins to have a general view of the many ways in which personality affects leadership; it seems also that the relationship between specific characteristics and leadership is indeed proven. The qualities of energy, intelligence, achievement motivation, task orientation and sociability do seem to be among the variables that have to be taken into account, though it may be that these characteristics do not play the same part in all situations and indeed that, in some cases, they may be mutually exclusive.

What is perhaps most important of all is that, in sharp contrast with most political scientists, and in particular with most earlier political scientists, psychologists have been concerned with leadership in general; they have also been concerned with 'ordinary' leadership, and not primarily with pathological cases. They are thus showing the direction that the analysis should take in the future, although a further and major step has yet to be taken: that of providing a general framework within which to locate and relate to each other the psychological and demographic bases of leadership. It is therefore important to turn now to this point and to see how far some elements of such a framework can already be delineated.

Towards a general model of the influence of personal factors on the impact of leaders

Detailed investigations often fail to show the precise role of personal factors in the context of leadership: yet the overwhelming intuitive impression is that this role is large and indeed glaring. Daily conversations remark on the effect that a leader may have because of his or her charm, appearance, oratory and popularity, but also intelligence, cunning or decisiveness. These comments, moreover, apply not merely to Churchill or de Gaulle, Roosevelt or Kennedy, Nasser, Nkrumah or Peron: they are felt to be valid, to a more limited extent, about many 'ordinary' national political leaders, as well as about many leaders who are neither national nor political. Clearly, there is an engrained belief that personality counts and probably counts for much. Compared with this 'commonsense', immediate, intuitive view, what is one to make of an analysis that concludes that personal characteristics may count to some extent, though the evidence is neither clear-cut nor definite? Should one assert that the impressions that prevail among the public are illusions and form part of a modern superstition which has transferred to leaders some of the miraculous powers once believed to be the privilege of saints? Or should one conclude, on the contrary, that academic studies are so obsessed with methodological purity that they fail to grasp what is obvious to the naked eye?

To answer this question, one needs to have a further look at the evidence. But before doing so it is worth noting that the problem stems in part from the standpoint from which it is considered. Political scientists consider leaders as a class, while the public considers them individually: an individual may seem exceptional by comparison with the rest of the population, but the difference may not be so large when leaders are compared with each other. If all leaders happen to be exceptional persons — which they are likely to be, up to a point at least, since otherwise most of them would not have become leaders — it may well be that leaders as a group are endowed with exceptional personal characteristics by contrast with the 'common man', and yet that there may be little difference when one leader is compared with another. Political scientists may thus consider all leaders and find that the range in the amount of personal influence is not very large, while 'ordinary' observers of politics may also correctly note that a given leader has a large impact at a given moment as a result of personal attributes. This feeling is reinforced by the fact that we focus typically on a small number of issues, so that the leader is being considered not merely by contrast with what ordinary citizens might achieve, but also with respect only to the issues that have been singled out for examination. It is not the whole set of personal attributes that is being assessed, but only that aspect of the personal attributes that resulted in the action of the leader who is being examined.[6]

Different conclusions may thus be legitimately drawn, depending on the standpoint. But, if it is not false to claim that the personal 'qualities' of a leader are 'exceptional' by comparison with those of the common man, and that they do have a marked impact on leadership effectiveness, it is surely worth considering the problem from this standpoint as well. One should therefore examine all the ways in which personal factors can affect leadership, as well as the part that various components of the personality are likely to play in different situations. One has to elaborate a model, as general as possible, of the different dimensions of the relationship between personal components and leadership impact.

In his *Personality and Politics*, Greenstein (1969) provides elements for such a model when he distinguishes between three aspects, which he calls 'phenomenology', 'dynamics' and 'genesis'. First, in what ways does — or could — this influence take place? What elements of the personality play — or may play — a part? Second, how does this influence vary over time? And third, what are the origins of this influence? This last question suggests that, in the chain linking dependent variables to independent variables, the personal attributes have first to be considered as independent variables with respect to the impact of leaders; but they then have to be considered as dependent variables and to be related to the independent variables that might account for their existence. At this point, too, questions relating to biographical or demographic characteristics have to be raised, as well as the role of 'deeper' elements of the personality. Thus, following Greenstein's distinction, we shall examine the ways in which personal elements may influence the impact of leadership; we shall then consider ways in which this influence may vary over time, and finally we shall look for the 'causes', or at least the 'antecedents', of these personal elements.

How do — or might — personal attributes affect the impact of leaders?

In the two preceding sections, we saw a substantial number of personal qualities playing a part in determining the role of leadership. Perhaps these qualities cannot be added to each other: there may be diminishing returns if the leader is 'too' intelligent, for instance; 'task-orientation' and 'empathy' or popularity may be to some extent antinomic. What would ideally need to be done is to match the qualities that might be required to the type of situations with which leaders are confronted. This cannot be fully accomplished, but what can be attempted is to determine the types of activities in which the leader has to be engaged in various circumstances; for instance, when have leaders to think analytically, to decide quickly, to court popularity? This, in turn, we can begin to assess by analysing the roles that leaders have to perform.

What, then, are these roles? First, leaders examine and analyse problems that they or others place on the agenda; second, they elaborate solutions to these problems; third, they adopt a solution which then becomes a decision; fourth, they 'sell' these solutions to a number of concentric circles of ever wider composition. Each of these activities requires different personal qualities if the stages of the process are to be fulfilled well.

In the first stages — the analysis of problems and the elaboration of possible solutions — leaders have to be able to grasp what is important and what is trivial, to weigh alternatives, to foresee possible outcomes. Of course, they are helped by advisers who have examined the questions beforehand and will suggest solutions; but they have to choose these advisers appropriately and yet not depend entirely on their advice, to assess the value of the solutions they propose, and to question the basis on which these solutions are made, thus detecting biases or mistakes. In the first two phases, then, the quality most required is manifestly intelligence.

In the subsequent stage — decision-making — the leader must be prepared to stop analysing the alternatives at some point and plump for one of the options. Decisions must not be taken too rapidly, before the problem has been adequately analysed, but they must not be postponed too long either: action has to be taken with respect to the problem at hand; other problems have also to be examined. Not all problems are equally urgent, admittedly, and intelligence is required to appreciate correctly the moment when the decision has to be taken. But decision-taking is not primarily a matter of intelligence: it is a matter of will power and courage. The leader has to have the emotional ability to stop the debate in his mind and take a particular side. This he will do if he has a strong desire to achieve results: 'motivation towards achievement' is thus probably the central quality needed. Too much intelligence might even be counterproductive when decisiveness is required, as some psychological studies referred to in the previous section showed: the level of analysis must not go beyond a certain point as the motivation to achieve results might then be impaired.

The leader must then 'sell' the decision taken to a number of groups in society. To simplify, these groups can be divided into three main categories: the immediate entourage, the bureaucracy, and the public at large. The immediate entourage includes many who have participated in the preparation of the decision. In this respect, the qualities required of the leader will be the same as those that the leader has to display in taking the decision; indeed, the decision may well often be taken in the context of meetings with members of this immediate entourage. But the leader must also display qualities of cunning and stubbornness, in view of possible objections, tactical or substantive, that may be made by members of the entourage. He or she is likely to be, at least at times, under considerable pressure to change the decision; he or she is also likely to find immediate subordinates divided on the solution proposed. Thus a strong motivation to achieve results is synonymous with determination. The rational calculation that characterizes the analysis stage gives way to the 'tough' one-sidedness needed to take and maintain a definite course of action.

The second type of group to which the leader must pay attention consists primarily of the administrative apparatus of the state, though it also includes other bodies in charge of implementation, some of which may even be private or semi-public. Of course, the ability of administrators to carry out decisions depends in large part on the quality of the personnel (including its willingness to obey) and on the efficiency of the organization; but in all situations it also depends on the extent to which the leader devotes some attention to what happens to the decisions he or she has taken and follows through the process of implementation (or sees that others follow it through on his/her behalf). Difficulties of implementation will always occur and have to be smoothed down.

These can be minimized only if the leader displays an ability to understand administrative processes and shows at least some attention to details. This is what is referred to by suggesting that he or she must be 'task-oriented'. This type of personal quality is manifestly different from the intelligence required in analysis or the determination needed to decide: task orientation must entail some interest in considering the concrete problems posed by the application of a decision and some willingness to 'descend' from the general to the particular. Yet this is also dangerous: over-devotion to detail takes up time that might be more profitably used to consider other problems. Among US presidents, the style of Carter, who was fond of looking at details, is often contrasted to that of Eisenhower or Reagan.

Yet task orientation must not be viewed merely as a negative trait: where the bureaucracy is inefficient or when much is demanded of the administration, for instance if new policies are pursued, greater attention to detail may be a prerequisite for success. Thus it may well be, going beyond the conclusions drawn by Fiedler outside the political field, that task orientation is an essential ingredient even when problems are not simple, though it has to coexist, in complex and difficult situations, with intelligence and determination.

Task orientation also competes with the quality most required with respect to the third set of groups to which national political leaders have to relate, namely, the public at large. All leaders need to be 'sociable', but national political leaders need particularly to be so endowed; some situations require them to be popular or, in the conventional sense of the expression, 'charismatic'. It is indeed in terms of their sociability that leaders tend to be judged most frequently, since the way in which they relate to the public is through activities designed to increase their popularity. As a result, the public may stress unduly the role of sociability and underplay the part played by other personal qualities. However, as Fiedler points out, sociability is likely to conflict with task orientation; the two qualities are unlikely to be jointly possessed by the same leader to a high degree, and the time spent on one particular aspect is at the expense of time spent on the other. National political leaders must not therefore concentrate too heavily on courting popularity.

A wide range of different qualities is therefore required of national leaders, who are unlikely to possess them all to the same high degree. Nevertheless, they do still have to be exceptional. Hence the view that leaders have also to be endowed with greater than average energy, since only if they are energetic can they be expected to be alert to problems and to engage all of their personality in the questions at hand. But energy is not enough; it has to be added to the other qualities with which leaders must be endowed, even if society is calm and demands limited. When the demands are large and tension great, on the other hand, satisfactory 'candidates' are likely to be uncommon. Perhaps it is not surprising therefore that revolutionary leaders should rarely be found, and even more rarely be found able to sustain for long the strain of the revolution.

The dynamics of the evolution of the personal attributes of leaders
Leaders need to possess a large array of personal attributes if they are to be successful; but demands are likely to vary over time, while the 'supply' of these qualities is also likely to change, even for the same leaders. The situation in the country will alter as different problems arise; and with age and experience, the ability of the leaders will not remain the same. Thus, leaders who are task-oriented and may be adequate or indeed good if what is required by society are limited or piecemeal changes may not be able to rise to the occasion if tension increases and analysis, determination and sociability become necessary. Even if there is no sudden and major change, a gradual modification of societal demands may result in very different qualities being required of the leader. Leaders whose goals were aiming at managing society or introducing limited changes may be faced with growing societal pressure and with conflicts among segments of the society which could not be handled piecemeal: Britain in the 1970s is a case in point among Western countries. Thus, leaders who are adequate at the start of their tenure may be increasingly ill-equipped with changes occurring in the demands of society. This is true as far as internal affairs are concerned; it is perhaps even truer with respect to external pressures. Eden was thus unable to cope with the strain of the Suez crisis in 1956 though he had been a satisfactory minister and prime minister previously.

Meanwhile, the leaders themselves change over time. By and large, their capacity to act effectively is likely to improve at first, as a result of better 'training'. They learn their job gradually and become better performers. The problems they face are often similar, and they need therefore less intelligence to discover the appropriate solution. They are also gradually better able to assess the extent to which their decisions are implemented correctly and rapidly; they may not need to intervene to the same extent in administrative details (though some may still be inclined to do so, if they are task-oriented). Even the process of taking decisions may become less difficult and less emotionally exhausting, while actions designed to maintain or increase popularity may also require less energy on the part of the ruler.

Such 'improvements' in the relationship between leaders and the various groups in society are also likely to result from a better anticipation of the leader's reactions on the part of those who relate to the ruler, especially among the immediate entourage, but also within the whole bureaucracy and the public at large. Advisers will come to know what the leader wishes to achieve; they will receive signals about the kind of decisions likely to be taken. Administrators will become aware of the extent to which the leader insists on a given degree and speed of implementation. The public will come to expect a particular style on the part of the leader; this style may be regarded positively or negatively, but if the reactions are positive the leader may need to devote less energy to maintaining popularity in order to achieve a particular result.

It has been argued, however, and indeed with apparent empirical evidence, that 'new' leaders may be in a better position in terms of their greater ability to achieve policy changes (Bunce, 1981). This would seem to result from the possession by new leaders of a certain 'capital', based on popularity, fear (for instance, if a coup has taken place) or the fact that it would be politically difficult, if not impossible, to replace immediately a newly appointed ruler. But leaders may enjoy more prestige on coming to office and yet become better able over time to deal with the problems they have to face. Some new leaders benefit from a 'period of grace', during which critical judgement is temporarily suspended or toned down. This does not mean that the leaders themselves are, during that period, better at analysing problems, taking decisions, following these through the implementation process or courting popularity: it merely means that they are less likely to be castigated if they are wrong. They are faced with an altogether easier environment, so to speak; the qualities they need to display are identical to those they will have to display in future, but the price that has to be paid is, momentarily, somewhat reduced.

Whether this period of grace occurs commonly or not, leaders do seem to become gradually better equipped at handling the problems with which they are confronted: their psychological qualities are sharpened and they use them more appropriately. But this improvement is not continuous or indefinite. In the first place, if leaders lack certain qualities that are required in a given situation, their inadequacy will then become apparent. Second, 'on-the-job' training in analysis or task orientation will reach a peak. Leaders are also likely to relax their attention, as they become convinced of their ability to handle effectively certain types of questions: they are likely to be less careful as similar situations arise, for instance in carefully analysing the parameters of a problem before taking a decision; or they will become over-confident about their popularity. Being more sure of themselves, of their judgement and of their capacity to 'deliver' results, they will be more likely to make mistakes. Alternatively, they will avoid problems which they feel (consciously or not) are difficult to solve, with the result that tension within the polity is likely to increase. This is how, as we saw, conflicts may develop in society. Overall, leaders' reactions to events will thus tend to become 'routinized'; new problems will no longer provide occasions to learn.

The 'routinization' of the leaders' responses has often been noticed: it results in large part from the drain on energy experienced by leaders who maintain an 'undivided' attention to the problems that arise. Whatever reserves of energy they might have possessed at the start, these are not indefinite, nor can they be reconstituted at the rate at which they are consumed. Of course, the consumption of energy will vary. Leaders who are markedly task-oriented will be more quickly exhausted. But this will also be the case if many new policies are launched or if many problems 'accidentally' occur. Indeed, leaders must remain ready to face new problems, and if they have consumed most of their energy in earlier years they will not be able to do so. There will be a marked decline in their ability to rule, possibly even a total breakdown of their motivation to achieve success; whatever their original goals, they may become managers because they no longer have the strength to act in any other way.

Thus a plateau will be reached. Rulers will not improve on their ability to handle problems beyond a certain point. In many cases, moreover, one can even expect a deterioration. This results in part from the 'routinization' of the leader's responses, as we saw; but it may well be precipitated by ageing, which intuitively does seem to affect many national leaders who have been in office for long periods, especially those who are physically old. It is true that some leaders in their seventies show considerable buoyancy, but even the most active 'grand old men' show signs of physical decline at the end. This was manifestly the case with Churchill and Adenauer; Franco and Brezhnev also seemed very diminished in the last years of their rule. Yet the effect of ageing, though less dramatic in the case of other long leaders, is also significant, although it may be not as well documented; indeed, when it is associated with illness, as with Eisenhower, ageing can affect relatively younger leaders as well.

There is thus an evolution of the effect of personal characteristics on leadership. This evolution results from the combination of two distinct movements which affect the environment on the one hand, and the leader on the other. The psychological qualities of leaders will first improve, then reach a peak, and eventually deteriorate. Meanwhile, the environment confronts these leaders with situations that require different psychological qualities. In the external area, unforeseen problems may arise for which leaders are not well equipped; internally, the situation may become more difficult to handle and the leader's qualities may no longer be those that are most relevant. If the emergence of a new situation is added to the remark that the ability of leaders is likely to deteriorate when they have been in office for long periods, it seems permissible to conclude that, over time, leaders are likely to be increasingly ineffective: this, of course, is a general, but not a universal, trend. But it does seem that, while a very rapid turnover results in the inability of rulers to control the environment of which they are temporarily in charge, a long period in office also seems to be naturally characterized by a diminished capacity to use even those qualities that leaders initially possessed.

The genesis of the personal influence of leaders

Not much is known of the reasons why a given leader may be task-oriented, courting popularity, achievement-motivated or 'intelligent'; but some of the analyses described earlier in this chapter suggest two possible lines of investigation: the role of demographic variables, and early socialization patterns.

Demographic variables — education, family and occupational background — were found to be generally associated with leadership, though more in the sense that they distinguished leaders from non-leaders than in helping to determine whether one given ruler was likely to have greater influence than another. This apparent lack of any direct link between demographic variables and leadership effectiveness, however, may be due more to the absence of systematic analyses than to the absence of a relationship, since we also noticed that family characteristics seemed to have at least some influence, and since studies of leadership undertaken by psychologists recognize the importance of these variables.

The difficulty, however, comes from the fact that it is not clear in what way demographic variables, and in particular social background variables, can directly play a part in affecting leadership effectiveness, save in that, as we pointed out, leaders coming from a certain group may be unwilling to act against the interests of this group. But an indirect influence appears easier to detect: the social background of a leader may contribute to the shaping of the psychological characteristics of this leader. Thus, personal attributes could still be recognized as the elements by which leaders make an impact on society, although the nature of these attributes — the particular configuration of the personality — would also be affected by the demographic variables.

For instance, while it may be problematic whether someone who comes from the middle class is more likely to be achievement-oriented merely because of the fact that he or she has a middle-class background, it seems less controversial to suggest that the values, the cognition, even the emotional balance of this leader will be affected by the social background. As a result of upbringing, the potential ruler may be more or less likely, first, to seek power in order to achieve results and, second, to show determination once in office. Similarly, certain types and levels of education seem intuitively to result in leaders being endowed with important psychological attributes. Indeed, some schools, in particular prestigious private schools, have long claimed that one of their main functions is to train the character and to provide their pupils with leadership skills; this is particularly the case of better-known English public schools. Military schools, similarly, emphasize the character-training aspect of their role. While there is no direct evidence that children having undergone such an education are indeed 'different' from what they would otherwise have been (evidence that seems very difficult to collect, in any case), it seems inconceivable that there should be no effect at all on the character or intelligence of those who attended these schools; at a minimum, these children will have received a better training and therefore will have been able to improve any latent qualities they had. Thus there is little doubt that demographic variables, from background to career, constitute a significant element in the extent to which leaders can exercise certain skills, even if the origin of these skills is not directly linked to this background.

Demographic variables constitute essentially the social part of the history of individuals; family history also constitutes part of that social history, but one that is usually so intense that it can, and probably often does, shape the deepest elements of the personality. This is why, as we saw, many political scientists have been inclined to look at very early childhood and at the relationship between parents and children to account for aspects of the personality. As we saw, they have tended to concentrate on the more pathological cases, partly because these seemed more important, and partly because the (often evil) influence of these leaders appeared to be accounted for by this early experience. But the influence of early childhood is general; and, indeed, as Barber's (as well as the Georges') analyses of the lives of US presidents clearly show, this type of inference can be made with respect to all types of leaders, even if they are 'normal' or 'ordinary'.

It is of course not yet clear how childhood experiences affect the psychological attitudes that leaders are likely to possess; but we know from general psychological studies that the personality of individuals is deeply marked by early socialization. It also appears that the relationship with parents and other members of the family will affect a wide range of personal attributes — intelligence perhaps, the need for popularity probably, and the motivation to achieve results almost certainly.

The ways in which this influence is exerted are obscure, as obscure as the ways in which demographic variables have an impact on the personality. The analyses on which findings are based so far suggest interpretations that are plausible. Because they are *ex post facto* and drawn from individual cases, these scarcely provide a genuine foundation for general hypotheses; indeed, it will probably be a long time before studies are undertaken to determine the precise conditions under which certain types of relationships do or do not result in some psychological characteristics prevailing among potential national political leaders. Yet, and as with demographic variables, it seems highly unlikely that the relationship between parents and children should not have a major effect on the character and intelligence of these children. Early socialization experiences can therefore legitimately be regarded as an important antecedent in the development of the personal qualities of leaders, alongside demographic variables, with which they are indeed linked, since social background is closely dependent on family background.

Of course, early socialization experiences do not provide 'the' reason why leaders possess some psychological attributes, any more than do demographic variables; differences among children cannot be wholly explained, even though, as we saw, the family experience of a younger child differs from that of a first child; similarly, persons with analogous social backgrounds or analogous education may well possess different psychological attributes. We must recognize that we still do not know the fundamental origin of these attributes or, to take Greenstein's expression, the real 'genesis' of the personal qualities of leaders. But an exploration of the backgrounds and early lives of leaders does at least provide important information about the ways in which what may be 'innate' qualities are orchestrated or crippled, strengthened or weakened.

Conclusion

For a theory of the role of personal components of leadership effectiveness to be elaborated and tested, much more is needed than can be achieved at present. We must be able to measure the impact of leaders in general, in the first instance; on the psychological side of the analysis, we need to achieve a strikingly more sophisticated understanding of the personality, of its various elements and of the relationship between these elements. We have also to know about the dynamics of development of the personality, from its origins to the moment when the leader achieves power and during his or her period in office. We must be able to measure, or at least assess with some degree of precision, the relative part played by the various components in determining the leader's influence. Such results are unlikely to be obtained in the very near future: we have therefore to be content with a number of 'drillings' in a little-known field.

Yet some points are clear. It would be inconceivable that the qualities that compose the personality did not matter, assuming that leaders do make a difference in the societies they rule. This seems to be true not only of those exceptional leaders (good or bad) who have a personality well out of the ordinary, but of other leaders, who also need to possess special personal characteristics, whether of intelligence, determination, task orientation, 'sociability' or, perhaps above all, energy. The many findings, however disparate and discrete they may be, point in that direction. The extraordinary characteristics that are required of leaders, moreover, have the effect of making these leaders different from most citizens, while also making it difficult for rulers to possess, for long periods, the qualities needed to cope with the environment they wish to control and to make the society agree with the goals they want to pursue. Precisely how much personality counts may remain a matter of debate for many years to come; but that the personality of leaders plays an important part in the way leaders shape our lives is a subject on which there does not need to be controversy.

Notes

1. For a comprehensive analysis of these biographies and 'psychobiographies', see Runyan (1982).
2. See for instance the studies of R.C. Tucker (1973) on Stalin and those of E. Erikson on Luther (1959) and Gandhi (1969).
3. See the study of A.L. George and J.L. George (1956) on Woodrow Wilson.
4. Noland (1966: 232), quoted in Renshon (1984: 240).
5. See in particular Robins (1977) and Renshon (1984).
6. I wish to thank Professor R. King, of Cornell University, for this point.

The influence of institutions on political leadership

Leaders as we saw in the previous chapter have personal influence, but they also hold a position, and, first and foremost, a title, which carries prestige and power. If it is most unlikely that personal characteristics have no impact on the effectiveness of leaders, it is equally unlikely that the position that these leaders hold has no impact. So much has been written about the positions of national leaders that it would be peculiar indeed if these writings all concentrated on an illusion; the whole thrust of political science in the field, which is devoted to the determination of the best possible arrangements designed to organize the powers and the status of leaders, cannot be based on a total misapprehension. The examination of the characteristics of the positions that leaders hold is one of the main areas of normative and empirical analysis, and it must be concluded that there is prima facie a very strong case for believing that these positions 'make a difference'.

As a matter of fact, and as might be expected in the field of leadership, the problem is not so much to determine *whether* these positions count, but to determine *how much* they count. The evidence in this respect is as elusive and difficult to evaluate as it is in relation to personal characteristics. We may know 'intuitively' that the prestige of a presidency, for instance, enables a leader to exercise some influence as a result of that position; but we do not know how to measure this influence in comparison, for instance, with positions held by other national leaders. Moreover, we know 'instinctively' that there are institutional consequences, ramifications — tentacles of that position, so to speak — which give the holder some influence in the polity. A leader is powerful not merely because of the symbols and the powers attached to the job, but because he or she can, as a result, control or at least influence many sectors of the political system. But this power, which results from the position of national leader, is all the more difficult to measure since it is so pervasive.

It is as if the leader could press a number of buttons which would result in a number of reactions within many different groups. Because they hold a position of national leadership, for instance, rulers will usually be able to appoint members of the government; they will also be able to 'instruct' the bureaucracy to act in a certain way; finally, they will often have power within the dominant party and thereby will be able to try to mobilize the population towards their policies. They will use these powers to a greater or lesser extent, to be sure. Personal ability will play a part; but the existence of these 'tentacles', these channels of influence, will place the leaders in a privileged position, not because of their own qualities, but because of the position they hold.

The analysis of the effect of the position of the leader needs to be conducted in some detail, because there are considerable variations from country to country and over time. Leaders may or may not be able to appoint their cabinet at will, for instance; the bureaucracy may be more or less efficient; the party in power may or may not be well organized. More generally, institutions and other arrangements that shape the position of leaders should be examined at four levels; first, the status of leaders — the prestige that stems from the position itself — varies; second, there are differences in the powers of leaders over the selection and control of the government and immediate 'entourage'; third, there is the bureaucracy, whose main task is to advise on and implement decisions and which is more or less at the disposal of leaders; and fourth, there are the means by which leaders can influence the population and which give them greater or lesser leverage — political parties, for instance.

The measurement of the potential effect of these institutional arrangements in helping or hindering leaders has obviously to remain rather crude, at any rate at this point in the development of our tools of analysis. It is not possible, for instance, to be precise about the extent to which a political party can strengthen the hand of a leader; nor is it possible to state exactly how much a ruler gains by being able to appoint and dismiss ministers at will or by having a strong bureaucracy. But certain broad conclusions can be drawn. What needs to be done before these questions are examined, however, is to assess in general whether institutions set up by constitutions, laws or other 'voluntary' decisions tend on the whole to help or restrict the power of leaders, and whether these are 'freer' in the exercise of their functions if they rely primarily on customs, conventions and other 'natural' developments in the polity. We shall therefore devote the first section of this chapter to this point, before looking successively at the status of leaders and at the 'instruments' they possess at the level of their 'entourage', their administration and the population as a whole.

Are leaders helped or hindered by the existence of constitutional and other 'man-made' arrangements?

Institutions have often been set up to reduce or circumscribe the power of leaders; on the other hand, the existence of well established arrangements may ensure that the leaders' decisions can be more smoothly implemented and accepted by the population. Overall, then, do leaders benefit from the existence of constitutional or other 'man-made' arrangements, such as bureaucracies and political parties?

There are three main factors that seem to suggest that the power of leaders is reduced by the presence of man-made institutions. First, institutions introduce greater predictability in political life. At one level, leaders appear to gain because they know that, if they press the appropriate button, certain consequences will follow. But they are not alone in having this knowledge; all others know, or at any rate quickly discover, that certain consequences flow from certain institutional arrangements. Thus, while leaders may gain from being (relatively) certain that given effects will follow from their actions to the extent that there is a structured 'system', the gains are somewhat offset by the fact that others, also knowing what will occur, may take appropriate action to counter these effects.

Second, the structuring of the position of leader does not necessarily result in the leader acquiring greater autonomy; on the contrary, institutional arrangements may be such that they limit leaders' opportunities to act or to influence the population. This is what many political theorists have pressed for in their writings, and many constitution-makers have attempted to achieve: namely, to reduce the power of leaders through the introduction of institutional arrangements and procedures. In such a case, the structuring of the system does not help leaders to make an impact; on the contrary, they would make a greater impact if there were no structuring at all. Indeed, many have attempted to shrug off the constitutional impediments that were imposed on them.

Third, attempts at introducing arrangements that might help the leader may not be successful. The comparison between political communication and electrical circuits is valid only up to a point; in fact, leaders are not in the fortunate position of expecting their decisions to be implemented by pressing a button: all they can hope for is that some of these decisions will be partly implemented in the fairly near future. The 'lines' linking leaders to the bureaucracy and the population are full of faults and 'short-circuits'. Thus, from the point of view of leaders, the 'system' is often inefficient, badly structured and badly organized. This is not only because of deliberate opposition, but often — perhaps mostly — because the system is simply unresponsive or only partly responsive. This lack of responsiveness, in turn, is due largely to the fact that we do not know how to make the system effective. There are thus manifest limits to the degree to which leaders are able to rely on institutions, arrangements and organizations around them to have the desired impact.

In part because the institutional arrangements may be loaded against leaders and in part because institutional 'engineering' is, to say the least, a very imperfect science, the development of a set of political and administrative structures will not necessarily provide leaders with greater opportunities to achieve results: there may be, on the contrary, greater constraints. However, the absence of structures consciously designed and established to facilitate or restrict the exercise of leadership does not mean that there would be no arrangements at all: if there were no political institutions set up by law or constitution, there would be 'natural' means by which leadership would be organized and leaders would relate to the rest of the nation. A political party may be a man-made device which can markedly advantage a leader or limit his impact; but, in the absence of political parties, leaders would relate to the population by other means, for instance through tribal or other groups.

Thus, the case of the leader who would have to rely on purely personal attributes is very rare, so rare as to be purely theoretical; for it to occur, there would have to be no social groups in the country, no customs, no rites by which leaders come to power, stay in office and relate to their entourage, the bureaucracy or the people. When there are no man-made structures, natural arrangements will take their place; more correctly, man-made political institutions will gradually be superimposed on and will supersede natural arrangements. But these natural social groupings continue to be influential; indeed, man-made political institutions are sometimes, if not often, purely formal and remain little implemented or not implemented at all. The interplay between man-made and natural arrangements is an instance of the classic intertwining between constitutional or legal mechanisms and behavioural patterns.

Man-made and natural arrangements are unlikely to have the same type of effects on leadership, however. Man-made arrangements, for instance, are more likely to be set up in order to restrict the power of leaders than are natural arrangements, although natural arrangements may have the effect of restricting the role of leaders, by accident rather than by design, in some fields. It is therefore necessary to examine the range of situations that might occur, from those in which man-made structures are weak and almost non-existent to those in which they are highly developed, in order to see whether the impact of leaders is likely to depend primarily on the existence of one or the other type of arrangements. A mapping of the ways in which man-made and natural structures can affect leadership will provide an indication of the extent to which the position of leaders and its ramifications can vary from one society to another. We will then know better the limits of the opportunities that may be given to leaders and of the constraints under which they may have to operate.

The possible impact of leaders in the absence of man-made structures

In theory at least, national political leadership could emerge in a context in which there were no structures specifically designed to organize the political system, though, as we just noted, natural arrangements will necessarily exist. How, then, would the position of leaders and its ramifications within the polity come to be characterized?

In such a case, first, the personal status of the leader may be vastly enhanced, as there may be no limitations on the conditions under which the rule is exercised. Of course, in many cases in which there are no constitutional or legal constraints, traditional arrangements may limit somewhat, though usually to a minor extent, the conditions under which leaders rule. For instance, succession arrangements are likely to exist, one common principle being that of primogeniture; or there may be limitations on the duration of the monarch's rule, though more frequently the position is held for life. These are instances of limited restrictions, typically resulting from tradition, which can be described therefore as 'natural'.

But there may be no limitations at all: the leader's status and personal position are then purely the result of the particular situation and the particular individual. Such cases occur frequently, even in the contemporary world, whereas the absolute monarchy is in marked decline. An example of unrestricted status is that of the leader whose accession to office and whose tenure is based on no pre-existing arrangements. Many military rulers who come to power by a coup are in this group; in such a situation we know in advance neither who will achieve office (although chiefs of staff may in practice be the most likely candidates), nor how long he will remain in office (Blondel, 1980: 157). The position is entirely uncertain; there are no rules at all, a state of affairs which may however be viewed by leaders as less propitious than that of the absolute monarch.

While the personal status of leaders therefore may not be regulated at all in some cases, there are even more situations in which the relationship between leader and entourage is not constrained by any pre-existing arrangements. There may well be no rules or customs determining who will become members of the government, how long these members will remain in office, what their powers will be or their relationship with the leader. There may of course be unwritten precedents that are being adhered to: traditional monarchs, for instance, may find it difficult not to include some of their relatives or some of the members of the major families of the realm; those who come to power by a coup may find it difficult not to reward some of their co-conspirators by giving them a place in the government. But this need not be the case for very long: the absolute rulers may later be able to dismiss ministers at will and replace them with whomever they want. A military or revolutionary council may have to be set up, but this can be emasculated, and many of the members forced to resign; the council itself may even be abolished (Blondel, 1982: 89–93). As a matter of fact, even in more 'regular' regimes, there are often no rules or traditions forcing leaders to appoint specific individuals or representatives of specific groups. In practice, it is not unusual for many leaders to come close to a position in which they can choose the members of their entourage at will; moreover, there are frequently no rules governing the relationship between the leader and the members once they have been appointed.

Leaders never have quite this same freedom with respect to the bureaucracy or the population at large. They cannot select the members of the national civil service at will; nor can they organize it entirely the way they wish. They may of course demote and promote some officials, especially at the top; they may introduce changes in the modes of operation of the bureaucracy; they may expand or restrict the scope of activities of civil servants. But their discretion is limited naturally in a number of important ways. First, as leaders cannot in practice replace the whole bureaucracy, they are clearly dependent to an important extent on the capabilities of the existing staff. Second, any changes that they introduce will result in costs as well as benefits: a bureaucracy cannot be upset without losing some of its efficiency, at least in the short term. Third, and most important, leaders are continuously dependent on the bureaucracy, whether it is a pre-existing corpus or one they have re-formed; they have to accept delays, conflicts and difficulties in the implementation of decisions.

There are thus inevitable constraints with respect to the bureaucracy. The absence of established political procedures does not give leaders total freedom, either, in their relationship with the population. On the contrary, there may be few opportunities to influence the population and thus to make an impact. The natural bonds that tie individuals together may constitute handicaps. If a society is primarily tribal, for instance, the chiefs will be the main means by which members of the tribe can be influenced. The national leader will therefore exercise influence only if he is a chief; otherwise, he will have to work hard to convince others or attempt to break up the tribal organization and establish man-made structures in order to avoid the consequences of natural structures. The same applies to ethnic groups, religious groups and any other natural communal organization.

Thus, when there are no man-made structures in a polity, national leaders often will not be able to exercise any marked influence on the population. While their status may leave their duration in office and their power to appoint their entourage unrestricted, they will encounter severe limitations with respect to their ability to control the bureaucracy and influence the population. A state of affairs in which there were no man-made rules determining the position of the ruler and its ramifications would be by no means 'ideal' from the leaders' point of view.

The possible impact of leaders in the context of man-made structures

With man-made institutions and arrangements, the balance of advantages and disadvantages becomes different. By and large, man-made arrangements reduce the freedom of rulers in terms of their personal status; they may reduce also discretion in terms of the ability of rulers to select and control their entourage; on the other hand, they may increase the capabilities of leaders vis-à-vis the bureaucracy, and they can often give leaders greater opportunities to exercise direct influence on the population.

Man-made institutional arrangements are often the result of demands to restrict the role of the national executive: consequently, one of their main aims is to ensure that the position of the chief executive becomes less exalted and less secure. But there are variations in the range of these restrictions and the extent to which they are fully applied or are circumvented in practice.

Institutional arrangements are also likely to introduce some restrictions in the ability of leaders to select at will the members of their entourage. This is not always the case, however: by and large, constitutional and other legal arrangements have focused rather less on governments and ministers than on leaders.

The effect of constitutional and other man-made rules can be very different with respect to the power of leaders over the bureaucracy. Typically, of course, national political leaders are less free to choose, promote and dismiss members of the civil service, as complex procedures are likely to be established, giving civil servants some de facto autonomy: this means some decrease in leaders' possible impact. But the introduction of these rules also diminishes the ability of administrators to act arbitrarily. The development of an *esprit de corps* is likely to result in the emergence of an ideology of loyalty to the state; while this loyalty may not be directed towards the person of the leader as such, it will help him or her indirectly. Moreover, the key variable may be a different one: what is likely to be most important is the technical ability and organizational efficiency of the bureaucracy, and these qualities are likely to be fostered by the development of more structured arrangements.

Finally, the impact of leaders vis-à-vis the population as a whole is likely to be increased by the creation of man-made structures. These tend to centralize the polity and strengthen the state. One should not exaggerate their influence, however: attempts to 'wipe out tribalism', for instance, have often been unsuccessful. But at least leaders can create instruments that will establish direct links with the population. This is what occurs with political parties, which often enable politicians to bypass ethnic, religious or other groups, even when the parties originated from these groups.

Not all the man-made structures strengthen the position of the leader, admittedly; some, indeed, are designed to reduce the power of leaders, parliaments and congresses at the national level, and other elected bodies at the local and regional levels. But these institutions also contribute to a 'nationalization' of politics and to a decline of the structures that existed, so to speak, independently of the state and independently, therefore, from the national leadership. Thus, even these institutions constitute instruments that rulers can use to their advantage.

The development of the state thus tends to increase the leaders' impact on the population. Leaders also thereby obtain greater opportunities to press for their goals. In traditional systems, they are severely constrained by the immemorial customs which must not be altered; they often tend to concentrate on foreign affairs, as was pointed out in Chapter 2 above. Internally, they lack the procedures to bring about reforms and the political mechanisms, such as parties, through which to 'sell' their new proposals to the population. Thus, not surprisingly, European monarchs attempted to set up institutions designed to enable them to introduce changes at the individual or collective level.

In modern systems, on the contrary, although leaders are markedly constrained, they do have the potential to act. Laws and regulations are mechanisms that can be used to determine the scope of change, while bureaucracies, parties and other groups can help to implement these proposals. National leaders are therefore far from being necessarily 'worse-off' when man-made institutions are introduced, though their impact is likely to be smaller in some respects than where there are no constitutional or legal rules. What they lose in stature and in power over the personnel is often compensated for by a greater freedom of manoeuvre in substantive matters. We need therefore to look more closely at the four levels of possible constraints and opportunities before being able to discover the extent to which leaders are helped or hindered by the political institutions that exist in society.

The status position of leaders and the impact
of leadership

Limitations on the status of leaders result primarily from constitutional and legal rules, as we saw; but these limitations can vary markedly. They may aim, for instance, at ensuring that the life of a leader be not vastly different from that of the common man: attacks against the mode of living of kings have been made partly on this ground. They may organize substantial rotation at the top in order to provide more opportunities for aspiring leaders. In ancient Rome, consuls and other magistrates served for one year only; many constitutions state that the chief executives may not serve more than one or two terms; Swiss presidents rotate every year; and in Yugoslavia the principle of rotation has been generalized.

There are thus reasons of equality or 'democratic participation' behind the limitations that are introduced; but the more common purpose is to reduce the power of leaders, that is to say, to diminish the influence that the position, in itself, might automatically carry. Thus, the tenure is subject to periodic reappointment; or the appointment is made continuously accountable to other bodies. Sometimes the functions of national leadership are split between two or more individuals. Of course, these provisions are not foolproof, both because it is possible to circumvent them and because other factors often interplay. Nor is it possible to measure precisely their effect, even in the best of circumstances; but it is worth at least describing them in broad terms.

Shared leadership

One type of limitation has consisted in decreasing the prestige of leaders, thereby diminishing the tendency of populations to obey rulers simply because they are in power. Thus, the pomp and pageantry attached to the office have been reduced in many countries, especially in republics, though probably appreciably less than might have once been envisaged.

This has been achieved indirectly in many cases by splitting the position of the head of state from that of head of government. Historically, the division often came about for other reasons, in particular because monarchs needed help in political and administrative fields; this is also why 'shared' leadership has frequently been instituted recently, especially in the Third World. In practice, however, when the head of state has a primarily formal function, as in most Western European countries and much of the Commonwealth (about 30 countries, or a fifth of the total), prime ministers may be spared the burdens of having to be present at purely symbolic functions, but their person is also less revered, while the head of state often continues to have social prestige, but may be devoid of any effective power. (This is not always the case, since there is frequently a need for residual functions of arbitration.)

Although these prime ministers thus have less prestige, it does not necessarily follow that their impact is more limited as a result. There may be some indirect evidence to substantiate the point, however, if we consider the choices made by a number of prominent politicians. Some have preferred to be heads of state to being prime ministers, when given the opportunity to choose: one of the best-known cases was that of de Gaulle in 1958. The examples of Karamanlis of Greece and of Soares in Portugal are less clear-cut, since they were also prepared to abandon some of their effective power, as had previously occurred with de Valera in Ireland; and while Adenauer did consider for a while the possibility of becoming president instead of chancellor, he abandoned the idea when it became clear to him that he could not be a 'strong' president in the context of the West German model.

A number of non-Western prime ministers, however, both in Commonwealth countries and in previously French Black Africa, chose to become presidents; some even abolished the position of prime minister, at least for a period. This happened in Ghana, Zambia and the Ivory Coast, among others; in Sri Lanka and Guyana, the model of the strong president was introduced in the late 1970s and early 1980s. In all these cases, it must be presumed that the leader believed he could achieve more as president than as prime minister. There is therefore probably a widespread belief, especially in the Third World, that the title and the pomp of the office have some importance.

The right to censure the leader and the impact of leadership

One reason why the position of prime minister may appear less prestigious than that of president is that it is less secure. Typically, prime ministers can either be dismissed by the head of state or be forced to resign by the legislature (and presumably can avoid the first of these threats only because of the existence of the second). This surely suggests a relatively weak position, as well as a probable reduction in the duration of tenure. Indeed, the division of the executive between head of state and head of government in nineteenth-century Europe could be viewed as based on a trade-off by which the long duration of monarchs would no longer matter, since the prime minister's power would be exercised for a shorter period.

The practical situation is not as clear-cut, however. First, the procedure of governmental responsibility to parliament has indeed achieved some reduction in the duration of leaders; but this reduction is not unique to parliamentary systems. It is true that long-term leaders tend now to be found primarily among the few remaining effective monarchs, among the founders of new states and in communist countries. But the duration of parliamentary prime ministers is not on average shorter than that of other leaders; in fact, it is typically longer than that of leaders in most other regimes, authoritarian or liberal (Blondel, 1980: 177–91).

Second, the effect of parliamentary accountability is far from being one-sided. The right to dismiss the national leader is in practice sometimes formal; often, it is merely residual and is exercised in extreme circumstances only. Indeed, the real effect can be the converse from the one that was sought. For instance, the prime ministers of many Commonwealth countries and a number of continental European countries probably benefited from the fact that parliament could dismiss them: they were better able to organize the legislature to their advantage by establishing their control over that legislature by means of a dominant party.

Thus, under some conditions at least, the threat of parliamentary dismissal of the prime minister has the paradoxical impact of increasing the power of that leader; and this situation must be considered in the light of the predicament of other leaders. These can be dismissed, whether they are under legal or constitutional threats or not; constitutions may constitute a hurdle against 'irregular' transfers of power, but these hurdles are frequently overcome. The practical difference therefore may be small between the case of a leader whom parliament may dismiss and that of another who may be constitutionally safe but is in real danger of being overthrown by a coup or a revolution — in fact, the probability of coups is larger where there are no legal means of dismissing the leader during his or her period of tenure. The possibility of dismissal by parliament therefore operates as a safety valve, not as a mechanism that effectively ensures more frequent turnover.

Admittedly, in a few parliamentary systems leaders are dismissed rather frequently, and sometimes very frequently indeed. The best-known — and the most extreme — case was that of France before 1958, although Belgium, Italy or Finland, as well as (to an extent) democratic Portugal, constitute more limited instances of the same phenomenon. In the French case certainly, and in the other examples probably, short tenure appears generally associated with limited impact. But the real cause of short tenure, in these cases, lies not in the constitutional position giving parliament the right to censure the leader, but rather from the uncertainty, and indeed fragility, of the tenure, which in turn results from the characteristics of the party system and the configuration of the political forces. For the coupling of the duration of leadership with parliamentary confidence means that, while rulers may suffer from the lack of parliamentary cohesion, they may also benefit from, and indeed reinforce, parliamentary cohesion where it exists; and when this cohesion exists, the impact can be large and the duration of tenure substantial. The responsibility of leaders to parliament thus does not result in a restriction of the strength of leaders: its effect should probably be seen in a tendency to translate, but with some exaggeration, the characteristics of the configuration of the political forces.

Fixed duration
The third way in which the status of leaders may be undermined is through the imposition of rules limiting the duration in high office to a fixed and usually rather small number of years. Fixed duration is usually viewed as an alternative to the power of dismissal by the legislature, since leaders who operate under the threat of dismissal typically hold office indefinitely: that is, for as long as they continue to be supported by the legislature and the dominant party. This support may be suddenly interrupted by an electoral defeat, but it need not be, and some prime ministers — in Canada, Australia or Sweden — to mention only Western examples, have been in power for very long periods, far longer than presidents of the United States or other 'constitutional' presidential systems would be legally entitled to remain in office (Blondel, 1980: 221–4).

If there is a fixed tenure rule — one or two terms of office, for instance — and if each of these terms is only of four, five or six years, there is a clear constraint on presidential 'horizons'. These constraints therefore have psychological consequences. The president is unlikely to be markedly involved in projects that will have a pay-off only after many years, especially if these projects entail immediate sacrifices. This is true, of course, of other types of leaders, but there is a further inducement for fixed-tenure rulers to be inclined to operate in the short to medium term: citizens, particularly those who are politically active, knowing that a president's term will end at a given point, become less inclined to follow his guidance as the end of his term approaches. The notion of the 'lame-duck' leader is directly associated with fixed-tenure positions, though one may occasionally find 'lame ducks' in other systems as well (for instance, if a ruler is appointed to prepare an election). Thus, on the one hand, the leader who operates under a fixed-term rule may not be inclined to use his or her potential to the full: he or she may therefore make less of a 'difference' than might naturally have been the case; on the other hand, citizens may be less inclined to obey a fixed-term leader at the end of his or her tenure to the same extent that they would otherwise, since citizens then do not know how long he or she will continue in power.

It would be valuable to be able to assess the precise extent to which the impact of leaders is affected by fixed-term duration: in the absence of any clear measurement, one can merely speculate on possible effects on the basis of indirect evidence. First, as was pointed out in the previous chapter, the impact of leaders probably does not remain the same over time. Rulers may be generally less effective in the very early period (though some might benefit from a 'state of grace' on coming to office); they may then become more successful; but later still their power may decline. Of course, the curve is not identical for every leader; some may not peak in this fashion. If, however, a duration of about five or six years is the optimum for most leaders and in most situations, the fixed terms that are imposed by many constitutions may seem ideal for the average ruler.

Indeed, the fixed term might even constitute a spur towards more effective action during the years when the leader knows that he or she will be in office. In principle, an indeterminate term may enable leaders to keep long-term considerations in mind; however, as leaders know that their continuation in office depends on there being a sufficient level of popular satisfaction, whether they operate under a fixed term rule or not, those whose tenure is indeterminate may find that greater pressures are exercised precisely because the opponents do not know when the current leadership will change. Conversely, pressure may be reduced in the case of fixed-term leaders, who may therefore be more inclined to pursue their goals without exaggerated concern for immediate popularity, since their opponents know in advance when they will have to leave office. But the evidence on this point, as we shall see, is at best very mixed.

A term of five or six years may thus be beneficial for the majority of rulers whose energy is nearly exhausted at the end of their period in power. The system does lack flexibility, however. One cannot accommodate the case of the ruler who might still be effective after a decade in office; more important, perhaps, there may be situations that demand greater continuity in office, especially during periods of nation- or regime-building, as in Germany after 1949, probably in France after 1958 and almost certainly in many of the new states after independence. Of course, there needs then to be a (rather unusual) empathy between leader and society, as did occur in the case of Adenauer in Germany and probably with de Gaulle in France, but this does not happen often. However, a short fixed term, which is not renewable or is renewable only once, does not enable leaders to cope with such cases. Perhaps this is why such provisions have not existed in Black Africa or have been set aside when they did exist; perhaps this is in part the reason for the institutional instability of Latin America, where, on the contrary, provisions for fixed terms are typically in force (Blondel, 1980: 168–71).

For, indeed, fixed-term systems have been associated with marked institutional difficulties. As a matter of fact, these regimes have been unable to ensure that leaders remained in office for the whole of the period for which they were appointed. The duration of leaders in parliamentary systems is longer than the world average, as we saw; on the other hand, the duration of presidents elected for a fixed term is on average shorter and typically is shorter — sometimes much shorter — than the term allowed by the constitution. Thus, postwar US presidents have been in office for five years, on average, while they could have been leaders for eight. This is a shorter duration than that of Western European and Commonwealth prime ministers; but it does at least take place in the context of regular succession. In Latin America, on the other hand, while presidents are elected for terms of four to six years and in many cases are not entitled to seek re-election, the average duration in office has been only about three years. This is largely because many presidential terms have been shortened by coups or forced resignations.

Thus, the fixed term system does not ensure that leaders remain in office for the whole of the prescribed period; it does not prevent some of these leaders from being as short-lived as are short-lived prime ministers in some parliamentary systems; and it may not even reduce tension in the polity and thus prevent coups from occurring. Leaders in these systems may not after all have the opportunity to govern in an assured manner, even during the relatively short period in which they are entitled to rule.

The impact of leadership is affected by the conditions under which the position can be exercised, but the effect is somewhat different from that which the arrangements suggest. Leadership in the contemporary world has, on the whole, less prestige, less pomp, less of an aura around it than it had in the past. This probably contributes somewhat to a reduction in impact. Contemporary leadership is also, on the whole, of shorter duration than in earlier periods, except in communist states and (but to a decreasingly important extent) in strong monarchies and among founders of states. To the extent that constitutional or legal arrangements play a part, this reduction has resulted, on the whole, from two different mechanisms: the fixed-term tenure of presidential systems, and the indeterminate tenure of prime ministers who may be dismissed by the legislature. That these arrangements correspond to a felt need is indicated by the fact that, where they do not exist, and even where they do, coups and other 'irregular' forms of pressure result in the resignation of many leaders. But the effect of shortened tenure on the role of leaders remains unclear, because many long-serving leaders may have expended most of their strength by the time they leave office; also, because they are typically forced to concern themselves with short- and medium-term actions, the impact of leadership during the years in which they are in office is not appreciably modified by the arrangements designed to limit it. Leaders are not markedly restricted in their scope of action and their ability to press for goals by the characteristics of the position they hold, while that position gives them enough prestige and, typically, enough time in office to be able to pursue these goals with determination if they are inclined to do so. While modern institutions may not provide leaders with a permanent 'carte blanche', they give many of them, and for a period of some magnitude, almost the same 'carte blanche' as their 'strong' predecessors had in the past.

The power of leaders over their entourage and the impact of leadership

When we turn to the examination of the politicians who are close to the leaders, and in particular to the national government, we move from an assessment of the direct effect that institutional structures may have on rulers to a more indirect influence. The question then is, how far may leaders be helped or hindered by the actions of others? Yet the object is not to look at the general effects that political bodies may have on decision-making: what has to be examined is a somewhat narrower problem, closely related to the impact of leadership itself; namely, the extent to which institutional mechanisms provide a framework that affects the ability of leaders to implement their goals.

The first type of institutional mechanisms that needs to be considered is that which regulates the power of leaders vis-à-vis their closest associates, their entourage and, in particular, the members of the government as well as special assistants and advisers. Prima facie at least, variations in the composition and powers of this group would seem to affect the impact of leadership; rulers who are entirely free to choose the members of their entourage, for instance, would seem potentially more powerful than those who do not have this freedom. Differences in the constitutional or legal powers of individual ministers would also seem to play an important part. In reality, however, differences are not as clear-cut.

The impact of leaders and the appointment of the national executive

Almost everywhere, national leaders have at least some discretion in the choice of their entourage, a discretion that is always greater with respect to the personal staff than to members of the government. But the amount of this discretion varies markedly and in many subtle ways. One can thus identify a number of broad types along what is obviously an underlying continuous dimension. At one extreme are the cases of leaders who are almost entirely free to choose the ministers and other members of the 'inner circle'. They are, of course, never wholly free: some political or technical constraints always make it imperative to choose at least some members from among specific groups and to maintain certain key people in their posts longer than the leader might wish; but one may consider as (in practice) free those rulers who can select their ministers and their personal staff from a wide variety of groups in society. Many types of leaders can do so: strong monarchs, founders of new states and many authoritarian presidents, whether civilian or military, are in this position. This type of discretion is found also in some liberal systems: US presidents are among the leaders who have the greatest freedom to choose their 'inner circle'.

In other countries leaders are appreciably more restricted, both in theory and in practice. Among the many forms that these restrictions can take, a 'middle' position is fairly common, namely, one that gives leaders the freedom to appoint ministers, distribute portfolios among them and ultimately dismiss them, but restricts the choice, exclusively or predominantly, to a particular and indeed rather narrow group, for instance a parliamentary party, or perhaps the top elements of the military or the elite of the civil service. Many types of leaders are in this category, including prime ministers of parliamentary systems in which there is a dominant party, some military rulers and some civilian presidents, at least in constitutional systems. This is the case, for example, in Venezuela and Colombia. Sometimes leaders have a little more choice, for instance because they can select some, but only some, of the ministers from outside the group of established politicians: this is the case in Fifth Republic France.

By and large, at least since the 1970s, communist systems also belong to this category. Their leaders experience limitations in two ways. First, ministers — and indeed the top members of the party hierarchy — are selected from among lower echelons of the administration or the party on a regular seniority basis; the high degree of specialization of most ministers results in there being a vertical ladder which leaders have to recognize. Second, others participate in the selection process — members of the politburos, for instance, as well as the members of the party secretariat who are in charge of personnel. These constraints did not exist in the early period, whether under Stalin in the Soviet Union or in the immediate postwar period in Eastern Europe; but the 'normalization' of political life in the 1960s and 1970s resulted in the de facto development of 'rules' of conduct which severely restricted the appointment powers of communist leaders, who are now appreciably more constrained in this respect than US presidents.

Finally, at the extreme end of this continuum, some leaders have almost no power at all to select or dismiss ministers. This may occur occasionally in single-party governments if the caucus of parliamentarians, rather than the chief executive, decides who shall be ministers: Australian Labor governments have been constituted partly on this principle, and even British Labour governments have moved some way in this direction. But the more usual case is that of multi-party coalitions in which leaders have to agree in advance on both the content of the policies and the members of the government. Not all coalition executives are organized in this way, but many are, especially in continental Europe. At the limit, as in Switzerland, no choice is exercised at all by the leader; indeed, it might be claimed that, strictly speaking, there is no single leader in that country and that the Federal Council as a whole exercises the leadership function.

Unquestionably, therefore, there are marked differences, both in theory and in practice, in the extent of freedom that leaders have in selecting and dismissing members of their entourage. What the consequences of this freedom are for the impact of leaders is not so clear. The right to choose ministers suggests that leaders can have their way and are truly 'above' their collaborators: their chosen ministers and aides may therefore be more loyal and may pursue more keenly the goals of the rulers. Yet it does not follow that they are automatically more effective in achieving these goals.

There are two main reasons why one may have at least some doubts with respect to achievements. First, a leader who has complete or near-complete freedom to choose may select pliant rather than effective subordinates. Some, J.F. Kennedy for instance, may wish to hear different points of view and appoint their collaborators accordingly, but others do not, and prefer to be surrounded by sycophants: in such a case, little is achieved. Second, and more important, ministers and other aides will truly help the leader if they have the right skills; unless the selection process results in the appointment of persons who are influential among the bureaucracy and indeed in the population, leaders may gain little, but the choice of such ministers may then result in severe constraints being placed on the leaders.

Thus, differences in the appointment powers enjoyed by leaders need not necessarily result in corresponding differences in effectiveness: leaders who are free to choose their subordinates are probably often obliged to decide whether to plump for loyalty or greater effectiveness. Thus, constraints on appointment powers may exist in practice, whatever leeway the constitutional and legal mechanisms leave to the leaders.

The power of ministers and the impact of leaders

Ostensibly, at least, a leader who has limited power to select and dismiss members of the government seems more likely to have to agree to, or at least to discuss, the views of these ministers than a ruler who can constitute his entourage at will. But the power of ministers can be further enhanced as a result of constitutional or legal provisions which state that governmental decisions have to be taken jointly by the whole executive. In many countries, especially in Western Europe, the principle of collective responsibility obtains: cabinet decisions are deemed to be decisions of all the ministers. This seems to constitute a major limitation on the possible impact of leaders; while 'hierarchical' government — liberal or authoritarian — seems to leave the chief executive free to pursue his or her goals, the egalitarian principle that is embedded in the parliamentary system appears designed to reduce the personal role of leaders in policy-making.

Yet, if the legal differences are large, the practical distinction between hierarchical and collective governments may not be as great. A few governmental systems are located at both ends of the continuum; but in most cases there is probably relatively little difference between the effective powers of ministers in systems that are legally hierarchical and legally collective. On the one hand, in many governments that are formally hierarchical or near-hierarchical, ministers exercise substantial influence. This is true in liberal presidential systems, to begin with. In the United States, the strength of the president is counterbalanced by the strength of the various departments, which are fortresses in their own right. The heads of the departments are thus often the spokesmen for these departments; the system is decentralized, 'polyarchical' — anarchic, even — rather than hierarchical. In other liberal presidential systems, especially in those that have lasted for a substantial period, there are often party coalitions or factions within the ruling party and these have to be accommodated; the president cannot issue orders to the ministers and expect that these orders will be automatically followed.

There are also serious doubts as to whether the 'hierarchical' structure prevails in many of the other systems where the leader is ostensibly 'above' the ministers, such as traditional monarchies, many military regimes or authoritarian presidencies. It is true that a leader who comes to power may be able both to appoint whom he wishes and to determine a policy line; but it is also true that the requirements of administration often make it necessary for the leader to listen, to compromise and to 'give in'. Some ministers may also become, for a while at least, indispensable: what they propose to the leader is then automatically accepted. It is as if, with time passing, governmental decision-making processes inevitably become more routinized and leaders are constrained not so much by the theoretical arrangements of the system, but by the very network that they themselves organized. Only if they decide to break that network, to destroy the mould and recast it, so to speak, can they again take the initiative fully and ensure that their decisions are given precedence. This can be done by some authoritarian leaders — and is more likely to occur with them than with liberal presidents. But the result is then more a question of personality than of organization; or, rather, the workings of the organization naturally lead to a substantial degree of influence being exercised by ministers, unless leaders take it upon themselves to see that their own influence prevails.

The case of communist states is informative in this respect, for these started typically on the basis of very authoritarian and hierarchical leadership arrangements and have become, by and large, markedly more collective. Except in a few instances such as North Korea and Romania, where a very strong personal ruler has been in power, leaders cannot operate a fully hierarchical system; some degree of consensus has to be obtained among the oligarchies that are constituted by politburos as well as (to an extent at least) by the presidiums of councils of ministers. This also results naturally from the seniority system which prevails and in effect replaces the elective mechanism. Thus, even in authoritarian systems, national executives tend not to be strictly hierarchical and at least some ministers have *de facto* powers over important segments of the public policy process.

These practical changes do not turn these governments into collective organs, admittedly. But, conversely, parliamentary governments usually are no longer collective, either. Only in a few of them is decision-making shared widely and fairly equally. Switzerland is the main example here, while some multi-party governments approximate this formula; overall, at most half a dozen governments are truly operating on this basis. Elsewhere among parliamentary systems, the leader is markedly above the rest of the ministers and much of the decision-making takes place by means of bilateral discussions between the leader and the relevant minister, with the leader alone exercising influence over a wide range of fields. This was true of very well-known statesmen such as Churchill, Trudeau, Adenauer, Schmidt and Palme; but it is also true of others in the large majority of the countries in which collective government is held to prevail.

The reasons for the distinction between theory and practice are numerous and are often mentioned. First, the standing of prime ministers in the party and in the country is markedly above that of the rest of the government: leaders are the ones who win or lose elections, not their ministers, and the effective structure of the executive reflects that political fact. Moreover, the collective principle may no longer satisfy the requirements of modern decision-making or indeed the psychological and socio-psychological conditions under which ministers exercise their functions, although this conclusion is controversial and the evidence cannot be said to have been collected systematically. What is clear is that the formal structure does not stop the trend towards hierarchical rule in cabinets. Where barriers to this type of rule exist, they result from the general characteristics of the party system and of the group configuration, as well as from the personality of the prime minister and from the crises and other accidents that may occur from time to time in the polity.

The structure of the government itself therefore probably has a relatively small part to play in increasing or decreasing the impact of leadership. First, the complexity of modern government makes it difficult for leaders to operate on the basis of a true hierarchy; if they do, this may be at the expense of the effectiveness of their rule since, in order to ensure compliance, they have repeatedly to modify the composition of the government and interfere in the activities of ministers, thereby creating a climate of suspicion which in turn reduces rather than increases the effectiveness of their entourage and the credibility of the executive. Second, and conversely, leaders seem rarely to be fully constrained by the collective will of their collaborators; this occurs only when not merely the governmental arrangements, but the whole character of the political system, creates a need for a high degree of consensus at all levels, as in Switzerland. The entourage does increase the influence of leaders, as these need 'arms and legs' to be able to make a mark on the polity; but variations in the way decisions are taken in the inner circle are certainly not as large as the formal structure suggests. On the one hand, most leaders can mobilize the government towards their goals; but on the other, and especially when the regime becomes established, leaders cannot expect to order members of their entourage about as if they were mere subordinates. The nature of the executive as an organization imposes constraints on leaders which the leaders cannot escape, or can escape only at considerable risk and at the cost of considerable efforts.

The character of the bureaucracy and the impact of leadership

If governments are the arms of leaders in their effort to make an impact on society, bureaucracies are the tools, the instruments *par excellence*, which leaders have to use and on which they have to rely. This is the widely accepted view of public administration, a view that has to be correct, at least negatively; for without the bureaucracy leaders and governments would not have a direct impact on the societies they rule. Thus the question that arises is, how much can the bureaucracy help to ensure that leaders and politicians make an impact on their societies? This help has to be viewed in the general context of a question that needs to be considered realistically, that is to say, on the understanding that there is necessarily some gap between politicians and administrators, that administrators cannot be expected merely to implement, and that variations in energy and drive on the part of administrators will have to exist.

The general conditions governing implementation in public bureaucracies

The 'help' that bureaucracies can give leaders depends, to a very large extent, on whether the goals that are being pursued are realistic. Assuming that they are, one can identify four factors within the civil service which will affect the impact of leaders. The first of these is competence: the administrative personnel must be trained to handle the questions that leaders want them to solve. There have to be good general administrators, including lawyers, managers capable of running services, and economists; there have to be highly skilled technicians, in engineering and medicine, in agriculture and in industry. Clearly, the emphasis depends on the demands made by the leaders; but competence is manifestly an essential variable, one that requires a considerable outlay in infrastructure and personnel long before policies are put forward.

The second condition relates to administrative organization. Limited results will be achieved if the internal organization of the services is either too light or too heavy. Co-ordination within the service must therefore be good, as horizontal links may be as important as the vertical hierarchy. Optimization between conflicting aims must be achieved; and one must avoid the kind of bottlenecks that arise when some agencies perform better than others — a situation that frequently appears to characterize communist bureaucracies.

Third, the links between the bureaucracy and the leader and government must be close and effective; civil servants must also be expected to be reliable. The magnitude of the problem, however, depends on what is demanded of civil servants: if greater demands are made, morale may decline. The difficulty stems fundamentally from the differences between the careers of civil servants and those of politicians; when politicians are recruited from a very different world, misunderstandings are likely to occur. The fostering of the loyalty of civil servants by a variety of means — but not at the expense of initiative-taking — is a manifest requirement if bureaucracies are to provide a significant help to leaders in achieving their goals.

Fourth, bureaucracies must be closely linked to the population, so that difficulties of implementation are reduced to a minimum.

Administrative bodies should have branches in the provinces, a development that is costly and also creates communication problems within the bureaucracy as well as between the leader and the bottom echelons of the hierarchy in outlying districts. Hence there are considerable debates about the relative value of a decentralized system (likely to lead to a better understanding of the needs of the population) and a system concentrated in the capital (which will follow more closely the decisions of the leader).

These four conditions cannot easily be fulfilled: some of the demands are contradictory, and the overall cost may be prohibitive. Indeed, we still do not know how to realize some of these aims as we are unsure of the techniques that might be utilized to achieve the desired results. In practice, improvements are likely to occur piecemeal, by trial and error, rather than on the basis of grand principles, many of which were shown in the past to be vague and impractical.

Problems posed by modern bureaucracies are compounded by the social and economic difficulties prevailing in their countries. The competence of the personnel, for instance, depends on the level of educational attainment in the nation at large; for instance, it is widely believed — and there is evidence to support this belief — that civil servants in the Third World are more 'corrupt' than civil servants in the West. If they find that their pay is too low, they will attempt to 'cash in' on the power their position gives them. Yet, if the society is poor, it is not clear that pay can be markedly increased.

Generally speaking, the poorer the country, the less efficient the bureaucracy is likely to be, although other variables, such as ethnic or religious cleavages, are likely to interplay. Yet it is where social and economic problems are most serious that the need to rely on the bureaucracy to effect change is also the greatest. At one level, admittedly, there are more demands on the bureaucracy in advanced industrial nations: the elaborate social welfare systems, as well as the complex economic regulations that characterize these states (even the most economically 'liberal' among them, such as the United States), require a sophisticated and large civil service. To this extent demands do rise, but the efficiency of the bureaucratic machine also improves in the context of general socioeconomic development.

However, social welfare mechanisms or economic arrangements are more elaborate in advanced industrial societies not because other societies do not 'need' such provisions, but because they cannot afford them and are not able to implement them. Thus the weaknesses of the bureaucracy in Third World societies are in part the cause, and not merely the consequence, of the underdevelopment of social welfare and economic provisions. Demands on the bureaucracy are kept low, to be sure; but an increase in these demands would lead to an improvement of the conditions of populations and should therefore be fostered: this is indeed gradually occurring.

Moreover, leaders of Third World states are often naturally inclined to want to modify the conditions under which society operates and to expand the activity of the bureaucracy in order to bring about social and economic improvements. They are therefore putting pressure on the bureaucracy to achieve results, while the structure and personnel may well be unable to achieve these results. The demands on the bureaucracy are therefore likely to be large, with negative consequences on the morale of the civil servants and on their overall performance. There is thus a major contradiction between the relatively low effectiveness of bureaucracies in less developed countries and the demands that are often made in an attempt to improve the conditions of their societies.

Types of societies, types of bureaucratic effectiveness and the impact of leadership

Leaders of all countries are thus faced with structural problems with respect to bureaucracies, although the problems and the constraints are different from one type of society to another. By and large, these constraints suggest that each country can be expected to attain, at a given point in time, only a certain level of effectiveness in implementation. Of course, leaders — and in particular leaders who wish to achieve goals that are appreciably more 'activist' than those of their predecessors — often wish to do more; to an extent at least, they can try and bend the 'muscles' of the bureaucracy; but their expectations will remain largely unfulfilled.

Variations in administrative 'overload' in different societies

Much emphasis has been placed on the overload of administrative bodies in Western countries, as popular demands go beyond what the administrative machine can process; overload is a universal problem, however, as demands tend almost everywhere to go beyond what administrative structures can do in relation to the levels of competence of the staff, the organization of the services and the character of the links with the government and the population. In the West, overload results from the large number and complexity of the programmes, as well as from efforts to innovate or reform these programmes; but innovation or reform can be implemented only if there is some slack in the administration. Communist states have experienced this difficulty to a major extent; and in the Third World problems are most acute, as problems of competence, organization, venality and a lack of links with the population are most serious. Thus, bureaucracies of the Third World should be expected to be 'overloaded', unless the leaders (primarily traditional leaders) wish merely to manage their societies; as most Third World leaders want to do more, they are likely to be hampered, rather than helped, by their bureaucracies.

Can the leader improve the conditions under which bureaucracy operates?

Admittedly, the capacity of a bureaucracy is not fixed and it is possible for leaders to improve its effectiveness. Leaders have attempted to do so for centuries, the Roman Empire, France and Prussia being among the nations in the West best known for their highly developed bureaucratic systems. But changes are necessarily slow, while demands for change in the public services appear to become greater in the modern period.

New leaders have at their disposal two types of instruments with which to improve (somewhat) the general conditions under which bureaucracies can be expected to help their rule to be more effective. One type is personal: leaders can use their prestige, their following in the nation and within the bureaucracy itself, to obtain greater loyalty and zeal on the part of civil servants. This strategy has some value, especially in the early period. It is probably part of the advantages that leaders enjoy during the 'state of grace' which often characterizes the early months. But this is only a temporary strategy; structural change has to occur in the administration, a policy that is often precluded, however, by the socioeconomic conditions. Any 'activist' leader will indeed try to introduce some changes: the simplest and most obvious of these consists in putting forward measures designed to improve the loyalty of administrators, while sanctions will be threatened against those who do not comply; suggestions are made that corruption will be eliminated and that 'enemies' of the new government will be prevented from undertaking their 'under-cover' activities.

But these measures are more spectacular than effective, unless they are pursued with great tenacity and are indeed accompanied by policies systematically designed to train other civil servants who might replace those who will be eliminated. For leaders will not achieve a change in the competence of the civil servants by trying to make the personnel do what they are not able to do or by making administrators behave in ways in which they have not been accustomed to behave. Communist leaders may have been able — but only to an extent — to modify the characteristics of the activities of bureaucrats in the countries in which they came to power; but this was only after many years of considerable pressure, much change of personnel and a general transformation of the socio-political climate. Having modified the country's general ideology, these leaders were then able also to modify somewhat the attitudes of civil servants. Yet this had only a limited success: the 'superior' characteristics of the East German bureaucracy have more to do with German traditions than with the impact of communism.

The more effective transformations are those that are concerned with, besides changes in the recruitment and training of the personnel, a systematic examination of the ways in which the linkage with the government, the organization of the service and the linkage with the population can be improved. But the inevitable trade-offs that have to be made, both within and between these elements, suggest a combination of systematic analysis and a clear recognition that 'improvements' can be obtained only up to a point and at a limited pace. The civil service cannot suddenly 'swim' within the population as 'fish in water', to draw from the Chinese communist remark directed at the role of the party; this can be done only gradually, especially when prejudices against the bureaucracy are large and an 'anarchistic' or anti-state tradition prevails. Thus, leaders must recognize that their efforts at modifying the structure of the bureaucracy will have pay-offs only in the relatively long term, and that the implementation of their own policies cannot entirely depend on these reforms, which at first might be disruptive.

Of course, these activities are unlikely to be successful unless they take into account the situation in which the bureaucracy finds itself and in particular the socioeconomic and political characteristics of the country. Since the 'ineffectiveness' of the administrative apparatus is likely to be greater where the socioeconomic infrastructure is weaker, only an improvement in this infrastructure can achieve the desired results; and an improvement in the political infrastructure, which we shall examine in the next section, is also an essential part of the operation. But, as an improvement in the socioeconomic infrastructure requires the intervention of leaders and governments by means of the bureaucracy, the only internal way out of the dilemma is by means of a series of integrated joint moves designed to ensure that one type of intervention is fully in harmony with all the others. Developing countries can also count to some extent on expatriate civil servants; because they are not part of the prevailing culture, these may help to improve the characteristics of the bureaucracy. But they are usually out of place in the environment, and at best are a temporary remedy to the difficulties of the 'developmental' strategy pursued by the leaders.

Bureaucracies are an important element in the process by which leaders can see their goals realized; but the constraints and hurdles are numerous and cannot be overcome easily, let alone rapidly. These hurdles do not stem mainly from the fact that bureaucracies do not 'want' the goals of leaders to be implemented: they are not in any case homogeneous. Nor are they inherently ineffective; if they are, unsatisfactory conditions (including the lack of training opportunities) are likely to be the cause. Leaders have to accept that the bureaucratic tools at their disposal cannot enable them to achieve more than a certain amount over a specified period of time; they can improve these tools somewhat, but only somewhat, and also over time. The impact of leadership depends on the structure of the bureaucracy. Leaders are not powerless to move the machinery and the structures, but the extent of their power is, and to their own detriment, often overestimated.

The impact of leadership and the structures of the political system

Unquestionably, the fate of the policies of leaders depends also on the response of the population, which should not merely not object but indeed be supportive. In this respect, however, it is often believed that the extent of support that can be generated among the citizenry depends largely on the existence of appropriate structures and institutional mechanisms within the polity. If these structures do not enable leaders to put across their goals and 'mobilize' the population, opposition will be large and may be a determining factor; if, on the contrary, the structures enable leaders to propagate their goals, it is then believed that these goals can be achieved (provided, admittedly, that there is no external interference).

This 'voluntaristic' and 'optimistic' view about the role of structures has led to widespread efforts by leaders holding different ideologies to set up organizations, principally political parties, to serve as channels of communication and as instruments designed to foster support. Yet evidence seems to show that the results are often disappointing. This is sometimes attributed to the unsatisfactory development of these parties and organizations; it is sometimes also attributed to the persistence of other structures which are felt to provide a home for attitudes and mentalities opposed to the leader's goals. Thus it is prima facie somewhat unclear whether, indeed, leaders can set up effective structures which will markedly help them.

To attempt to ascertain this matter, let us examine successively the part that three types of structures play: those that develop 'naturally' within the society and are especially strong in traditional and developing countries; those that are 'man-made' but are not set up by the leader and prevail in Western societies; and those that leaders create and which characterize both communist countries (or at least, characterized them at the start) and many Third World societies.

'Natural' structures and the impact of leadership

'Natural' structures can be defined as those that have existed in the polity for a sufficiently long period for their origins to be indeterminate. They tend therefore to be constituted by groups of a social rather than primarily a political character; but they have an important political impact, especially because of the strength of the bonds of loyalty that exist within them. They include in particular tribes, ethnic groups and religious bodies; in some of the older industrial countries, Britain for instance, working-class organizations often have a similar character.

Natural structures have two main characteristics, which are interconnected: they can count on a massive loyalty of members of the group; and the linkage between the group and the members is based on emotional rather than rational ties. Members belong to these natural structures by being born into them and by growing up with other members of the group. They therefore create intense patterns of relationships which are usually exclusive. The link is based not on ideas or goals, but on emotional ties; the groups exist not because of what they do, but merely because of what they are. They develop a culture and an ideology which regulate the behaviour patterns of members and are implemented by means of moral pressure and, if there is transgression, by coercion. But this 'ideology' is concerned more with the maintenance of the cohesion of the group than with any achievements or purposes; at the limit, there are no other aims besides the continuation of the group's existence.

The relationship between the members and leaders of the group is based on similar bonds of loyalty. The procedures by which leaders are selected emerge gradually. Chiefs or elders in tribes, ethnic groups or religious bodies are appointed by mechanisms which, in principle at least, are no more questioned than the codes of conduct that regulate the relationship between members, and the leaders can count on a loyal following. There are clear limits to the power of leaders, however, and these are provided by the rules and customs of the group. The chief or elder cannot go beyond these traditional powers. Consequently, policy-making is somewhat limited; in particular, it does not normally include the power to modify the customs-regulating behaviour among members of the group.

The bonds of loyalty existing within these natural structures affect the position and power of national leaders in societies, such as those of the Third World, where groups of this kind prevail. Typically, national political leaders can benefit from the allegiance of members to the extent that they are themselves leaders of a 'natural' group (if they are chiefs of a tribe or heads of a religious organization) or else enter into strong alliances with the leaders of these groups. But the bond is manifestly stronger in the former situation; if the national leader 'floats above' the natural groups, so to speak, he or she is likely to have to make compromises, and these are equally likely to be temporary or periodically questioned.

Given the character of these natural structures, and given also that the configuration of these structures is unlikely to coincide with national boundaries, the probability is that national leaders will tend to suffer rather than benefit from the existence of strong traditional groups. First, national leaders will be opposed, or even ignored, in their efforts at nation-building. Tension may grow and armed clashes may occur (and these are likely to be helped from outside by 'sympathetic' leaders who may belong to the same tribal, ethnic or religious groups as those that are 'oppressed'). Second, national leaders cannot expect to be able to develop a complex set of policies on the basis of the loyalty of natural structures: they will intermittently or even continuously find it difficult to press their goals either on their own group or on the other groups with which they are associated. The goals of the national leader will be viewed with suspicion; they will be considered as encroachments on traditions. The disruption of tribal, ethnic or religious groups will be seen as the ultimate or even proximate consequence of the national leader's actions.

Thus, the 'help' that natural structures give to national leaders is rather limited. It is likely to decrease as time passes unless these leaders decide not to modify internal relationships within the nation, a posture that has been adopted by some African rulers. If they are managers or adjusters, national leaders are likely to be accepted by the leaders and members of the natural structures; they can then benefit, to an extent, from traditional loyalties. But, if they wish to achieve more and pursue policies of social change, they will be hampered by the natural structures. They need therefore to turn to other structures in order to find support.

Man-made structures and the impact of leadership
Most political structures, in the narrow sense, are 'man-made'; leaders and other politicians have long felt the need to build institutions that will help them come to power and stay in office. Man-made institutions of course extend well beyond the political arena conceived in the strict sense, but many of these have also been conceived and used by politicians. Thus one can distinguish between three broad types of man-made structures: the formal political institutions, such as assemblies, local governments, courts and indeed national executives; the informal or unofficial political bodies, such as political parties; and the other unofficial organizations that are connected with or play a major part in political life, such as trade unions, women's organizations, youth organizations and other interest groups.

Of course, these organizations are set up with aims that are appreciably broader than the purpose of supporting leaders or even helping to recruit a political elite; indeed, some have the specific aim of limiting the scope of activity of leaders and of supervising their activities. But, in all cases, and unlike natural structures, they are typically set up for a purpose — for instance, that of organizing the political system according to certain principles, as with formal state institutions, or in order to defend a section of the community, as with interest groups. Thus, these man-made institutions experience support and loyalty not because of the emotional relationship that may exist among the members, but because of the expectation that certain results will be obtained. The ties linking man-made structures and the majority of members are thus more specific, more instrumental and, consequently, often weaker.

The distinction between natural and man-made structures is not always as sharp, admittedly. Efforts are sometimes made to capture the patterns of relationships that exist within natural structures for the benefit of newly created institutions. Groups organized for the defence of minorities, for instance, are in part based on the loyalties that exist naturally among those who belong to the same ethnic group; voluntary organizations based on one church owe part of their growth and continued support to the underlying natural loyalty existing among parts of the society to that religion. Political parties can benefit from a similar transfer of loyalty from tribal, ethnic, religious or class-based groups. State institutions have a similar base, as national feelings are used to boost support for the man-made organization that the state constitutes.

The linkage between man-made institutions — which promote goals — and natural structures — which result from patterns of relationships — is neither universal nor complete, however. Many man-made structures correspond only partly to patterns of relationships, since the goals they promote, for instance, cover only a section of the natural group or, alternatively, extend beyond that group. This is often because the leaders of the man-made structures aim at the support of a broader segment of the population, the natural structure providing a base that is numerically too small or geographically too circumscribed: religious-based parties thus have typically attempted to extend their influence beyond the confines of the faithful. More generally, the distinction between natural and man-made groups has tended to increase as the latter have promoted policies applicable to the whole nation and not merely to one section.

For man-made groups are typically national in character, or, if their geographical coverage is limited to a region or district, they are none the less concerned with an administrative division of the state and thereby, indirectly, with the organization of the state. To this extent, as was pointed out in the first section of this chapter, man-made structures contribute to the 'nationalization' of politics and thus help leaders to combat the sectional tendencies that characterize natural structures.

Consequently, however, man-made institutions often may not acquire the same strong loyalty as natural structures; in a conflict between natural and man-made structures, therefore, citizens may support more strongly the natural structures than those of the state, be they the formal organizations set up by the constitution or informal bodies such as political parties or interest groups.

The help that national leaders receive from man-made structures is therefore dependent on the extent to which these structures are able to fight successfully and eventually to roll back the natural structures in which patterns of loyalty go, as we saw, to chiefs and elders. If this happens, national leaders will profit from the development of man-made structures, whether constitutional bodies such as assemblies or 'unofficial' organizations such as political parties. There is a price to pay, however, as these structures are often set up in order to restrict the power of leaders: representative assemblies may help to 'nationalize' politics, but they also attempt to make rulers accountable; political parties may help to provide leaders with a national following, but they also oblige these to pay attention to other influentials within the party, regionally and nationally. The game of politics becomes more national; it ceases to be based on traditional loyalties; but leaders become the prisoners, so to speak, of the type of linkage created by the man-made structures. Thus, when there is a streamlined two-party system, as in many parts of the Commonwealth, national leaders may temporarily command great influence; but where multi-party systems prevail as in parts of continental Europe, national leaders often have little or no opportunity to stand markedly above those who are the decision-makers in each of these parties.

The impact of leadership and the setting up of new structures by the leaders themselves

The widespread desire of national leaders to attempt to surmount these limitations leads them to set up new structures, 'personalized' political parties for instance, which would be at their command. Were they to be successful in this enterprise, they would be able to circumvent the sectional effect of traditional groups without having to endure the limiting consequences of established parties and powerful assemblies. But the task is difficult, for what needs to be done is to establish a party that, together with ancillary organizations, can command widespread support in the population and help to provide effective backing for the leader's policies.

In reality, new organizations run the risk of being more formal than real; they may be active at the centre, but have few 'feelers' at the periphery. To meet this problem, authoritarian monarchs of the past set up bureaucracies and implanted them in the provinces, not just to administer the country, but to counter the traditional support of the aristocracy. In the twentieth century the military has sometimes been used for this purpose; more commonly, single parties have been viewed as good instruments to reduce the power of traditional groups (tribal, ethnic or religious) and to muzzle representative mechanisms in addition to any 'modern' groups which might restrict the power of the leader; for political parties seem especially well suited to develop ramifications within the nation, at the workplace and within communities, and thus to harness a large support for the national leaders.

The technique of the personalized party has been widely adopted; it has been particularly popular in the post-independence period in Black Africa. Military leaders have also started single parties to overcome the limitations of the military as a means of providing and shaping support in the community. But the success of these ventures has often been smaller than anticipated. A popular leader may use some of his own support to build a new party; but it is questionable whether he can then obtain from the party added opportunities to strengthen his impact. For the build-up of real support for the party is slow; the effort must be sustained by large numbers of active followers. Many personalized political parties of the 1960s and 1970s have fallen far short of their expectations: they have been empty shells or a mere coating of the natural structures of tribes or ethnic groups.

There are exceptions, but these correspond to cases where the party is truly a collective enterprise — and thereby goes beyond being of help to the leader alone. This has been obviously the case with communist parties. It is also the case with the Mexican PRI, which has substantially reduced, by incorporation, the role of natural structures; but the PRI is not the 'puppet' of the Mexican president, who cannot use the organization as a means exclusively devoted to the propagation of his goals. Other personalized parties have followed the same fate. The Gaullist party is no longer the 'poodle' of its leader; the Peruvian APRA did not succeed in enabling its founder to come to the presidency; while the Peronist party in Argentina had greater effect in bringing its founder back into power than in helping to propagate policies when he was in office.

Thus, while structures existing within the community, both natural and man-made, significantly help rulers to establish themselves and to channel support in the nation, political parties created by a leader depend on the popularity of this leader. They orchestrate the founder's voice, but only if the founder is prepared to give the party a large base and share with his or her followers some of the opportunities. The effect of the new structures is thus neither miraculous nor solely for the leader's benefit. New parties may help to reconstruct the political system, to reduce the weight of natural structures or to modify the configuration of man-made structures: to this extent, they may be valuable and indeed important. But they usually take too long to mature to be of significant help to the founder. By helping to build them, leaders may make an important contribution to the characteristics of leadership in the country in future generations; they rarely make a very large contribution to their own support, which must already be large if the party is to have a real chance of survival. In matters of institutional creation and development, there are no more short-cuts than in matters of social development in general: paper organizations deceive only those who wish to be deceived.

Conclusion

The position of leaders is markedly affected by institutional arrangements; but, because of the diverse ways in which this influence occurs, rulers are rarely able to benefit fully and exclusively from a set of advantages without being constrained in a number of directions. We examined these effects at four levels: the personal situation, the entourage, the bureaucracy, and the citizenry. In all cases there were costs as well as benefits, and these came from man-made arrangements as well as from natural developments. Leaders may try to improve their position by setting up new structures; but they cannot ensure that their organizations will be sufficiently lively to help them markedly. They need to have a large personal following to launch a political party or increase the effectiveness of the bureaucracy, for instance; and it is not clear that they gain markedly, in the short term at least, by having set up that party or expanded administrative structures.

We cannot of course measure the costs and benefits precisely; but an impression can be given, if not for individual rulers, at least for the main types of leadership arrangements that exist in the world today. These fall broadly into six categories: traditional monarchies, authoritarian civilian presidencies, military presidencies, communist systems, constitutional presidencies, and parliamentary–prime ministerial governments. In the first three of these systems leaders have considerable personal scope of action and, by and large, considerable scope to appoint the members of their entourage; but they usually receive limited help from the bureaucracy and often are hampered by the strength of the 'natural' structures — the traditional tribal, ethnic or religious groupings — although, especially in authoritarian presidencies, single parties are often set up by the leader and may, in some circumstances, provide some extra support. In communist systems leaders may (typically) be able to count on long tenure, but their power to appoint their entourage is relatively limited; on the other hand, they receive much support from the bureaucracy and considerable help from the party. In Western systems, too, the bureaucracy is usually a strong instrument at the disposal of leaders, and, more than occasionally, so is the dominant party, though there are also many instances of weak or sharply divided parties. By and large, however, leaders often have limited control on the selection of their entourage, except in some presidential systems and especially in the United States; and their personal position is less secure than in most other regimes, though there are variations, and some prime ministerial systems have provided prime ministers with considerable personal support. Thus, gains and losses among various types of leaders in the contemporary world compensate each other to an extent; types of costs and types of benefits differ from one regime to another, but the overall balance sheet may not be very different.

There are considerable variations in individual cases, however, as there are special circumstances in a particular country, for instance if parties are well organized but sharply divided; external factors also play a part in enhancing, if only for a time, the position of the leader vis-à-vis the nation, the bureaucracy or the entourage; and some leaders, especially the founders of states but occasionally others, may be in a position to establish institutions that will in turn help them to increase their impact on society and indeed the impact of their successors also. In mentioning these cases, however, we are beginning to move from the specific role of position to one in which personality is added to position to produce an overall effect. Some leaders are able to use their own skills and popularity to build institutions which may help to strengthen their role in the subsequent years of their tenure; other leaders do not have strong institutional instruments at their disposal. The differences among the majority of leaders are perhaps smaller than might have been expected, partly because the 'mix' of resources that leaders receive is so varied that one can enjoy an advantage on one aspect and a loss on another. Substantially more analysis is required on this point; but if one excludes the cases at both extremes, where all the structures combine to help leaders or hamper their activities, many rulers at least appear endowed with a number of institutional 'talents', and it is up to them, with their personal qualities, to make these talents fructify.

6
The future of the study of political leadership

Throughout this study, we have felt the need for a more precise assessment of the characteristics of national political leadership. We found that the judgements passed are often vague and the evidence inconclusive. This vagueness and inconclusiveness fuel controversies of principle, such as those relating to the question of whether leaders make a difference. Intuitively, it would seem that there are considerable variations, from some rulers who leave almost no mark at all to many who have some effect, and a few who alter society to a very large degree. Yet it seems difficult to progress from these impressions to hard evidence: the indicators that we might use are somewhat imprecise, and operationalization seems consequently difficult.

Part of the problem posed by the assessment of leadership stems from the need to improve the conceptualization of the problem. The main purpose of this book has been to look more closely at these questions in order to identify the elements on which attention should be focused if one is to assess political leadership. Given that what is essential is to determine the part that leaders play, the first priority must be to discover variables by which to compare both the actions of leaders and the reactions of society; an effort has then to be made to distinguish the part played by personal factors from that played by the structural resources at the disposal of rulers. What a close examination suggests is that there are indeed ways of describing the impact of leaders in some detail and that there are also ways by which personal attributes and institutional supports can be listed and classified.

Ultimately, however, the assessment has to be more precise. We need to do more than discover what the impact *might* be, or what influence some personality traits or some institutional factors *might have*: we need to be able to measure what this impact *is* in concrete situations, and how different factors *do* interplay in the particular context of given sets of leaders. But such a measurement can be undertaken only if the variables that are to be measured are amenable to precise operationalization. This is likely to occur to an extent; indeed, on some aspects, it has already been done. In other respects, however, progress is likely to be slow, as substantial efforts need to be made to discover new variables that are amenable to better measurement.

The aspects of leadership that are measurable and, to an extent, already quantified

If we consider the field of leadership en bloc, it may seem utopian to assert that measurement is possible. The most important analyses, or at least those that are best known, tend to be qualitative; they are devoted primarily to general considerations of the characteristics of leadership or to a description of individual cases of (usually outstanding) leaders. A precise measurement seems, at best, remote.

This is of course a valid conclusion, but only in so far as we consider the field of leadership as a whole. In order to examine the problem in its most general manner, we have considered first in some detail the question of the possible impact that leaders can make, since only if leaders can be expected to make some impact is it meaningful to examine the problem of leadership at all. We noticed that there were methods that might result in a more precise assessment than currently appears possible, but we also recognized that the task was complex. As there seemed to be a prima facie case for concluding that leaders, as a category, do make some impact, even if this impact is not as large as is sometimes believed, we proceeded to consider its origins. We found that personal characteristics had begun to be explored, that they could be (to an extent) classified, but that, so far, there had been relatively few attempts to go beyond classification, at least with respect to national political leadership. Similarly, we found that leaders had institutional and other structural resources — and handicaps. It was possible to list many of these, but it seemed also that these institutional and structural instruments had not been examined closely with a view to assessing how much these helped or hampered leaders; the general direction of their impact could be ascertained, but the precise effect of each of them, or even of most of them, remains at best vaguely perceived.

Yet, if, instead of looking en bloc at these three problems of impact, personal variables, and institutional instruments, we consider the aspects of each of them separately, some measurement seems possible and is even already in common use. Institutional variables may be hard to measure in general, but the duration of leaders in office is intrinsically and readily measurable; the personal variables that relate to social background and career and even some of those that relate to personality can also be assessed precisely. And, if the impact of leaders seems in general difficult to measure, one corner of the problem — that of the popularity of rulers — is known with great precision in some countries.

The role of structures and the question of the duration of leaders
Among institutional resources at the disposal of leaders, the strength of the personal position is, as we saw, an important factor. Duration in office is an element of the personal position; whether this duration is pre-determined or indeterminate can be significant, though behavioural constraints affect markedly, as we also saw, the legal arrangements. Thus *expectations* of duration in office are perhaps the most significant variable: they affect leaders, politicians and the public at large. Italian or

Japanese prime ministers are unlikely to operate on the assumption that their tenure will extend beyond a few years, whereas British, Swedish or West German leaders can expect to be constrained mainly if not only by unfavourable election results, which they will endeavour to counter, and communist party secretaries can probably count on being in office for at least a decade and possibly for life.

Expectations of duration exist also in countries whose political institutions are less stable. In the Third World, while founders of states normally could count on staying in office for periods as long as those enjoyed by communist leaders, second-generation leaders are not so fortunate; in particular, because of military coups, rulers rarely stay in office for more than a few years. Indeed, expectations can also be different from legal duration even where leaders are elected for a fixed term, especially in constitutional presidencies. In many Latin American countries, as we saw, presidents often have to resign or are dismissed before the end of their legal term.

Of course, duration is only one variable among others with which to measure the institutional resources at the disposal of leaders. But it is an important one, as is shown by the efforts made by those who drafted constitutions either to reduce duration, as in eighteenth-century America, so as to diminish the power of the chief executive, or on the contrary, to extend tenure, as in mid-twentieth-century Germany and France, in order to give leaders a leverage they did not have under preceding periods of democratic rule.

This variable is obviously eminently quantifiable, and it therefore can give a precise assessment of the realistic expectations that leaders can have in a variety of countries. Yet so far, few attempts have been made to exploit this indicator to the full. The analysis of leadership has tended to be conducted as if duration in office were indefinite, or as if there were no time constraints placed on great numbers of leaders. This may have been permissible as long as the analysis was based on regimes in which monarchs were hereditary and stayed in power until the end of their lives. Since, however, hereditary monarchy has remained relatively widespread only because the large majority of the monarchs have become symbolic, and since most of the other leaders who are formally appointed for indefinite periods cannot stay in office for more than a few years, questions of duration, and of expectations of duration, are highly relevant and deserve to be explored fully.

On other aspects of the institutional support of leadership, admittedly, a precise measurement is more difficult. Yet, three possible improvements can be made. First, information is available or can easily be made available on the extent to which others, besides the leader, participate effectively in policy elaboration. There is substantial information about the operation of 'shared' or 'dual' leadership systems, in which a president (or party secretary in communist states) delegates to a prime minister a segment of the decision-making process, particularly with respect to internal matters. The techniques of measurement that we have at our disposal may not enable us to locate the dual-leadership systems precisely on a continuous dimension ranging from all-power-to-the-president to all-power-to-the-prime-minister, but it is at least possible to divide shared executives into four or five types, depending on whether the distribution of powers leaves almost all, a majority, a substantial portion, little, or very little of the decision-making to the 'second-tier' leader. Given that variations over time can easily be plotted, it is possible also to see how far changes in this distribution of power appear to affect the impact of the top leader and indeed of the whole leadership 'duumvirate'.

About the same level of information is available with respect to the relationship between the leader and the 'entourage', especially the cabinet. We still do not know the extent to which cabinets are collective or hierarchical so as to be able to plot each of them, at various points in time, on a continuous dimension; but we do know whether a given cabinet is fully hierarchical, fully collective, or located on at least one of three other points on this dimension. We can, moreover, assess whether the position of a particular cabinet–leader relationship (near-hierarchical, near-collective, or intermediate) has varied: we can therefore, as with shared leadership, assess to what extent the impact of leaders at a given point in time appears to have been affected by the relationship between cabinet and ruler. We noted in Chapter 5 that, as a matter of fact, the variations may be reduced somewhat as a result of the need that leaders experience to appoint subordinates to fulfil specific essential conditions, for instance subordinates who have technical competence. As information on the background of leaders is available, and as similar information can be obtained on the background of ministers and other members of the 'entourage', it is possible to determine whether there is a relationship between technical competence and hierarchical or collective government; one can also subsequently determine what effect, if any, these two variables have jointly on the impact of leaders.

The opportunities to measure precisely the role of the bureaucracy are appreciably more limited. It is still impossible to operationalize on a world-wide basis the relevant characteristics of administrative bodies — competence of the personnel, organization of the departments, linkage with the government, linkage with the population — not because such characteristics cannot be, in principle, described precisely, but because information on most of these aspects is still too scarce with respect to the large majority of countries. The most that can be hoped for at this point is to elaborate a number of dichotomies.

There is better world-wide information on some at least of the political structures linking leaders to the population: a more precise measurement of the role of these structures can therefore be attempted, though the complexity of the network is such that many of the 'measurements' are likely to be tentative. The best-known structures are, of course, the political parties. It is possible to assess the effect of the party system and therefore to provide distinctions about the extent to which both the system as a whole and one party in particular help leaders to make their goals better known and more acceptable to the population. One can also distinguish among systems without parties, systems where parties are weak, and systems in which parties are truly significant institutions; one can evaluate, in the case of a single-party system, whether that party is both effective and principally at the disposal of the leader, and, in the case of systems of more than one party, whether there is a dominant party on which the leader can rely or whether fractionalization is such that there is little hope for the leader to count on being able to use the party to exercise significant influence. It is not possible at this stage to rank countries by means of a precise measurement; but one can at least identify a number of discrete points at which the various political systems can be located on a dimension ranging from 'no help' to 'substantial help' being provided to the leader by the political party.

It is more difficult to assess the role of other structures, both because their characteristics are often less well known and because the way in which these structures should be viewed as alternative or complementary to each other has not been analysed, let alone measured. It is not clear, for instance, whether a tribe has more effect than an ethnic or a religious group, or than the military or, indeed, a political party. But it is at least possible to assess in broad terms the extent to which 'natural' structures play a part in the distribution of influence across the country. It is also possible to determine whether the military, where it plays a significant part, extends widely across the nation or is concentrated primarily in the capital and a few other cities.

These assessments can at least lead to three- or four-point scalings. Moreover, it may even be worthwhile to attempt to elaborate a compound index which would take into account 'natural' structures, parties and the military. Rankings on such an index could then be related to the impact that leaders have on society. Any conclusions that would be drawn from such an analysis would manifestly be tentative; but even such tentative conclusions would constitute a sizeable improvement over the present state of knowledge in the field. These efforts would also undoubtedly constitute a spur for further efforts towards the elaboration of classifications and rankings which would gradually provide a precise picture of the extent to which political structures help leaders to make an impact on their societies.

*The role of personal variables and the assessment
of the background of leaders*

Another set of eminently measurable variables is constituted by the background of leaders, which relates not only to sex, age, educational, regional, religious and occupational characteristics, but also to more specifically political indicators such as party political affiliation or parliamentary career. Assuming that we do not know whether certain psychological traits result in certain types of leadership, and whether these psychological traits are more likely to be found among people, say, of a certain age or social milieu, we cannot know whether the persons who have this type of background become leaders *because of* certain psychological characteristics; but we can at least know whether or not these leaders turn out to have certain leadership characteristics. We may not know, for instance, what psychological effect age may have; but it is not irrelevant to learn whether leaders who come to power at a certain age have certain characteristics in common as leaders. Is it the case, for example, that, because communist rulers tend to be old and to stay in office for a long time (indeed, often after a long period of preparation near the top), their leadership is thereby affected? There are enough cases of old rulers across the world to enable us to ascertain the possible effect of age on the character of leadership.

What has been missing so far is a systematic documentation of social background variables with respect to leaders and government ministers. The data that have been collected show that leaders are almost exclusively male, mostly middle-class and mostly well-educated (Blondel, 1980: 115–34). Finer analyses, based on a more precise documentation and a more sophisticated treatment of the data, would make it possible to follow closely the different types of career paths, and would help to relate these personal characteristics to the activities of leaders.

The analysis of personality factors is more difficult to undertake, as improvements depend largely on developments in the field of psychological analysis. But two aspects can already be studied. First, further advances can be made with respect to exceptional and, in particular, revolutionary leaders. The studies of Rejai and Phillips (1979, 1983) show that it is possible to document a number of 'traits' of these 'exceptional' leaders. For these at least, it is therefore becoming possible to determine psychological characteristics with precision and in a comparative framework; it is consequently becoming possible to assess both the role of background on psychological characteristics and the influence of these psychological characteristics on the impact that 'exceptional' leaders are found to have on their societies.

Second, progress can also be made, this time for all types of leaders, along the lines of the characterizations of Barber (1977) and Heady (1974). Contemporary leaders can be classified according to a number of important variables, such as energy, intelligence or the ability to handle subordinates and to be appreciated by the population. The result may not be a complex scaling, but some groupings at least can be achieved and it may be possible to determine the role of 'activism', or of a 'positive' orientation among leaders. Although the distinctions are still rather crude, they throw some light on the relationship between personality and leaders' backgrounds and they provide indications of the relationship between the personality of leaders and the impact of these leaders on society. It will, for instance, be possible to determine whether 'managers' tend to have different psychological characteristics from leaders who pursue other types of goals, and whether 'cautious' leaders, that is to say, leaders who wish to achieve less than society would wish them to do, differ from 'ambitious' rulers — those who wish to achieve more than society would wish them to — because of the characteristics of their psychological make-up.

The impact of leaders and the assessment of popularity and popular demands

There is, however, little value in attempting to measure even one important aspect of the personal characteristics of leaders and the institutional framework within which these leaders operate if it is not possible to measure also the impact of these leaders. Here too, however, a precise assessment can be made, for some countries at least, in two important respects: the popularity of leaders among the population, and the attitudes of citizens to various issues. Popularity is different from impact, to be sure. It is a compound index which results from policies and images, from external and internal activities, from style as well as content. But popularity does take goals into account, even if these are diffracted in a peculiar manner. Moreover, as popularity can be examined in conjunction with popular standpoints on issues, one can begin to discover elements of the relationship between the perceived characteristics of leaders and societal demands. When leaders are popular, one can assess the extent to which societal demands correspond to this popularity; when they are not, one can assess the distance between the perception of the leaders' characteristics and the demands that the population wishes to press for.

There are geographical limitations to these analyses, admittedly. First, only in those countries where opinion polls are conducted and published can leader popularity and popular demands be assessed with precision. But it is no longer the case that only a few countries have public opinion polls, although the countries where these are conducted are drawn disproportionately from among the highly industrial and most liberal. The quality, and therefore the reliability, of the material also varies, though it has manifestly improved over the last decades. It is highly likely that the number of countries in which polling takes place regularly will increase gradually; it already includes, alongside Western liberal democracies, many Latin American and South and South East Asian nations. It is therefore possible to measure with precision levels of popularity and types of societal demands, to discover variations over time, and thus to compare curves of success or failure among public opinion of many leaders in liberal democracies and at least a substantial number of Third World polities.

One can go further, moreover. Much information could be obtained if a sustained effort were undertaken. To begin with, there is information on the goals of most leaders. Sources of various kinds tell us what these leaders wish to do and to what extent they are attempting to implement their programmes. This is true for the large majority of countries. In fact, the cases about which little information exists are confined to two types of situations: those of transient leaders, who emerge rather frequently in some countries, especially in Latin America, and those of leaders of closed countries, which are typically small and very traditional, though some communist countries occasionally fall into this category. In practice, neither of these two groups is very important: the transient leaders usually have no time to implement any goals, and the instances of closed countries have become very rare. In practice, therefore, the paucity of information affects only some time comparisons.

Not only are goals known at the time leaders come to office, but changes in goals over time can also be monitored, although leaders may not always want to proclaim that they have had to make a 'U-turn', at least not when they have been forced by circumstances to do so against their ideological bent and their original pronouncements. But a close examination does indicate whether a change has taken place, even though the precise moment of the move may not always be clear even in the mind of the leader; in practice, this matters little from the point of view of the analysis.

Thus, with respect to the collection of data on the goals of leaders, the problem is primarily to undertake the rather laborious task of identifying what the goals have been and whether changes have occurred over time. It is true that the assessment is hampered by conceptual and methodological problems, a point to which we shall return. But we saw in Chapter 3 that it was possible to group and organize the goals of leaders according to two variables: the scope of intervention, and the extent of changes proposed. It may not be possible, or at any rate easy, to assign to each leader a precise position on the two-dimensional plane that these variables define. In the first instance, we proposed in Chapter 3 that leaders be located at one of nine positions. Without being unduly ambitious, it would seem possible to achieve a little more and to locate leaders at one of four or five points on each of the variables, once data on goals began to be collected systematically. If this were possible, a substantial improvement in the measurement would be achieved.

The impact of leaders cannot be measured only by considering the goals that they pursue: these must be contrasted, as we saw, with the demands of the population. For many countries we do possess adequate information in this respect. These are the countries in which opinion surveys are conducted periodically in order to assess both the popularity of leaders and the stands taken by citizens on a variety of issues. Indeed, as changes in these societal demands are monitored by opinion polls, and as the analysis of the leaders' goals enables us to plot changes in these goals over time, it is possible to look at the evolution of rulers' impact in the light of the modifications of goals.

The analysis of leadership thus can be assessed more precisely than is being done at present, with the help of data that are already available but have not been collected systematically so far, and with the help of rankings which can be undertaken without any need to improve substantially on current levels of operationalization. We can circumscribe both the goals of leaders and societal demands, and therefore assess the impact of these leaders with a substantial degree of precision for many countries and in broad contours for the large majority of the rest. There are greater hurdles with respect to the personal and structural origins of this impact, admittedly; yet, even there, progress can be made beyond what is already readily measurable, which as we saw is substantial, on the basis of information available. Can it also be hoped that further progress will be made beyond this point, and that the analysis will become truly precise in the relatively near future?

Conceptualization, measurement and the study of political leadership

The assessment of what is possible in the future depends not only on improvements in data collection and in techniques of analysis, but also on efforts at conceptualization and operationalization, the outcome of which is difficult to predict. We have therefore to examine the obstacles and assess whether these can be expected to be overcome. It seems that the least serious obstacles relate to the measurement of psychological characteristics, while improvements in the assessment of structural resources and of the impact of leaders raise appreciably more serious difficulties.

The measurement of the psychological characteristics of leaders

So far, relatively little has been achieved in the measurement of psychological variables. This is due mainly to the fact that political scientists and psychologists have not yet devoted much attention to the elaboration of rankings which could be applied to political leaders.

Large numbers of 'traits' have been identified, as we saw in Chapter 4; but studies have been too specialized and have had little regard for the accumulation of knowledge. Moreover, these traits are often too detailed to be of general use in comparative analysis: one should, at least in the first instance, concentrate on a small number of broad characteristics. This is the strategy that Barber (1977) and Heady (1974) have begun to follow, and one that could be extended to cover the traits that, for instance, Rejai and Phillips (1983) have investigated in their analysis of revolutionary leaders.

Political scientists cannot undertake this kind of enquiry without the help of psychologists, who have to provide the relevant techniques and who can replicate these analyses among whole populations in order to discover differences between leaders and non-leaders. But, given that psychologists have already engaged in studies of leadership on a substantial scale, the problem is not so much to elaborate new techniques as to apply existing techniques widely and systematically.

Political scientists also need to collaborate with psychologists for the analysis of the personal characteristics of the leaders themselves. Tests cannot be administered to national political leaders in the same way as to random samples of the population: one has therefore to analyse the psychological characteristics of leaders, as Rejai and Phillips did in their investigation of revolutionary rulers, by inferring the personality structure from behavioural patterns. For the vast majority of contemporary national political leaders, such an analysis is possible, given that so much is known about their past and present life and in particular about the way they tackled problems, reacted to crises and undertook to be followed and obeyed by subordinates and the population. The task is manifestly long and arduous, though Rejai and Phillips have shown that it can be undertaken successfully. What is clear is that there are no technical impediments to the enquiry. One can therefore conclude that the personality of leaders can be assessed in some detail, and distinctions can be drawn between leaders and non-leaders on the basis of existing methodological tools and available information.

The measurement of the structural resources of leaders

There are more serious problems with respect to the measurement of the structural resources of leaders. The information that needs to be collected is vast, and the framework of analysis is unclear. Ideally, we would need to know, for each country and for each leader, both the strength of these structures and the extent of help that they can provide for the ruler. As a matter of fact, what we know about these structures is vague. We could improve our grasp of the characteristics of bureaucracies if a systematic effort were made to examine the organization, competence and linkages of these bodies with the government and the population. We might also be more precise about the help that political parties can give leaders. But it seems quite unrealistic to hope to be able to categorize precisely the part played by 'natural' structures, not even by such 'modern' institutions as the military, in part because the influence of these bodies is less clearly defined, and in part because empirical enquiries are unlikely to be conducted on a sufficiently large scale. The most that can be hoped for is a gradual improvement of the information.

Yet the main difficulty lies in the absence of a conceptual framework for the analysis of the help that structures can give to leaders. We need, first, to be able to assess what part each structure plays in the polity, for instance in order to mobilize the demands of the citizens; we need to discover the extent to which political parties as well as other institutions are followed by the citizens. In effect, we have to be able to measure the 'weight' of each structure in the polity. In reality, there are so far no means of doing so. We may feel intuitively that the communist party in communist states is 'very strong' in that it extends its tentacles widely within the population; but there is no satisfactory means by which one can compare this 'strength' with that of some Western parties, for example. One can list figures of membership, one can point out that most of the important decisions of the state are taken by the party, but one cannot go beyond that and arrive at a compound index which would suggest that the weight of the CPSU is greater by a specific number of points than that of the Social Democratic Party in Sweden.

Nor is this all. Having assessed the relative weight of all the structures in the polity, we would also need to assess the part played by the leader within each of the relevant structures. This assessment, too, is impossible at present. We may be sure that the secretary of the Communist Party of the Soviet Union has a large say within that party, while in most cases the US president has relatively little influence within his own party. But this does not amount to a precise assessment; nor are there signs that these assessments will improve markedly in the foreseeable future. Our knowledge of the influence of leaders within political parties will remain somewhat limited. The instruments by which we could measure this knowledge are not clearly defined, as we have to rely on general impressions; and, because the instruments that we use are so blunt, it is very difficult to expect that we shall be able to go beyond simple comparisons.

There will be some improvements, to be sure, as there have been manifest improvements in our knowledge of party life, of the role of 'natural' structures and of the activities of the military in the course of the last decades. But progress will be gradual and relatively slow; neither the process of information-gathering nor the effort at better operationalization will lead to more than partial results in the course of the coming years.

The measurement of the impact of leaders

With respect to the assessment of the impact of leaders, information-gathering raises some difficulties; but problems of conceptualization and operationalization are even more serious. On the one hand, one can expect to obtain gradually better information about leaders' goals and societal demands; the number of countries in which public opinion surveys will be conducted will increase, and it will become difficult for leaders to resist the pressures made by those who wish to find out what the population wants. The leaders themselves, even in communist countries, are likely to be anxious to discover, by means of surveys, which policies are popular or unpopular. They may not find it very useful to know their precise level of influence within their party or within the bureaucracy, but they are likely to want to ascertain how the population reacts to their policies. Thus they themselves will contribute to the information-gathering process with respect to societal demands.

On the other hand, problems of conceptualization and operationalization will remain. We may be able to classify goals and demands into a number of categories, but, although the variables truly have an underlying continuous character, it seems difficult to operationalize the measurement on a continuous basis, as with the analysis of the role of institutional resources from which leaders can benefit. We have identified two dimensions, namely, scope of intervention and extent of change, in order to assess leaders' goals and societal demands. Analytically, we know that the intervention of leaders in the affairs of the nation can be greater or smaller and that the change that is proposed can also be greater or smaller; we know, therefore, that these are real dimensions. In practice, however, there are no clear indications as to what a 'unit' of change or a 'unit' of intervention can be, as is the case for power, which is also based on underlying dimensions and yet has not been measured on a continuous basis.

As is well known, this difficulty has been perceived for a long time to be one of the main drawbacks experienced by political scientists in comparison with economists, who can use the continuous variable of money to assess the extent of change that occurs with respect to a large number of indicators. One solution has been to borrow from economics the continuous variable of money, and thus to give monetary values to the effect of power, change or governmental intervention. At present, this seems to be the only way to proceed if one wishes to obtain a continuous variable. It is true, moreover, that the effect of power, or of change, or of governmental intervention is to affect the monetary value of many characteristics, in particular the budgets that leaders propose and implement. Yet there are serious problems for the analysis, since these monetary indicators grasp only a fraction — indeed, a small and varying fraction — of the problems that are being measured; in particular, if we use monetary indicators, some aspects of governmental intervention are privileged in comparison with others. Thus, while it might be possible to find satisfactory monetary equivalents to the growth of governmental intervention in some sectors — economic of course, but also social — it is manifestly more difficult to discover monetary translations of ideas of innovation in other areas. The result is likely to lead, in many cases, to major distortions: constitutional amendments, changes in the status of certain groups, cultural reforms, regional reorganizations, indeed, some forms of economic restructuring cannot adequately be translated in monetary terms.

Thus, so long as there are no means of discovering 'units' with respect to change and governmental intervention, the determination of leaders' goals and societal demands will lead at best to ordinal measurements. There will be improvements, to be sure: it will be possible to increase the number of 'points' on the scale and thereby to discover a substantial number of locations on the two-dimensional space for both leaders' goals and societal demands; and it will be possible to improve the measurement of impact by comparison with our existing knowledge. But it is unrealistic to believe that we can obtain, in the foreseeable future, a truly precise measurement of the effect of leaders, any more than we can expect to be able to achieve a precise measurement of the role of structures in helping leaders to make an impact on their society.

Conclusion

The measurement of leadership can be improved, but within limits. There is already a substantial amount of precise assessment and even of quantification. Substantial progress will be made as and when there is a better realization of what can be obtained with the data that are already available or can be collected without a massive task, and with the help of the conceptual tools that are at the disposal of scholars. We can obtain a general idea, indeed a relatively precise idea, of the overall impact of leaders; we can have at least some information about the personal characteristics that may account for this impact; and at least some of the structural resources that are at the disposal of leaders can be assessed and compared.

Not only can the various aspects of leadership already be measured and even quantified to some extent, but better information and a better examination of the relevant variables will improve this measurement further. Admittedly, as far as one can see, the measurement of leadership cannot be expected to go beyond the discovery of relatively complex ordinal distinctions with respect to the factors that play a major part.

Leaders' goals and societal demands, the weight of structures and the support that these structures give to leaders — even the psychological characteristics of rulers — have to be conceived as existing along dimensions on which we can only discover a number of discrete points. This means that the analysis of the relationship between the variables is also hampered by substantial limitations.

But we must be clear about the nature of these limitations. They do not make the analysis of leadership impossible; they are not such as to make it unrewarding to look for relationships between the impact of leaders and the personal and institutional factors that appear to account for this impact. The present state of affairs is not fixed, moreover: not only is it likely that instruments will be improved as efforts are made to operationalize concepts, but one can already begin to see ways in which leaders can be classified and compared. Consequently, the characteristics of leaders will become gradually better known. The more precise measurements that are necessary to achieve a better assessment will constitute a spur towards further refinements in the understanding of leadership itself.

7

Conclusion

In the course of the last few decades, views about political leadership have begun to change. They are changing in part because the role of leadership itself has altered as a result of the major emphasis given, in the contemporary world, to social and economic development; they are changing also because, as a result, leadership has come to be viewed more positively, more constructively, than in the past; and they are changing, though more slowly, because a close examination of the impact of leaders has made the traditional dichotomy between heroes and 'ordinary' leaders seem increasingly unrealistic, as increasingly unrealistic as seems the dichotomy between those who believe in the 'great men' theory of history and those who feel that 'leaders do not matter'.

Perhaps the most important change results from the fact that, in our societies, leadership has come to be concerned principally with the improvement of social and economic conditions. Of course, this role of leadership is neither entirely new nor wholly exclusive. In the past, too, rulers have had to be concerned, to some extent, with the economy and with social life; this has been viewed as fundamental in a number of countries ever since the seventeenth century. But even before mercantilism became widespread, social and economic interventionism occurred, at least sporadically, in many polities; consuls and emperors had to ensure that sufficient quantities of grain were delivered to Rome. This economic and social role was not viewed as a primary, let alone principal, function of leaders, however; more important, it was not viewed in the context of a dynamic process of development of society. By and large, for western European leaders at least, up to and including the nineteenth century, the most important problems were to maintain peace at home and to ensure that the country was protected externally. For some, the maintenance of internal order had to be the main preoccupation; for others — probably the majority — the main task was to defend their country against the ambitions of other rulers — or else to attempt to increase the size of their territory.

Of course, neither of these functions has disappeared in the twentieth century. International relations, peaceful or not, continue to be a major preoccupation for many leaders, and not merely those of the largest nations. As a matter of fact, the feeling remains that involvement in world affairs is in some sense more 'exalted' than the 'mere' preoccupation with what de Gaulle, echoing Louis XIV, called the 'intendance', which covered the whole area of social and economic affairs: only a few countries — and above all those that were shattered by the second world war, namely Germany and Japan — were for most of the subsequent decades economic 'giants' and international 'dwarfs'; and even in these countries, the preoccupation of leaders with foreign affairs tended to grow as the memory of the 1945 defeat gradually faded away.

Moreover, the 'flight into foreign affairs' is not merely the result of a feeling that it becomes a leader to be able to deal with world problems, or indeed that it is necessary to fight colonialism, imperialism or even communism on a world front, as Nkrumah, Tito, Nasser and many other Third World leaders did. The concern with foreign affairs is also an opportunity, consciously realized or not, systematically exploited or not, to achieve results on the home front by providing a diversion from the daily preoccupations of citizens, and by fostering a sense of national identity and pride in the country's achievements. 'Nice little wars' have in the past often been regarded as a means of strengthening leaders at home; the same aim has been sought in the contemporary world by many leaders, even though specific motivations may often have been complex.

The reason why external and internal purposes have often been mixed stems of course in large part from the fact that leaders have been as unable as ever to ensure internal order and maintain themselves in office. Coups, rebellions and guerilla warfare have affected large numbers of countries — not surprisingly, given the creation of so many new states, often with highly artificial boundaries, during the recent period. Thus, in a large majority of Third World countries at least one leader has been displaced by a coup, and in many repeated disturbances have occurred; several communist states have had to quash rebellions by military might, including Soviet might; and in Western countries, although by and large regimes have been stable and the immense majority of leaders have come to and left office in a regular manner, many of these leaders have been confronted with tense internal situations arising from strikes or ethnic or regional discontent, often fuelled by student protest. These, directly or indirectly, resulted in the fall of several leaders, including L.B. Johnson, de Gaulle and Edward Heath.

Yet, while foreign affairs and internal order continue to be subjects of major preoccupation among contemporary rulers, they have ceased to be the main focus of attention. Perhaps more important, social and economic problems are almost universally perceived as the underlying cause of internal unrest and, indeed, of a substantial proportion of external troubles as well. Strikes are directly the result of economic difficulties, and ethnic and regional disturbances are at least in part the result of a sense of economic deprivation and social discrimination, as are other types of rebellions, riots and even armed internal conflicts. Indeed, whatever the 'root cause' of the internal disturbances that leaders have to face, the fact that it is believed, by both the public and the leaders, that the cure has to be found by economic and social means is an essential factor in placing these means at the centre of the functions that leaders have to fulfil.

But economic and social problems are not merely at the centre of the preoccupations of leaders; nor is the lack of concern with development widely interpreted as the main reason why leaders fall. The most crucial point is that social and economic development is viewed as a process which has to take place at a sustained rate if it is to achieve results, a process that, at the same time, creates tensions while development is taking place. These tensions have to be overcome if success is eventually to be achieved. Comparisons thus have to be made with medicine or even surgery. The patient has to undergo treatment; the cure often entails sufferings, indeed for long periods, before an improvement is noticed. But, unlike most illnesses for which a cure has been found, the process of development entails not just sufferings, but almost indefinite pain. In fact, because there is no equivalent to death in the case of societies, the illness of countries can mean that little or no progress will occur if the 'cure' that has been chosen is not appropriate. Thus, socioeconomic development problems resemble those of medicine only in so far as they are often as intractable as those of physical illness; but because they can be more prolonged, because words such as 'agony' or 'collapse' are inapplicable to the body politic, the predicament of political leaders is more difficult than that of doctors and surgeons. The emergence of a widespread desire for social and economic change in the contemporary world has confronted national rulers with difficulties that their predecessors never had, even those who, as enlightened despots of the eighteenth century, started to uplift their societies. Modern political leaders do not choose to be concerned with the continuous improvement of their societies: they *have* to take this concern on board or they may not stay in office. The population often demands that their lot be improved and, even if they do not, the leaders themselves believe and are repeatedly told by others that it is their duty to achieve social and economic progress.

Almost certainly, this change in the principal role of leaders provoked the transformation of attitudes towards leadership that has been noticeable in the course of the last few decades. For if leaders are to be essentially concerned with the 'cure' of social and economic ills, and if this role entails the continuous guidance and direction of the population, it is simply not possible to dismiss leaders as either unimportant or dangerous, as many of the classical political theorists did, or as playing a crucial but exceptional part, as Weber's model of authority suggested. On the contrary: leadership has to be viewed as continuously playing a positive part in developing society. Efforts have therefore to be made to ensure that leaders do fulfil this positive role. This entails, in the first instance, a precise determination of the personal qualities and institutional support that are most appropriate.

It is understandable that judgements on leaders and on leadership should have so often been negative in the past and even to the present day. So many rulers have been tyrants and despots that the natural reaction has been to try to reduce their power by setting up institutions that acted as many hurdles against encroachments by the 'executive' power. Consistent with this view, the prevailing effort was directed towards discovering how people could ensure their protection against leadership, not towards determining how leaders could be made best use of. The focus was on the girders, not on the characteristics of the engine, as leadership was viewed as a fire consuming everything in proximity, except for the distant — and utopian — future when rulers might be expected to become 'philosopher-kings'.

Weber's analysis helped to change this approach. In the special case of societies in crisis, the German sociologist showed that leaders could be the central point of a new legitimacy. In this he went further than even those among the classical theorists, who recognized that some exceptional leaders could play a crucial part in helping to bring about the new institutions of the state. For Rousseau's legislator was merely a catalyst. He embodied the views of the people, was better than the people, perhaps: his function was to make the population see the light. Weber's charismatic leader genuinely constructed the polity. He brought together what was divided into many fragments and what, without him, would have remained in fragments.

But Weber's standpoint was partial, because it was concerned only with the extraordinary periods of crisis during which legitimacy had broken down. To account for the contemporary situation one has to go further, and view leadership as one of the key instruments by which society can gradually be transformed by producing the 'doctors' thanks to whom the 'illnesses' of the country might eventually be cured or at least gradually improved. So far, this approach to leadership has not had its 'grand' theorist, in the way that Machiavelli can be said to have theorized about the traditional usurper and Weber about the national saviour. But the well-known twentieth-century leaders, good or evil, have gradually helped to determine the profile of such a ruler, a profile in which the most important aspect appears to be a daily concern for the improvement of society, where long-term developments are balanced with the recognition of current problems, and where technical and economic progress is associated with a major interest in the well-being of citizens.

It may seem unrealistic, and indeed perhaps absurd, to claim that this vision of the ideal ruler emerges from the ugly 'mistakes' that occurred in the twentieth century with respect to some leaders. Mussolini, Hitler and Stalin are names associated with excesses only; so are the names of some of the dictators who emerged in the Third World. But other leaders have more than compensated for these 'mistakes'; in addition to Roosevelt, Churchill and Nehru, even some of the more ruthless leaders such as Mao, and some of the more humane 'populists' such as Nasser or Bourguiba, Tito or Nyerere, have contributed to the build-up of a composite image, indeed of an 'ideal-type', an ideal-type which the reality of contemporary leaders only approximates, but whose characteristics can be identified. This identification is essential, because it makes it possible to see what personal qualities and institutional types of support are needed if leadership is to fulfil the continuous and positive role that social and economic development — indeed, the survival of the world — manifestly require.

Lenin once said that the energy of the working class had to be harnessed for the revolution, and that the party, like the piston of a steam engine, was the means by which this energy could be stored and provide maximum power. A similar remark could be made about leadership. What is required is the discovery of mechanisms by which the energy of leaders can best be used to the advantage of mankind — not so much by building girders or other protective arrangements, but by finding an outlet and a direction in which the mind, and also the emotions — indeed, the whole personality of leaders — can most profitably be used.

Institutional mechanisms remain important, but, first, they have to be assessed in a realistic way and, second, they should not be organized so as to block the activities of the leaders: they must be geared to the most efficient use of the resources that those leaders can command in order to make an impact on society. This is why it is essential to analyse the ways in which, as we saw, the position of the leader, the structure and powers of the entourage, the characteristics of the bureaucracy and the linkages between leader and population can best provide the leader with expert advice, smooth communication and feedback — in short, with a general ambience which helps and comforts the ruler, rather than with a climate of suspicion and worry. Little is gained by creating hurdles which the leader is adamant to overcome, or by setting up institutions which only block the ruler's goals because they are inefficient.

The French system of government has often been viewed as a monarchy tempered by anarchy; but anarchy does not compensate for monarchy. The monarch does not become more responsible. Those who set up institutions must recognize and accept that leadership is necessary, to use Tucker's expression, to 'diagnose', to 'prescribe a course of action' and to 'mobilize' (Tucker, 1981: 15ff.). The institutions must be geared to these purposes — indeed, must be organized in the best possible way to achieve these purposes.

Thus, the institutions surrounding the leader must be based on the premise that there is to be trust in the leader, trust in the leader's willingness to act as a leader, and trust in the leader's competence to act in this manner. For this to occur an effort must also be made to ensure that leaders have the qualities required for the job. Plato called for education, but an education that would be special for those who would have the 'calling' of leadership. The education of leaders does not have to be based on this highly selective process. What is needed is that the choice of leaders be based on the recognition that certain qualities — intelligence, energy, decisiveness, ability to deal with subordinates and the population, and probably many others — are required if leaders are to be effective. Hence the crucial importance of knowing more about these qualities, not just in general but in specific situations; for what is demanded of a saviour is not identical to what is demanded of an 'innovator' or a reformist. We need to understand the personal characteristics, the syndrome of 'traits', that best fit a given leadership requirement. The purpose of institutional arrangements is to support, occasionally to steer, the activities of leaders; but the source of the leaders' 'activism' is the leaders themselves. It is through a better knowledge of the characteristics of this 'activism' that one can expect to obtain gradually a better realization of the 'ideal-type' of the positive political leader who is needed for the development of contemporary societies.

In such a context, it becomes almost as ludicrous to discuss whether nations determine their leader or leaders mould their nations as it is ludicrous to attempt to determine whether leaders are either 'heroes' or mere cyphers. The traditional dichotomies were based in part on the utopian desire to achieve instant miracles; they were reinforced by the somewhat more realistic image of the successful warrior who, by his victories, gave the nation a prestige and a power that seemed hitherto impossible to attain. These were the images conveyed by Alexander, Caesar and Napoleon, though the contributions of these 'heroes' also markedly mortgaged the future of their nations. As long as leadership was viewed primarily in terms of war and peace, and thus as a poker game in which the winner would take all if his luck was, indeed, very unusual if not miraculous, there was at least some logic in analysing the effect of leaders in terms of a dichotomy.

Of course, even in this case the dichotomy was exaggerated: there never was a war to end all wars. There were only some warriors who were luckier or better able to mobilize more resources than others. Not only did these very lucky warriors usually end up in catastrophe, as did Alexander, Caesar and Napoleon, but many other generals were only moderately successful or had a variety of successes and reversals. Thus there is in reality no more room for a dichotomy in the field of war and peace than there is in the internal field.

In internal affairs, however, the 'rankings' are more clearly marked, in part because the leaders themselves have very different goals, which indeed may change over time, and in part because their impact depends on the extent to which the population is 'receptive' to these goals. This 'receptivity', in turn, depends on the mood and conditions of the nation and on the external circumstances within which these leaders operate. Thus, the question of the impact of leaders cannot be viewed in the form of the sharp contrasts that 'romantic' dichotomies, somewhat simplistically, have typically painted: there are, in reality, gradations and stages.

An assessment of the impact of leadership cannot therefore be made without a detailed knowledge of both the leaders' 'inclinations' and the characteristics of the environment. This is why it is prima facie unrealistic to believe that such an impact is either 'great' or 'non-existent'. This is also why it is unrealistic to believe either that the leader alone can shape the polity or that the effect of the leader's policies, indeed the policies themselves, are merely the product of the environment. What even a casual observation shows is that leaders vary markedly in the extent to which they affect the polity. This extent can already be assessed in broad terms; more precise measurements will no doubt gradually be made, as one examines more closely and comparatively the specific contributions of leaders to society, namely, the goals they pursue when they are in power. These goals can be compared, since what is relevant for the analysis of the impact of leaders is the extent to which rulers aim at changing the status quo, in breadth or in depth or, indeed, in both breadth and depth. Thus the countries of the world are ruled by leaders who wish to be managers or revolutionaries, saviours or innovators, or indeed wish to hold one of an infinite number of positions in the space determined by variations in scope of involvement and variations in extent of change.

A casual observation also indicates that demands differ from one society to another, even though there are further divisions within the population of each country. Leaders are thus confronted with citizens who may be satisfied by and large with the status quo or who may wish to see changes introduced, these changes being of a widely diverse magnitude. For instance, the people may be concerned primarily with a particular area or a small number of areas of government; at the other extreme, they may be intensely worried about the whole of the political, social and economic system; and there is an infinity of intermediate positions. These views, too, can be located on a two-dimensional space which parallels the two-dimensional space on which leaders' goals are placed.

By comparing the position of leaders with the changes that have occurred among the population during the period of their tenure, one can discover the extent to which these leaders have played a part in altering society. Although it is not yet possible to draw more than the broad contours of the impact of leaders, one can already see that it is unrealistic to expect them to be able to make a large and sustained transformation of society unless the situation is 'ripe'. Leaders and the environment are related in a 'systemic' manner; thus, what has to be assessed is how far a leader is able, given the nature of the demands of the polity that he or she rules, to alter to some extent the character of the demands, by accelerating or slowing down movements of opinion that exist in society.

But the recognition that leaders somewhat modify the environment with which they are confronted also means that the qualities and role of an individual leader should be judged not by the extent to which, for instance, large reforms are introduced, but by the impact he can make given a particular 'predisposition' of the environment. Effective leaders may therefore be found in every type of society. They need not be those who appear to be 'heroes', as these may, on the contrary, benefit from a situation that is favourable or may introduce policies that do not survive them and may be rescinded or bypassed under subsequent leaders.

The impact of leaders today, in most countries at least, is felt primarily in internal matters. But both the ambitions of leaders and the characteristics of their environment result in an involvement in external matters, which may sometimes be crucial to the survival of the nation. There are therefore also leaders' goals and societal demands with respect to foreign affairs, and these are related to internal demands primarily by the need of the population to feel that the country is protected and respected. Thus, societal demands with respect to external matters may be very limited, almost non-existent, where there is contentment with the place of the country in the world; but the leader may be confronted with a strong pressure for policy change if the citizens, by and large, have an acute sense that their national pride is hurt, or if the country is subjected to warnings or attacks on the part of other nations. The combination of internal and external demands complicates the calculus of leaders' goals and popular reactions, both by creating problems for rulers and by offering opportunities. The internal effect of a leader may also be increased or decreased because of an improvement or a deterioration in the feelings of citizens about the status of the nation in the world. On this point too, however, the impact of leaders must be measured in finite amounts, since, in the majority of cases at least, results are neither minuscule nor very large, especially over time.

We have therefore to become increasingly aware of the fact that, by and large, political leaders play a significant but bounded role in society. We have to abandon the practice of making rapid and 'radical' judgements separating the great from the inept; we have to look carefully at the large group of leaders who have substantial influence, given the point of departure of their actions and the external conditions they face. In this perspective, it becomes essential to know more about the psychological characteristics of leaders and especially about those characteristics that are suited to given situations, as it is also essential to discover institutional supports which 'orchestrate' the potential impact of leaders by helping to transform goals into policies and by improving communication with the population and feedback from the citizens. This is why the detailed study of the impact of political leaders and of the characteristics of political leadership is more than mere curiosity about the behaviour of the men and women who rule the world: it is directly and inextricably linked to the attempt to ensure that political leadership improves in the generations to come.

Bibliography

Aberbach, J.D., R.D. Putnam and B.A. Rockman (1981) *Bureaucrats and Politicians in Western Democracies*. Cambridge, Mass.: Harvard University Press.

Alexander, R.J. (1962) *Prophets of Revolution: Profiles of Latin American Leaders*. New York: Macmillan.

Baltes, P.B., and O.G. Brim, Jr (ed.) (1983) *Life-span Development and Behavior* Vol. 5. New York: Academic Press.

Barber, J.D. (1968) *The Lawmakers*. New Haven, Conn.: Yale University Press.

Barber, J.D. (1977) *The Presidential Character*, (2nd edn). Englewood Cliffs, NJ: Prentice-Hall.

Barkan, J.D., and J.J. Okumu (1979) *Politics and Public Policy in Kenya and Tanzania*. New York: Praeger.

Bass, B.M. (1981) *Stogdill's Handbook on Leadership*. New York: Free Press.

Bensman, J., and M. Givent (1975) 'Charisma and Modernity: The Use and Abuse of a Concept', *Social Research* (Winter), 42: 570–614.

Benze, J.G., Jr (1981) 'Presidential Skills', *Presidential Studies Quarterly*, (February) 11: 470–8.

Berger, P.L. (1963) 'Charisma and Religious Innovation: The Social Location of Israelite Prophecy', *American Sociological Review* (December), 28: 940–9.

Bialer, S. (1981) *Stalin's Successors: Leadership, Stability and Change in the Soviet Union*. Cambridge University Press.

Blake, R.R., and J.S. Mouton (1982) 'Theory and Research for Developing a Science of Leadership', *Journal of Applied Behavioral Science*, 18(3).

Blau, P. (1963) 'Critical Remarks on Weber's Theory of Authority', *American Political Science Review* (June), 57: 305–16.

Blau, P. (1964) *Exchange and Power in Social Life*. New York: John Wiley.

Blondel, J. (1980) *World Leaders*. London: Sage.

Blondel, J. (1982) *The Organization of Governments*. London: Sage.

Bogardus, E.S. (1934) *Leaders and Leadership*. New York: D. Appleton-Century.

Borgatta, E.F. (1964) 'The Structure of Personality Characteristics', *Behavioural Scientist* (January), 9: 8–17.

Breslauer, G.W. (1982) *Krushchev and Brezhnev as Leaders: Building Authority in Soviet Politics*. London: Allen & Unwin.

Bretton, H. (1966) *The Rise and Fall of Kwame Nkrumah: A Study of Personal Rule in Africa*. New York: Praeger.

Brim, O.G., and J. Kagan (1980) *Constancy and Change in Human Development*. Cambridge, Mass.: Harvard University Press.

Broder, D. (1980) *The Changing of the Guard*. New York: Penguin.

Browne, C.G., and T.S. Cohn (1958) *The Study of Leadership*. Danville, Ill.: Interstate Printers and Publishers.

Bunce, V. (1981) *Do New Leaders Make a Difference? Executive Succession and Public Policy under Capitalism and Socialism*. Princeton, NJ: Princeton University Press.

Burke, P.J. (1971) 'Task and Social-Emotional Leadership Role Performance', *Sociometry* (March), 34: 22–40.

Burns, J. McGregor (1963) *Roosevelt: The Lion and the Fox*. Cambridge, Mass.: Harvard University Press.

Burns, J. McGregor (1973) *Presidential Government*. Boston: Houghton Mifflin.

Burns, J. McGregor (1978) *Leadership*. New York: Harper and Row.

Carter, L., W. Haythorn and M. Howell (1950) 'A Futher Investigation of the Criteria of Leadership', *Journal of Applied Social Psychology* (April), 45: 350–8.

Cartwright, D., and A. Zander (eds) (1960) *Group Dynamics: Research and Theory.* Evanston, Ill.: Row, Peterson.

Cartwright, J.R. (1978) *Political Leadership in Sierra Leone.* Toronto and Buffalo: University of Toronto Press.

Cartwright, J.R. (1983) *Political Leadership in Africa.* New York: St Martins Press.

Castles, F. (1982) *The Impact of Parties.* London and Beverly Hills: Sage.

Clapham, C. (1969) 'Imperial Leadership in Ethiopia', *African Affairs* (April), 68: 271.

Clayton, R., and W. Lammers (1978) 'Presidential Leadership Reconsidered: Contemporary Views of Top Federal Officials', *Presidential Studies Quarterly* (Summer), 8: 237–45.

Cleaves, P. (1974) *Bureaucratic Politics and Administration in Chile.* Berkeley: University of California Press.

Cohen, D.C. (1972) 'The Concept of Charisma and the Analysis of Leadership', *Political Studies* (September), 20: 299–305.

Collier, D. (ed.) (1979) *The New Authoritarianism in Latin America.* Princeton, NJ: Princeton University Press.

Cronin, T.E. (1975) *The State of the Presidency.* Boston: Little, Brown.

Dahl, R.A. (1961) *Who Governs?* New Haven, Conn.: Yale University Press.

Daly, W.T. (1972) *The Revolutionary: A Review and Synthesis.* London and Beverly Hills: Sage.

Davis, J. (1929) 'A Study of 163 Outstanding (Russian) Communist Leaders', *American Sociological Review*, 24: 42–55.

d'Entreves, E. (1981) *Aquinas: Selected Political Writings.* Tolowa, NJ: Barnes and Noble.

Dogan, M. (1975) *The Mandarins of Western Europe.* New York: Halsted.

Downton, J.V., Jr (1973) *Rebel Leadership: Commitment and Charisma in the Revolutionary Process.* New York: Free Press.

Dye, T.R. (1971) *The Measurement of Policy Impact.* Tallahassee: Florida State University Press.

Edinger, L.J. (1964) 'Political Science and Political Biography: Reflections on the Study of Leadership', *Journal of Politics* (May and August), 26: 423–39 and 648–76.

Edinger, L.J. (ed.) (1967) *Political Leadership in Industrialized Societies: Studies in Comparative Analysis.* New York: John Wiley.

Edinger, L.J. (1975) 'The Comparative Study of Political Leadership', *Comparative Politics* (January), 7: 253–69.

Eisenstadt, S.N. (1963) *The Political Systems of Empires: The Rise and Fall of the Historical Bureaucratic Societies.* New York: Free Press.

Erikson, E.H. (1959) *Young Man Luther.* New York: W.W. Norton.

Erikson, E.H. (1969) *Gandhi's Truth.* New York: W.W. Norton.

Etzioni, A. (1965) 'Dual Leadership in Complex Organizations', *American Sociological Review* (October), 30: 688–98.

Evans-Pritchard, E.E. (1940) *The Nuer.* Oxford: Clarendon Press.

Eyestone, R. (1970) *The Threads of Public Policy: A Study in Policy Leadership.* Indianapolis: Bobbs-Merrill.

Fagen, R.R. (1965) 'Charismatic Authority and the Leadership of Fidel Castro', *Western Political Quarterly* (June), 18: 275–84.

Farrell, R. B. (ed.) (1970) *Political Leadership in Eastern Europe and the Soviet Union.* Chicago: Aldine.

Fiedler, F.E. (1967) *A Theory of Leadership Effectiveness*. New York: McGraw-Hill.

Fiedler, F.E., and M.M. Chemers (1975) *Leadership and Effective Management* Glenview, Ill.: Scott, Foresman.

Fishbein, M., E. Landy and G. Hatch (1969) 'Consideration of Two Assumptions underlying Fiedler's Contingency Model for Prediction of Leadership Effectiveness'. *American Journal of Psychology*, 82(4): 457–73.

Forrester, D.B. (1970) 'Indian State Ministers and their Roles', *Asian Survey* (June), 10: 472–82.

Friedland, W. H. (1964) 'For a Sociological Concept of Charisma', *Social Forces,* (October), 43: 18–26.

Friedrich, C. J. (1961) 'Political Leadership and the Problem of Charismatic Power', *Journal of Politics* (February), 23: 3–24.

Geertz, C. (ed.) (1963) *Old Societies and New States*. New York: Free Press.

George, A.L., and J.L. George (1956) *Woodrow Wilson and Colonel House: A Personality Study*. New York: Dover Press.

Gerth, H.H., and C.W. Mills (eds) (1958) *From Max Weber: Essays in Sociology*. New York: Oxford University Press.

Gibb, C.A. (1954) 'Leadership', pp.877–920 in Lindzey Gardner (ed.), *Handbook of Social Psychology: Special Fields and Applications*, Vol. II. Reading, Mass.: Addison-Wesley.

Glassman, R. (1975) 'Legitimacy and Manufactured Charisma', *Social Research* (Winter), 43: 615–36.

Goldman, M., and L.A. Fraas (1965) 'The Effects of Leader Selection on Group Performance', *Sociometry* (March), 28: 882–8.

Gonzales, E. (1974) *Cuba Under Castro: The Limits of Charisma*. Boston: Houghton Mifflin.

Gouldner, A.W. (ed.) (1965) *Studies in Leadership*. New York: Russell and Russell.

Greenstein, F.I. (1967) 'The Impact of Personality on Politics: An Attempt to Clear Away Underbrush', *American Political Science Review* (September), 61: 629–41.

Greenstein, F.I. (1969) *Personality and Politics*. Chicago: Markham.

Groth, A.J. (1970) 'Britain and America: Some Requisites of Executive Leadership Compared', *Political Science Quarterly* (June), 85: 217–39.

Gruder, W. (1971) 'Career Patterns of Mexico's Political Elite', *Western Political Quarterly* (September), 24: 467–82.

Gulembiewski R.T. (1961) 'Three Styles of Leadership and Their Uses', *Personnel* (July/August), 38: 34–45.

Gurr, T.R. (1970) *Why Men Rebel*. Princeton University Press.

Haddad, G.M. (1971) *Revolutions and Military Rule in the Middle East: The Arab States*. New York: Speller.

Halal, W.E. (1974) 'Toward a General Theory of Leadership', *Human Relations*, 27(4): 401–16.

Hamblin, R.L. (1958) 'Leadership and Crisis', *Sociometry* (December), 21: 322-35.

Hare, A.P. (1957) 'Situational Differences in Leader Behavior', *Journal of Applied Social Psychology* (July), 55: 132–4.

Hargrove, E.C. (1966) *Presidential Leadership Personality and Political Style*. New York: Macmillan.

Heady, B. (1974) *British Cabinet Ministers*. London: Allen and Unwin.

Herrmann, M.G. (ed.) (1977) *A Psychological Examination of Political Leaders*. New York: Free Press.

Hetzler, S. A. (1955) 'Variations in Role Playing Patterns Among Different Echelons of Bureaucratic Leaders', *American Sociological Reveiw* (December), 20: 700–5.

Hill, W. (1969) 'The Validation and Extension of Fiedler's Theory of Leadership Effectiveness', *Academy of Management Journal* (March), 12: 33–47.

Hirschman, A.O. (1963) *Journeys Toward Progress*. New York: Twentieth Century Fund.

Hocart, A.M. (1970) *Kings and Councillors: An Essay in the Comparative Anatomy of Human Society*. Chicago University Press.

Hoffman, S. (1967) 'Heroic Leadership: The Case of Modern France', in L.J. Edinger (ed.), *Political Leadership in Industrialized Societies*. New York: John Wiley.

Hollander, E.P. (1964) *Leaders, Groups and Influence*. London: Oxford University Press.

Hollander, E.P. (1978) *Leadership Dynamics: A Practical Guide to Effective Relationships*. New York: Free Press.

Hook, S. (1955) *The Hero in History*. Boston: Beacon Press.

House, R.J., and M.L. Baetz (1979) 'Leadership: Some Empirical Generalizations and New Research Directions', *Research in Organisational Behavior*. 1.

Hudson, M.C. (1977) *Arab Politics*. New Haven, Conn.: Yale University Press.

Hunt, J.G., and L.L. Larsen (eds) (1979) *Crosscurrents in Leadership*. Carbondale, Ill.: Southern Illinois University Press.

Huntington, S.P. (1968) *Political Order in Changing Societies*. New Haven, Conn.: Yale University Press.

Inkeles, A., and D.H. Smith (1974) *Becoming Modern: Individual Change in Six Developing Countries*. Cambridge, Mass.: Harvard University Press.

Jackman, R.W. (1976) 'Politicians in Uniform: Military Governments and Social Change in the Third World', *American Political Science Review* (December), 70: 1078–97.

Jackson, R.H., and C.G. Rosberg (1981) *Personal Rule in Black Africa*. Berkeley: University of California Press.

Kautsky, J.H. (1969) 'Revolution and Managerial Elites in Modernizing Regimes', *Comparative Politics* (July), 441–67.

Kellerman, B. (1984a) *The Political Presidency*. New York: Oxford University Press.

Kellerman, B. (1984b) *Leadership: A Multidisciplinary Perspective*. Englewood Cliffs, NJ: Prentice-Hall.

Kenneth, F. (ed.) (1975) *Militarism in Developing Countries*. New Brunswick, NJ: Transaction Books.

Kipnis, D. (1958) 'The Effects of Leadership Style and Leadership Power Upon the Inducement of an Attitude Change', *Journal of Applied Social Psychology* (September), 57: 173–80.

Korten, D.C. (1962) 'Situational Determinants of Leadership Structure', *Journal of Conflict Resolution*, 6: 222–35.

Koslin, B., and M. Moos (1951) 'Political Leadership Re-examined: An Experimental Approach', *Public Opinion Quarterly* (Fall), 563–74.

Krieger, L. (1970) *Kings and Philosophers, 1689-1789*. New York: W.W. Norton.

Lacouture, J. (1970) *The Demigods: Charismatic Leadership in the Third World*. New York: Alfred Knopf.

Laird, R.E. (1966) 'Some Characteristics of the Soviet Leadership System: A Maturing Totalitarian System', *Midwestern Journal of Political Science* (February), 10: 29–38.

Lande, C.H. (1965) *Leaders, Factions and Parties: The Structure of Philippine Politics*. New Haven, Conn.: Yale University Southeast Asia Monograph, no. 6.

Lasswell, H.D. (1960) *Psychopathology and Politics*. New York: Viking Press (first published 1936).

Lasswell, H.D., D. Lerner and C.E. Rothwell (1952) *The Comparative Study of Elites*. Palo Alto, California: Stanford University Press.

Leach, E.R. (1954) *The Political Systems of Highland Burma*. Cambridge, Mass.: Harvard University Press.

Lee, M.T. (1968) 'The Founders of the Chinese Communist Party: A Study in Revolutionaries', *Civilizations*, 13: 113–27.

Leighton, A. (1945) *The Governing of Men*. Princeton, NJ: Princeton University Press.

Lemarchand, René (ed.) (1977) *African Kingship in Perspective: Political Change and Modernization in Monarchical Settings*. London: Frank Cass.

Malloy, J.M. (1977) *Authoritarianism and Corporatism in Latin America*. University of Pittsburgh Press.

Marak, G.E., Jr (1964) 'The Evolution of Leadership Structure', *Sociometry* (June), 27: 174–82.

Marcus, J.T. (1961) 'Transcendence and Charisma', *Western Political Quarterly* (March), 14: 236–41.

Mazlich, B. (1976) *The Revolutionary Ascetic*. New York: Basic Books.

Mazlich, B. (1981) 'Leader and Led: Individual and Group', *Psychohistory Review* (Spring) :214–37.

Mazlich, B. (1984) 'History, Psychology and Leadership', in Kellerman (1984b).

Mazrui, A.A. (1970) 'Leadership in Africa: Obote of Uganda', *International Journal* (Summer), 25(3): 538–64.

McClelland, D. (1975) Power: The Inner Experience. New York: Irvington.

McFarland, A.S. (1969) *Power and Leadership in Pluralist Systems*. Palo Alto: University of California Press.

McKenzie, R.T. (1955) *British Political Parties*. London: Heinemann.

McKinlay, R.D. and A.S. Cohan (1975) 'A Comparative Analysis of the Political and Economic Performance of Military and Civilian Regimes', *Comparative Politics* (October), 8: 1–30.

McKinlay, R.D. and A.S. Cohan (1976) 'Performance and Instability in Military and Nonmilitary Regime Systems', *American Political Science Review* (September), 70: 850–64.

Micaud, C.A. (1969) 'Leadership and Development: The Case of Tunisia', *Comparative Politics* (July), 1: 468–84.

Mitchell, T.R. (1970) 'Leader Complexity and Leadership Style', *Journal of Personality and Social Psychology*, 116: 166–74.

Moos, M., and B. Koslin (1952) 'Prestige Suggestion and Political Leadership', *Public Opinion Quarterly* (Spring), 16: 77–93.

Morris, R.T., and M. Seeman (1950) 'The Problem of Leadership: An Interdisciplinary Approach', *American Journal of Sociology* (September), 56: 152ff.

Neustadt, R. (1960) *Presidential Power*. New York: John Wiley.

Nice, D.C. (1984) 'The Influence of War and Party System Aging on the Ranking of Presidents', *Western Political Quarterly* (September), 443–55.

Noland, R.L. (1966) 'Presidential Disability and the Proposed Constitutional Amendment', *American Psychologist*, 21.

Nordlinger, E.A. (1970) 'Soldiers in Mufti: The Impact of Military Rule upon Economic and Social Change in the Non-Western States', *American Political Science Review* (December), 64: 1131–48.

Odetola, O. (1982) *Military Regimes and Development*. London: Allen and Unwin.

O'Donnell, G.A. (1973) *Modernization and Bureaucratic-Authoritarianism*. Berkeley, Cal.: Institute of International Studies.

Ohl, C.M. (1981) 'An Exploratory Investigation of House's 1976 Theory of Charisma as Revealed in the Speeches of American Charismatic Leaders', Florida State University *Dissertation Abstracts International* (March), 41: 9-a.

Olson, M. (1982) *The Rise and Decline of Nations*. New Haven, Conn.: Yale University Press.

Paige, G.D. (1972) *Political Leadership*. New York: Free Press.

Paige, G.D. (1977) *The Scientific Study of Political Leadership*. New York: Free Press.

Pareto, W. (1963) *The Mind and Society* (4 vols). New York: Dover Press (first published 1916).

Perlmutter, A. (1981a) *Modern Authoritarianism: A Comparative Institutional Analysis*. New Haven, Conn.: Yale University Press.

Perlmutter, A. (1981b) *Political Rulers and Military Rulers*. London: Frank Cass.

Perrucci, R., and M. Pilisuk (1970) 'Leaders and Ruling Elites: The Interorganizational Bases of Community Power', *American Sociological Review* (December), 35: 1040–57.

Pressman, J., and A. Wildavsky (1973) *Implementation*. Berkeley: University of California Press.

Rabow, J., F.J. Fowler, Jr, D.L. Bradford, M.A. Hofeller, and Y. Shibnya (1966) 'The Role of Social Norms and Leadership in Risk-Taking', *Sociometry* (March), 29: 16–27.

Rappoport, A.S. (1910) *Mad Majesties*. New York: Brentano.

Ratnam, K.J. (1964) 'Charisma and Political Leadership', *Political Studies* (October), 12: 341–54.

Rejai, M. (1969) 'Toward the Comparative Study of Political Decision-Makers', *Comparative Political Studies* (October), 2: 349–60.

Rejai, M. and K. Phillips (1979) *Leaders of Revolution*. London and Beverly Hills: Sage.

Rejai, M. and K. Phillips (1983) *World Revolutionary Leaders*. New Brunswick, NJ: Rutgers University Press.

Renshon, S.A. (1984) 'Assessing Political Leaders: The Criterion of Mental Health', in Kellerman (1984b).

Robins, R.S. (ed.) (1977) *Psychopathology and Political Leadership*. New Orleans: Tulane University Press.

Roche, J.P. (1955) 'The Bureaucrat and the Enthusiast: An Exploration of the Leadership of Social Movements', *Western Political Quarterly* (June), 8: 248–61.

Rose, R. and E.N. Suleiman (eds) (1980) *Presidents and Prime Ministers*. Washington, DC: American Enterprise Institute.

Runyan, W.M. (1982) *Life Histories and Psychobiographies: Explorations in Theory and Method*. New York: Oxford University Press.

Rustow, D.A. (ed.) (1970) *Philosophers and Kings: Studies in Leadership*. New York: George Braziller.

Sayles, L.R. (1979) *Leadership*. New York: McGraw-Hill.

Schapera, I. (1956) *Government and Politics in Tribal Societies*. London: C.A. Watts.

Schwartz, B. (1983) 'George Washington and the Whig Conception of Heroic Leadership', *American Sociological Review* (February), 48: 18–33.

Schweitzer, A.R. (1974) 'Theory and Political Charisma', *Comparative Studies in Society and History* (March), 16: 150–81.

Searing, D.D. (1969) 'Models and Images of Man and Society in Leadership Theory', *Journal of Politics* (February), 31: 30–1

Selassie, B.H. (1974) *The Executive in African Governments*. London: Heinemann.

Selznik, P. (1957) *Leadership in Administration: A Sociological Interpretation*. New York: Harper and Row.

Shack, W.A., and P.S. Cohen (eds) (1979) *Politics in Leadership Perspective*. Oxford: Clarendon Press.

Shils, E. (1965) 'Charisma, Order, and Status', *American Sociological Review* (April), 30: 199–212.

Shils, E. (1968) 'Charisma', in *Encyclopaedia of the Social Sciences*. London: Macmillan.

Shogan, R. (1982) *None of the Above*. New York: New American Library.

Sills, D. (1968) *International Encyclopaedia of the Social Sciences*. Vol. 9, 'Leadership', pp. 91–113.

Smith, G. (ed.) (1971) *1000 Makers of the Twentieth Century*. Newton Abbot: David and Charles.

Stewart, L.H. (1977) 'Birth Order and Political Leadership', pp. 206–36 in Herrmann (1977).

Stogdill, R.M. (1974) *Handbook of Leadership: A Survey of Theory and Research*. New York: Free Press.

Stogdill, R.M., and A.E. Coons (eds) (1957) *Leader Behavior: Its Description and Measurement*. Columbus, Ohio: Ohio State University.

Suleiman, E.N. (1984) *Bureaucrats and Policy-Makers*. New York: Holmes and Meier.

Swearingen, R. (ed.) (1971) *Leaders of the Communist World*. New York: Free Press.

Thiselton, T.F. (1903) *Royalties in All Ages*. London: John C. Nimmo.

Tonnies, F. (1955) *Community and Association* (English edition). London: Routledge and Kegan Paul.

Toth, M.A. (1981) *The Theory of the Two Charismas*. Washington, DC: University Press of America.

Tucker, R.C. (1968) 'The Theory of Charismatic Leadership', *Daedalus* (Summer), 97: 731–56.

Tucker, R.C. (1973) *Stalin as Revolutionary 1879–1929*. New York: W.W. Norton.

Tucker, R.C. (1977) 'Personality and Political Leadership', *Political Science Quarterly* (Fall), 92: 383–93.

Tucker, R.C. (1981) *Politics as Leadership*. Columbia, Mo.: University of Missouri Press.

Weber, M. (1968) *Economy and Society*, (3 vols). New York: Bedminster Press.

Wildavsky, A. (1969) *The Presidency*. Boston: Little, Brown.

Wildavsky, A. (1975) *Perspectives on the Presidency*. Boston: Little, Brown.

Wildavski, A. (1984) *The Nursing Father: Moses as a Political Leader*. University of Alabama Press.

Willner, A.R. (1970) 'Perspectives on Military Elites as Rulers and Wielders of Power', *Journal of Comparative Administration* (November), 2: 261–76.

Willner, A.R. (1984) *The Spellbinders: Charismatic Political Leadership*. New Haven, Conn.: Yale University Press.

Willner, A.R., and D. Willner (1965) 'The Rise and Roles of Charismatic Leaders', *Annals* 358 (March), 7: 7–88.

Wishart, J.K. (1965) *Techniques of Leadership*. New York: Vintage Press.

Wittfogel, K.A. (1957) *Oriental Despotism*. New Haven, Conn.: Yale University Press.

Index

Aberbach, J.D., 79

Absolute (authoritarian) presidencies, 163, 179

Absolute systems, 29

Accession to power, 21, 29, 35, 37, 64, 74, 110, 111, 145, 152, 182, 186

Active vs. passive leaders, 27, 126, 127, 187, 200

Adams, 126

Adenauer, 14, 89, 90, 144, 157, 160, 166

Adjusters, 95, 101, 112

Administration, see Bureaucracy

Africa, 76, 90, 175
    South of Sahara (Black Africa), 27, 74, 75, 160, 178

Age, 117, 186

Alexander the Great, 91, 200, 201

Algeria, 77

Allport, 129

Amin, 74

Approaches, 1, 10–35, 36–80,
    classical political theory, 41–5, 65–7, 86, 197, 198
    economics, 47
    history, 39, 41
    institutional, 37, 46
    leaders-do-not-matter-thesis, 18, 19, 23, 27, 48, 195
    philosophy of history, 47
    psychology, 38–41, 115, 116, 119, 121, 126, 128–30, 133–6, 186, 190
    psychopathology, psychoanalysis, 121–4
    sociology, 37, 41, 47, 48, 116, 124
    social anthropology, 40

Apter, D., 49

Aquinas, 66

Argentina, 78, 117, 178

Aristotle, 41, 45, 63, 65

Asia, 75

Asquith, 119

Ataturk, K., 75, 90

Atlantic Area (the 'West'), 10, 18, 52, 67, 74, 75, 77, 109, 141, 159, 171, 173, 180, 187, 191, 196

Australia, 159, 164

Austria, 107

Authoritarianism (authoritarian leaders), 31, 75, 102, 158, 163, 165, 166, 177

Autobiographies, 115, 121

Barber, J.D., 27, 28, 38, 126–8, 146, 183, 190

Bass, B.M., 40, 130–4

Belgium, 158

Biographies, 115, 120–4, 126

Bismarck, 10, 70, 89, 90, 102

Blondel, J., 9, 85, 117, 152, 153, 158–60, 186

Bokassa, 74

Borgatta, E.F., 133

Boumédienne, 77

Bourguiba, 75, 76, 102, 199

Brezhnev, L., 14, 22, 144

Britain, 13, 21, 38, 69, 110, 118, 126, 141, 145, 164, 183

Bunce, V., 142

Bureaucracy, 8, 25, 32, 37, 43, 68, 71, 76, 81, 95, 139, 140, 142, 148–55, 163, 164, 167–73, 177, 179, 180, 184, 190, 192, 199

Burns, J.M., 1, 2, 10, 20–2, 27, 35, 39, 114

Cabinets 29, 167, 184 (see also Prime ministerial systems)

Cambodia, 74

Canada, 159

Cardenas, 90

Career, see Accession to power

Carter, 127, 140

Cartwright, J.R., 114

Castro, 59, 80

Ceasar, 200, 201

Central African Republic, 74

Centralization, 25, 101, 169

Chamberlain, 119

Charismatic leaders, 21, 24, 38, 39, 48–62, 135, 140, 198 (see also Weber)

Chief Executives, 37, 65, 154, 164

China (Popular Republic), 75, 89, 110, 172

Chile, 74, 91, 103

Churchill, 11, 18, 48, 88–91, 119, 134, 136, 144, 166, 199

Civil service, servants, see Bureaucracy

Cleavages, 103, 111–13, 169, 196

Colbert, 68

Collective leadership, 165, 166
Colonialism, 77
Columbia, 163
Comforters, 101, 103, 105, 106, 112
Commonwealth, 156, 157, 158, 161
Communist systems, 18, 23, 52, 70, 117, 158, 161, 163, 166, 168, 170–3, 179, 186, 188, 191, 192, 196
Comparative study, framework, 8, 11, 12, 17–19, 26, 27, 80, 82, 120, 186, 190
Comte, A., 47
Conflicts, 25, 37, 60–2, 167
  internal, 30, 63, 72, 109, 119
  external, 8, 30, 63–8, 71–2, 73, 104–12, 118, 141, 196, 200, 202
Conservative leaders, 32–4, 83
Constitutional presidencies, 6, 159, 179, 183
Coups, see Succession, irregular
Cromwell, O., 10

Dahl, R.A., 41
Definition, of leadership, 2, 3, 11–17
  components of, 16, 50
  conceptualization, 181, 189–94
  mobilization, 16, 17, 62, 200, 201
  diagnosis, 16, 17, 200
  prescription of course of action, 16, 17, 200
De Gaulle, 12, 14, 78, 88, 90, 91, 92, 95, 135, 136, 157, 160, 195, 196
Demographic characteristics, 11, 37, 38, 117–20, 130, 131, 133, 134, 136, 137, 144–6, 182, 184, 185
Demands, see Public Support
d'Entreves, E., 66
De Valera, 157
Development, see Socio-economic change
Disraeli, 70
Dogan, M., 79
Downton, J.V., 60
Dual leadership, 156, 183, 184
Duration, 9, 29, 51, 85, 152, 154, 156–9, 182–5
  fixed term, 159–62
  continuity, 15, 64
  stability, consolidation, maintenance, 64, 74

Eden, 141
Educational background, 43, 116, 117, 120, 145, 146, 186, 200
Educational policy, 69, 70

Effective vs. ineffective leaders, 132, 135, 136, 202
Effectiveness, success, 2, 72, 78, 117, 122, 123, 137, 144, 145, 148, 164, 167, 171
Egypt, 22
Eisenhower, 127, 140, 144
Eisner, K., 55
Emperor Charles V, 91
England, 68 (see also Britain)
Enlightened despotism, 68, 70, 70
Entourage, see Subordinates
Environment, influence of, 3–5, 7, 11, 15–19, 23–5, 29, 30, 33, 34, 40, 43, 45–7, 51, 52, 80, 81, 85, 96–114, 119, 128, 130, 134–6, 142, 144, 201, 202
Equatorial Guinea, 74
Erikson, E.H., 147
Ethiopia, 103
Ethnic background, 118, 186
Europe, 95, 155
  Central, 69, 89, 105
  Continental, 68, 158, 164, 177
  Eastern, 163
  North-Western, 14
  Western, 109, 156, 161, 165, 195
Evans-Pritchard, E.E., 79
Execution of laws, 66, 67
Experience, training, 142, 143

Family, early childhood, 118, 145, 146
Ferry, 70
Fiedler, F.E., 40, 135, 136, 140, 141
Finland, 158
Foreign affairs, 62–7, 70, 71, 73, 74, 77, 78, 83, 84, 88, 91, 92, 95, 98–100, 104–6, 111, 155, 195, 196, 202
Founders of new states, regimes, 60, 102, 158, 161, 163, 180, 183
France, 12, 13, 22, 35, 44, 46, 68–70, 74, 89, 91, 92, 101, 104, 110, 158, 160, 163, 171, 178, 183, 199
Franco, 103, 144
Frederic of Prussia, 69
Friedrich, C.J., 49, 55, 57

Gabon, 75
Gandhi, 122, 147
Germany (Dem. Rep.), 172
Germany (Fed. Rep.), 13, 14, 17, 55, 107, 111, 157, 160, 183, 196
George, A.L. & J.L., 38, 146, 147

Ghana, 157
Gibb, C.A., 40, 41,
Goals, 25, 29, 34, 63, 80−101, 107−14, 116, 122, 125, 141, 155, 160, 162, 164, 167, 168, 170, 172, 187−9, 192−4, 201, 202
Gomulka, 22
Good government, 65−7
Gorbachev, 14
Great Britain, see Britain
Great Depression, 70, 72
Great leaders, 10−15, 18, 34, 92, 94, 95
Greece, 22, 157
Greenstein, F.I., 38, 129, 138, 146
Grenada, 77
Groups, 25, 53, 95, 101, 111, 148, 151, 153, 155, 163, 173
  ethnic, 174−7, 179, 185
  interest, 46, 175−6
  religious, 174−7, 179, 185
  tribal, 174−6, 178, 179, 185
Guyana, 157

Heads of Governments as distinct from Heads of State, 156, 157
Heady, B., 126, 186, 190
Heath, 196
Hegel, 47
Heredity, 117, 183
Hermann, M.G., 40, 133
Heroes, 10, 11, 19−26, 47, 64, 66, 82, 86, 87, 93, 109, 120, 124, 195, 202
Hierarchal government, 165 (see also Collective leadership)
Hitler, 11, 22, 48, 86, 90, 91, 95, 122, 199
Hobbes, 3, 41, 43, 44, 63, 65, 66
Hoffmann, S., 114
Holland, 68
Hollander, C.P., 40
Huntington, S.P., 49

Ideal leadership, 17, 44, 199, 200
Ideal types of leadership, see Weber
Ideology, see Goals
Impact, 4, 5, 6, 11, 18, 23, 26−8, 48, 50, 51, 127, 136−47, 161, 162, 164, 168, 173, 181, 182, 185, 186, 192−3, 199, 201−03 (see also Role of leaders)
Implementation, 33, 81, 85, 98, 100, 140, 150, 153, 154, 169−72 (see also Bureaucracy)
Imposition, coercion, repression, 30−34, 75

Internal affairs, 62−7, 84, 88, 91, 92, 98, 100−12, 141, 195, 196, 201, 202
India, 117
Innovators, 95, 101, 103, 106, 112, 200, 201
Informal bodies, 175, 177 (see also Groups, Parties)
Institutional arrangements, 6, 7, 8, 14, 15, 25, 27−30, 34, 45, 46, 52, 85, 115, 123, 148−51, 153−80, 182, 199
Institutionalization, see Institutional arrangements
International environment, 77, 98−101, 105−7, 109, 112, 113 (see also Conflicts, external, and Foreign Affairs)
  isolation, 32−4
Iran 52, 90, 102
Ireland, 157
Italy, 17, 67, 158, 183
Ivory Coast, 75, 157

Jackson, R., 27, 29, 74
Janda, K., 9
Japan, 105, 109, 110, 183, 196
Jefferson, 126
Joan of Arc, 104
Johnson, 76, 78, 196
Jordan, 52

Karamanlis, 157
Kaunda, 59
Kellerman, B., 1, 2, 39
Kennedy, J.F., 22, 63, 127, 136, 164
Kenya, 75
King, R., 147
King of Morocco, 52, 77
King of Jordan, 52
Khaddafi, 59
Kruschev, 14

Lasswell, H.D., 38, 121
Latin America, 74, 161, 183, 188
Law-making, 66, 67
Leach, E.R., 79
Legislatures, assemblies, 37, 38, 122, 126, 155, 157, 159, 163, 164, 175, 177, 186
Legitimacy, 50, 51, 54, 55, 64, 65, 198
Lenin, 10, 21−3, 89, 91, 199
Limited presidencies, see Constitutional presidencies
Lincoln, 11
Lloyd George, 119

Locke, 41, 42, 45, 65–7
Longlasting leaders, 85, 105, 144, 158, 161
Louis XIV, 68, 195
Luther, 122, 147
Lycurgus, of Sparta, 10, 35, 42, 66, 67

Machiavelli, N., 36, 41–5, 63, 64, 67, 198
Macias, 74
Macmillan, 22
Maddison, 126
Managers, office-holders, 'mere'
    policymakers, 10, 12, 13, 19–26, 92–5,
    100, 101, 105, 106, 112, 143, 187, 201
Mao Tse-tung, 10, 23, 86, 87, 89, 91,
    103, 199
Marx, K., 45
Mazich, B., 22, 23, 39
McKenzie, R.T., 38
Measurement, 40, 181–94
Media, 25, 32
Mercantilism, 68, 195
Mexico, 178
Michels, R., 38, 47
Middle East, 76
Military, 75, 152, 153, 163, 165, 177,
    179, 183, 185, 191
Ministerial posts, ministers, 126, 141,
    165–7 (see also Entourage)
Mitterrand, F., 35
Models, 8, 80, 121
Monarchies, monarchs, 6, 13, 42, 43, 66,
    68, 89, 117, 120, 152, 155–8, 161, 163,
    165, 177, 179, 183, 199
Montesquieu, 35, 41, 42, 45, 65
Morocco, 52
Mosca, G., 38, 47
Moses, 89, 104
Mussolini, 199

Napoleon, 10, 22, 46, 47, 86, 87, 95, 200,
    201
Nasser, 59, 77, 78, 90, 136, 196, 199
National identity, 108–11, 196, 202, 203
Nationbuilding, 175
Nationalism, 32
'Natural' political structures, 151–4,
    173–5, 179, 185, 191
Nehru, 199
Neustadt, R., 38, 39
New leaders, 142
Nixon, R., 122, 127
Nkrumah, 59, 78, 136, 196

Noland, R.L., 147
Non-political leadership, 1, 40, 55, 56
North Korea, 117, 166
Nyerere, 59, 199

Occupational background, 116, 117, 120,
    186
Operationlization, 15, 57–60, 88, 181,
    189, 192
Opinion polls, 187, 189, 192
Oppositions, 29, 31, 76, 173
Ostrogorski, 38

Paige, G.D. 1, 2, 9, 28, 29, 36, 39, 50
Palme, 166
Paraguay, 34
Pareto, W., 21, 40, 47
Parliamentary systems, 29, 158, 161, 163,
    165, 166
Parliaments, see Legislatures
Parties, 16, 21, 25, 35, 38, 46, 148–51,
    155, 158, 159, 163, 166, 167, 172, 173,
    176–80, 184, 186, 199
Paternalistic leaders, 89–91, 93, 103
Pétain, 91
Peel, 69
Peron, 136
Personal characterstics, 19, 25, 28,
    115–47, 121, 181, 182, 198, 200 (see also
    background)
Personality, role of, 2, 4–6, 8, 21, 25,
    27, 28, 30, 34, 38, 45, 85, 124, 125,
    128–47, 166, 167, 180–2, 186, 194, 199,
    203,
    components, traits, 115, 121, 124–36, 137
    conceptualization, definition, 115, 116,
        124–9
    measurement, 189, 190
    types, 121, 124–8
Personalization, 61 (see also Charismatic
    leadership)
Personal rule, 48, 74
Peru, 178
Peter the Great, 68
Phillips, K., 11, 118, 124, 186, 190
Philosopher-kings, 43, 198
Pinochet, 91
Plato, 41, 43, 44, 63, 200
Plutarch, 20, 120
Pol Pot, 74
Popularity, 61, 62, 65, 71, 77, 111, 134,
    135, 141, 160, 178, 180, 187–9

Populist leaders, 90, 91, 93, 95, 106, 199
Portugal, 157, 158
Position, see Resources
Positive vs. negative leaders, 27, 126, 127, 187
Power(s) of leaders, 2–4, 14–17, 37, 42, 44, 148, 149, 156, 177
  power to appoint, dismiss other leading positions 148, 149, 152–5, 157, 158, 162–5 (see also Entourage)
Presidents, 11, 13, 14, 17, 29, 37, 38, 118, 126, 140, 146, 156, 157, 159
Presidential systems, 13, 14, 29, 37, 38, 41, 148, 161, 163, 165, 179, 191 (see also Absolute presidencies, Constitutional presidencies)
Prestige, status, 149, 152, 154–6, 161, 171
Prime ministers, 11, 21, 22, 37, 118, 126, 141, 156–9, 166, 167, 179 (see also Dual leadership)
Prime ministerial systems, 29, 161, 163, 179, 183
Progressive leaders, 32, 34, 84, 91
Protectors, 93, 94, 101, 106, 113
Public support, rejection, 7, 8, 16, 25, 30–4, 36, 43, 51–4, 56, 58, 60–2, 64, 71, 74, 99, 108, 134, 139, 140, 142, 148–55, 164, 168–70, 172, 173, 177–9, 184, 187, 189, 191, 192, 197, 199, 201–3
Putnam, R.D., 79

Rappoport, A.S., 122
Rational, legalistic bureaucratic leaders (rule), 21, 24, 50–3, 56, 60, 135
Reactionary leaders, 90, 91
Reagan, 77, 94, 140
Reformers, 95, 103, 106, 113, 200
Regime, see Institutional arrangements, Personalization
Regional, geographic background, 120, 186
Rejai, M., 1, 11, 118, 124, 186, 190
Religious background, 118, 120, 186
Religious bodies, groups, 174–7, 179, 185
Renshon, S.A., 147
Repression, see Imposition
Resources, 3–6, 25, 28–30, 181, 182, 199, 201
  institutions, 155, 180–3, 192, 198, 200, 203
  legal position, 5, 6, 13, 14, 17, 148, 149

measurement, 190–3
Results, see Impact
Retirement, see Succession
Revolutionary ideologies, 91, 103, 106
Revolutionary leaders, 11, 21, 33, 35, 75, 77, 89, 93, 103, 106, 111, 113, 118, 124–6, 186, 190, 201
Ricardo, 47
Robespierre, 86, 87
Robins, R.S., 147
Rockman, B.A., 79
Role of government, see Impact
Roles of leaders, 2, 36–80, 138
Romania, 166
Rosberg, C., 27, 29, 74
Rose, R., 79
Roosevelt, F.D., 11, 21, 22, 48, 109, 126, 136, 199
Roosevelt, T., 55
Rousseau, 35, 41, 42, 44, 45, 65, 66, 198
Routes to leadership, see Accession to power
Runyan, W.M., 147

Sahara, 77
Saviours, 88, 90–3, 102, 104–6, 112, 135, 198, 200, 201
Schapera, I., 79
Schmidt, 166
Schweitzer, A., 57
Scope of activities, 7, 8, 15, 34, 35, 45, 80, 93, 94, 175, 179, 181, 188, 192, 193
Secretaries of communist parties (in power), 14, 183, 191
Seligman, L., 1
Senghor, 76
Sex, 117, 186
Shah of Iran, 52, 90, 102
Shared leadership, 156, 165 (see also Dual leadership)
Shils, E., 49
Sills, D., 1, 40, 41
Shogan, R., 63
Soares, 157
Social background, 25, 116, 117, 145, 146, 186
Socialization, 11, 95, 119, 144, 146 (see also Background)
Social movements, 39
Socio-economic change, 62, 68, 73, 103, 170, 172, 195, 197–9

Socio-economic environment, 30, 32, 33, 47, 48, 71, 75–7, 169, 170 (see also Cleavages, Conflicts)
Socio-economic policy (-making), 62, 68–77, 195, 196
Solon, of Athens, 2, 66
Sorensen, T., 63
South & South-East Asia, 188
Southern Hemisphere, 73
Sovereigns, see Monarchs
Soviet Union (Russia), 14, 23, 39, 68, 70, 74, 107, 109–11, 163, 191, 196
Specialization, 93, 163
Sri Lanka, 117, 157
Stalin, 11, 14, 48, 86, 87, 103, 109, 122, 147, 163, 191
Stewart, L., 118, 119
Stogdill, R.M., 1, 2, 40, 130–3
Stroessner, 34
Subordinates, 6, 9, 16, 68, 71, 80–1, 139, 142, 149, 151–4, 162, 164, 167, 179, 180, 184, 199
  advisers, personal staff, 162–4, 184
  ministers, 71, 81, 162–4, 184, 186
Succession, 110, 152
  irregular, 110, 158, 161, 196, 197 (see also Military)
  regular, retirement, 66, 67, 158, 161, 196
Sukarno, 59, 78
Suleiman, E.N.B., 79
Sweden, 159, 183, 191
Switzerland, 29, 100, 156, 164, 166, 167

Taiwan, 117
Thatcher, 18, 77, 95, 100
Third World, 18, 29, 38, 39, 46, 49, 57–9, 69, 70, 74–6, 90, 102, 110, 156, 157, 169–74, 183, 188, 196, 199
Thiselton, T.F., 122
Titles of leaders, 148, 157

Tito, 196, 199
Tonnies, F., 53
Traditional leaders (rule), 24, 51–3, 60
Traditions, 7, 8, 149, 151–3, 155
Transfer of power, see Succession
Transforming leaders, 20, 21, 27, 35, 89, 91–3, 103, 105, 106, 111
Transactional leaders, 20, 21, 27, 35
Trudeau, P., 166
Tucker, R.C., 1, 16, 20, 39, 49, 147, 200
Tunisia, 102
Turnover, see Duration
Truman, H., 126
Typologies, 12 (see also, Presidencies, Prime ministerial systems, Dual leadership, Monarchies, Long leaders, Military)
Tyrants, 11, 20, 23, 86, 87, 198

Uganda, 74
United States, 17, 37, 38, 39, 46, 66, 74, 100, 109, 117, 118, 122, 126, 140, 146, 159, 161, 164, 165, 169, 180, 183, 191

Venezuela, 163
Voltaire, 44

War leaders, 18
Washington, 11, 126
Weber, 21, 24, 35, 37, 38, 40, 47–62, 88, 135, 198
Western Europe, see Atlantic Area
Wildavsky, A., 41
Willner, A.R., 54, 57–60, 79
Wilson, H., 21
Wilson, W., 38, 122, 147

Yugoslavia, 156

Zambia, 157